HIGHWAY

101 The History of El Camino Real

HIGHWAY 101
The History of El Camino Real

California's Historic Highways

Stephen H. Provost

CRAVEN STREET
BOOKS
Fresno, California

Highway 101: The History of El Camino Real
Copyright © 2020 by Stephen H. Provost. All rights reserved.

All photos by author unless otherwise noted.

Book design by Andrea Reider

Published by Craven Street Books
An imprint of Linden Publishing
2006 South Mary Street, Fresno, California 93721
(559) 233-6633 / (800) 345-4447
CravenStreetBooks.com

Craven Street Books and Colophon are trademarks of
Linden Publishing, Inc.

ISBN 978-1-61035-352-6

135798642

Printed in the United States of America
on acid-free paper.

Library of Congress Cataloging-in-Publication Data on file.

To the curious, the explorers, and the trailblazers

Contents

ACKNOWLEDGMENTS

Several people were instrumental in helping me make this work possible through their contributions, guidance, and support. Among them U.S. 101 historian Dan Young, who took me on a guided tour over the northern end of the highway, and of course, my wife and traveling companion Samaire Provost, who not only accompanied me on my photo trips up and down the state but served as my guide for the portion of Old 101 that passes through San Diego County, where she grew up.

INTRODUCTION

My previous book, *Highway 99: The History of California's Main Street,* took readers on a tour through the heart of California, down a road I traveled during my childhood. In 2012, I moved west from the San Joaquin Valley, where I'd lived most of my life, to the California coast and began driving a different highway: U.S. 101.

It parallels—literally and figuratively—old U.S. 99, but it has a history all its own that's just as rich and fascinating.

As with *Highway 99,* I've explored the history of the road itself as well as the people and places along the way who supplied it with a unique identity: people like Walter and Cordelia Knott, founders of Knott's Berry Farm just a mile off the 101; Florence Owens Thompson, the iconic "Migrant Mother" in Dorothea Lange's famous photo; Anton and Juliette Andersen, who started Pea Soup Andersen's in Buellton; and Alex Madonna, who laid hundreds of miles of California highway and built the distinctive Madonna Inn along U.S. 101 in San Luis Obispo.

Up ahead, you'll read about the signs along the highway, both porcelain and neon, and you'll learn about how the oil industry helped define the road.

I've followed a format similar to the one I used in *Highway 99,* dividing the book into two sections: the first topical, and the second a south-to-north tour of the road that will help you follow the modern route and retrace the old. Each of the chapters in Part II is named for what I considered to be the most recognizable stretch of highway in each area I've covered, although there are often other names for each section.

So hop in your vintage Model T or your modern Chevy Malibu, buckle up, and enjoy a ride down memory lane, a.k.a. U.S. Highway 101.

The open road awaits.

APOLLO 70

PART I:
THE STORY
OF OLD 101

1

BELLS, NO WHISTLES

How do you choose the path for a highway? It's a question we may not think about as we're rushing down the interstate, hurrying to get to whatever our destination may be: the office, a romantic dinner with our sweetheart, Christmas dinner at Grandma's house. But road builders had to think about it a lot at the dawn of the automotive age, when there weren't any paved roads to speak of.

When they charted a course for the first primitive highways, they had their own agendas. Many of them were businessmen who had a stake in getting people to the front door of their restaurants or retail establishments. What better way to attract customers than to create a highway that ran right outside that front door? That's what Carl Fisher, the brains behind Dixie Highway from Detroit to South Florida, did: He owned a lot of land in and around Miami, and he wanted to create a road that would bring snowbirds south for the winter.

In between, it would pass through established cities and towns, even if they weren't exactly in a direct line from Point A to Point B. The result, Fisher admitted, was the equivalent of a "four-thousand-mile wandering pea-vine."

Where there were no towns to speak of, highways often followed the path of least resistance. If they had to cross mountain ranges, they went around hills and through canyons. This was necessary in an age when highways were carved out using steam shovels and mules pulling Fresno Scrapers. More sophisticated machinery was still a long way off in 1912, when the nation still had just 250

A couple stands near a decorative bell between Ventura and Calabasas on El Camino Real in 1906, two decades before the road was signed as U.S. 101. *Public domain.*

miles of concrete road—before asphalt replaced concrete as the material of choice in building a highway.

Even when technology advanced, the cost of upgrading roads was often prohibitive—at least at first.

Cy Avery, the Tulsa man who was the force behind the legendary Route 66, put it this way in a 1955 interview with the *Tulsa World*: "Highways were routed around hills instead of through them, bridges were built eighteen feet wide, and section lines were followed despite the resulting right-angle turns because these made roads cheaper. There wasn't any big earth-moving machinery then, and we could build miles of road for what it would have cost to cut through one little hill. If we had made bridges two feet wider, we couldn't have built as many bridges. We had just so much money, and there was never enough."

The Cuesta Pass north of San Luis Obispo shows what happened when road builders took the long way around. If you look off to the west as you descend the steep grade heading south toward the city, you'll see a narrow band of concrete curled like a serpent around a low hill. This is a portion of the highway's original alignment. Early builders couldn't blast their way through the mountains, so they went around them, creating horseshoe bends such as Dead Man's Curve, a similar segment of concrete that was once part of U.S. 99 between Grapevine and the Tejon Pass. As the name indicates, these were treacherous segments of road. At about 15 feet wide, they offered barely enough room for cars to share the road as they headed in opposite directions: The slightest miscalculation at an unsafe speed could send a vehicle tumbling over the edge.

Then there were the hairpin curves on the Conejo Grade along the Old 101 in Ventura County, winding steeply downhill from Thousand Oaks toward Camarillo. And on the San Juan Grade heading out of Salinas.

Elsewhere, highways snaked their way through canyons and riverbeds—which proved a problem during the rainy season, when flash floods, like the road builders, like the highway builders, followed the path of least resistance. Roads washed out. Vehicles got stuck. It was one heck of a muddy mess. Again, the Cuesta Pass offers a good example: The modern freeway is elevated and runs along the side of the mountain, the earth beneath it held in place above the canyon by a huge retaining wall. The original road, which extends from the concrete horseshoe bend described above, is a few hundred feet below, at the base of the canyon. When it was built back in 1915, one report counted 71 hazardous curves along its length through the canyon and over the pass.

Many of the old highways, such as Highway 99 and portions of U.S. 101, followed established rail lines. If you're driving up 101 between Paso Robles and Salinas, take the San Ardo exit and follow Cattlemen Road north to San Lucas. You'll notice that the road parallels the Southern Pacific railroad tracks precisely.

The old road over the Cuesta Grade, just north of San Luis Obispo, can be seen in the foreground, against the backdrop of the modern highway's retaining wall. .

What does this have to do with U.S. 101?

At one time, Cattlemen Road *was* U.S. 101—before the federal highway was rerouted to its current location a few miles to the west. With many towns having been built along rail lines, it only made sense for newborn highways to follow the same course.

Other highways were carved out along old stagecoach routes, which in turn often followed even older Spanish or Native American trails.

Long before the first concrete was poured through Cuesta Canyon, a parallel path now officially called Old Stage Coach Road was in use. It lies to the west of both highway alignments, and it's paved now, so you can drive its nearly three-mile length in just a little more than 15 minutes. But back in 1876, when the county passed a $20,000 bond to construct a road of its own in the area, it took eight hours for a six- or eight-horse freight wagon to travel eight miles (that's right, 1 mph) to get from the Waterfall Saloon on the SLO side of the grade to the foot of the far side.

Old Stage Coach Road was also sometimes known as the Padre's Trail—and in fact, many of the earliest cross-country links weren't called highways or even roads but trails in deference to the dirt paths that had preceded them. There was the Santa Fe Trail from Independence, Missouri, to Santa Fe, New Mexico, which foreshadowed a segment of the famed Route 66. The Old Spanish Trail made its way across the continent from St. Augustine, Florida, to San Diego, a path later followed by portions of three federal highways: U.S. 70, 80 and 90. The Arrowhead Trail connected Los Angeles to Salt Lake City, while the National Old Trails Road ran from Baltimore to L.A. and also helped lay the groundwork for part of Route 66.

Then there was El Camino Real, which is a different story entirely.

HIGHWAY OF LEGEND

Those bells along U.S. Highway 101 may not clang for ears to hear, but even so, they tell tales that ring true: stories of an old footpath that linked 21 Franciscan missions established along the California coastline in the late 18th and early 19th centuries. Those stories resonated with Californians who, a century later, came up with the notion of giving motorists a chance to retrace the steps of the Spanish missionaries—with tread marks—in those newly popular contraptions called automobiles.

The challenge was finding the exact route of those old footpaths, a problem that proved to be all but daunting. They had been, after all, footpaths, and while it's possible to wear a trail through brush and tall grasses, that trail will be quickly lost once it's abandoned or obscured by

Participants in the Pasear Tour, a 2,000-mile tour of California, drove south from San Francisco to Los Angeles as part of their journey in 1912, stopping here in front of the San Buenaventura Mission. *Public domain.*

mud after a rainstorm. The fact is, the routes between the missions shifted frequently (just as their successor highway routes would do), so those who sought to reconnect the dots had to do a lot of improvising.

Their goal was not only to revitalize the historical landmarks, but also to draw the curious and historically minded to a road that would run from San Diego up through the San Francisco Bay Area. A pair of librarians from Los Angeles had formed the Society for the Preservation of Missions in 1892, but had found little support for their cause, raising only $90—a paltry sum even in those days—over three years to renovate the landmarks.

So they turned the project over to an entity known as the Landmarks Club, which, unfortunately, fared little better—especially when the Spanish-American War of 1898 turned that nation's sentiment decidedly against anything with a Spanish flavor.

The good news was that the war lasted less than four months and was over by summer, after which opposition subsided and the project began to pick up steam—thanks in large measure to the advent of the automobile.

The *Santa Cruz Sentinel* ran a story in the fall of 1901 that began with the definitive statement, "The old, old Spanish highway is to be reconstructed."

The effort, it maintained, was based on the belief "that the rehabilitation of the original El Camino Real from San Diego to San Francisco, making it passable for carriages, automobiles, bicycles or pedestrians, would prove an invaluable adjunct to the attractions and inducements offered tourists."

The term "tourist attraction" might not have entered the popular lexicon yet, but those two words were used in the very same sentence, leaving little doubt about the advantages of pressing ahead with the project.

The Landmarks Club put together enough donations to steady the walls at the San Fernando Mission and fix the roof tiles at San Juan Capistrano, but it was the prospect of creating a network for tourism that brought a key segment of the public on board: business. Harrie Forbes, a member of the Landmarks Club, began pitching the idea to various women's clubs, which helped it gain momentum. The name "El Camino Real" was chosen because it evoked a sense of history and prestige, in much the same way the transcontinental Lincoln Highway would draw upon the popularity of the nation's 16th president. Translated as the "The Royal Road" or "The King's Highway," it wasn't connected with any particular king, though Ferdinand VII was on the throne at the time when most of the missions were built. At that point, however, the paths connecting them were hardly highways in the modern sense—or any sense, for that matter.

Indeed, some members of the media scorned the entire idea as a fabrication. The *San Francisco Chronicle* labeled it a myth. And an *Oakland Tribune* editorial, published under the headline "El Camino Real a Fake," branded "the tale of a great highway traversing California from south to north" under Spanish rule as "pure fiction"— "not the work of Spanish hands, but of the Gringo imagination."

The motorcar would be the true royalty of the new road, or rather those few wealthy individuals who could afford the luxury of the still-novel horseless carriages. These deep-pocketed travelers had what the nascent tourism industry craved—money, and they had little desire to navigate a circuitous route through hills and still unpopulated valleys between the missions. In those days, cars broke down almost as often as they managed to run smoothly, and only the most adventurous of travelers was daring enough to wander far off the beaten path.

When the El Camino Real Association, formed in 1904, sought to establish how much of the original route was still in use, its members could identify only five miles of roadway that hadn't been overgrown with weeds or crisscrossed with private fences and property lines. Some of the missions were decidedly out of the way for road builders who wanted to maintain a reasonably direct route up the coast that included stops in most of the major towns. As a result, the San Carlos (Carmel), San Fernando, and San Miguel Missions were bypassed and relegated to spur roads.

But in the end, it didn't matter. Not just because of the highway's catchy, if somewhat fanciful name, but even more so because of the bells.

They were the brainchild of Harrie Forbes, who with her husband just happened to own the only bell foundry west of the Mississippi. Early California state roads were numbered, but weren't signed—much of El Camino Real was Legislative Route Number 2 (LRN 2), which ran from National City in the south to San Francisco in the north. But that number appeared only on maps, not on the road itself. And while the state's two auto clubs took up the task of placing porcelain road signs along main routes showing the distances between cities, El Camino Real got a more distinctive marker.

Forbes had been drawn to the mission bells as early as the 1880s: On returning to her Boston home from a honeymoon visit to California, she began making papier-mâché models of them. The imagery stuck in her mind when she returned to the state and became involved in the Landmark Club's mission projects, and she subsequently proposed that the bell become the symbol of the highway. The El Camino Real Association approved the idea, and Forbes fashioned the first cast-iron bell, which was suspended in 1906 from an 11-foot-tall guidepost shaped like a shepherd's crook outside the Plaza Church in Los Angeles.

The first bell erected in Northern California went up in Santa Clara three years later, and by the following year, 90 bells were in place along the emerging route. Emerging it

A mileage sign on the bell in front of the Los Angeles Plaza Mission around the turn of the 20th century tells visitors how far it is in each direction to the next California mission. *Public domain.*

This infusion of cash helped make the new Royal Road into something its semifictional namesake had never been: a continuous highway running up the California coast—and beyond into the Pacific Northwest states of Oregon and Washington. It was at this point that a new name for the highway started to gain resonance—one that played off the success of the Lincoln Highway, dedicated in 1913, which spanned the continent in fits and starts from New York's Times Square to San Francisco's Lincoln Park.

"Constantly, for many years, we have seen the name of Roosevelt linked with that of Lincoln," Phoebecus Smithicus of Oakland wrote on Page 16 of the *San Francisco Chronicle*, dated January 27, 1919. "We have the Lincoln highway, running east and west, the length of our land. Why can we not have, running north and south, from Seattle to San Diego, the Roosevelt highway?"

Indeed, in March of 1919, the *Oakland Tribune* reported the founding of the Roosevelt Highway Association in Oregon to tout a $2.5 million state bond for construction of the road in that state—provided Congress pitched in with an equal amount.

The Roosevelt Highway was one of many names that would become attached to various sections of the road, which went on to attain uniform federal highway status as U.S. 101 in 1926. Yet despite that apparent uniformity, it remained an amalgam of many wonderfully distinct roads. Like almost every highway on the map before the advent of the modern interstate system, it was actually a series of roads cobbled together, connecting towns as it traversed city streets and country roads in a hodgepodge of frequently shifting alignments, detours, and bypasses. And it took on a radically different character each time it passed from one geographic and cultural center to the next.

In San Diego County, it was known as the Pacific Coast Highway, a designation it retained along the coast as it passed through Orange County and Santa Monica as U.S. 101A. The "A" stood for "alternate," identifying it as an optional north-south route in the federal highway system that also included just plain U.S. 101 farther inland. The western alignment was later re-signed as State Route 1, a designation still shared with 101 at various points on its journey northward, notably for a

still was, because it was only in that same year (1910) that the State Highways Act provided money—$18 million of it—to begin paving the highway. But although as many as 400 bells were in place by 1915, much of the roadway between towns along the way remained unpaved and subject to washouts. The initial infusion of state funds hadn't been enough to cover the cost of paving all the roadways planned for California, so the legislature passed a $15 million follow-up bill five years later. An additional $20 million went into the pot in 1919, by which time the scope of the highway project had broadened to span the three contiguous Pacific Coast states.

stretch of more than 50 miles along the Central Coast and again where it crosses the Golden Gate Bridge.

In the freeway era, the inland route became known as the Santa Ana Freeway through Orange County, a portion of which was absorbed by Interstate 5 until it reemerged northward as the Hollywood Freeway and, swerving westward, became the Ventura Freeway. In its earliest days, it was the Rincon Sea Level Road between Ventura and Santa Barbara, the first drivable seaside highway along that stretch of coastline.

Later, the section of State Route 1 from Santa Barbara north to San Francisco—including the portion shared by U.S. 101—became known as the Cabrillo Highway, in honor of Portuguese explorer Joao Rodrigues Cabrillo.

In 1542, Cabrillo became the first known European to navigate the coast of what would one day be called California. But the name Cabrillo Highway (like El Camino Real) isn't nearly as old as the venerable name might suggest. It actually dates to the spring of 1957, when state senator Alan Erhart of Arroyo Grande proposed the designation for the stretch of road between San Francisco and the Mexican border.

To the north, U.S. 101 was the Bayshore Highway (later Freeway) from San Jose to San Francisco. Then, north of the Bay Area, it becomes the Redwood Highway, taking its name from the world's tallest—and, indeed, only—stands of old-growth coastal redwood trees through which it passes for the next 350 miles.

One of the highway's 400-plus bells stands guard on the Cuesta Grade.

SIGNED, SEALED, AND DELIVERED

Two words: Captive audience.

That's what drivers on U.S. 101 and other highway were—and still are. In a way, traveling the American highway is a lot like watching television: You have your big-budget specials (that gorgeous scenery), your regularly scheduled programming (gas stations and rest stops), and even test patterns in the form of traffic jams.

Then there are the commercials. In neon. In illuminated plastic. On billboards. On road signs, which are the public service announcements of the highway experience.

Even the kids who set up those neighborhood lemonade stands know the principle: More traffic equals more business. And where are you going to find more traffic than by the side of a road? Even better: a highway. No sooner had we taken to our newly built highways in that fantastic new contraption, the motorcar, than signs started popping up telling us where to go. Just try counting the number of arrows you see on a road trip; if you're on the road a while, they can easily number in the hundreds.

Traffic on the Santa Ana Freeway at its junction with the Ramona Freeway in 1954. © *California Department of Transportation, all rights reserved. Used with permission.*

The signs started out simple. In the early years of the 20th century, before the government took over the funding of highway construction, boosters banded together in "trail associations" to promote and maintain various roads. These groups consisted mainly of businessmen seeking to make money by routing the highways past their front doors. Road maintenance wasn't a matter of altruism:

TRAFFIC
MUST
YIELD TO
PEDESTRIANS

1 ↑   MORRO BAY   13
      HEARST CASTLE 43
      MONTEREY   136

PASO ROBLES 28
SALINAS   127   101 ↑
MONTEREY   146

State Route 1 and U.S. 101 share the same roadway for miles along the California coastline. This sign is posted near one location where they diverge in San Luis Obispo. .

The better the roads, the more likely drivers were to use them—and the better business would be.

Signs telling you what road you were on or how far it was to the nearest town helped, too. In the early years, a maze of more than 250 trails appeared across the country, and they weren't the expressways or freeways of today. They utilized country lanes and city streets, sometimes making it difficult to stay on course. A wrong turn from Broadway onto Main Street, and you might find yourself miles off track. To make matters more "interesting," there were places where two of these early highways shared the same road. Two might merge or diverge without notice, and drivers wouldn't know which way to go.

The Apache and Old Spanish Trails shared the same stretch of road with the Atlantic-Pacific, Evergreen, and Lee Highways in southwestern New Mexico—a phenomenon that would persist after the federal highway system was established. For instance, the route now known as Interstate 10 east of Los Angeles once carried signage for U.S. 60, 70, and 99. Even today, segments of U.S. 101 are co-signed as State Route 1.

As if the overlapping routes weren't bad enough, trail associations competed with one another for traffic, sometimes adopting confusingly similar names. If you were traveling through Kansas, you could take the Old Santa Fe Trail, touted by an association formed in 1911 to promote the historic route. Or you could instead follow the New Santa Fe Trail, brainchild of a group formed a year earlier to boost a road that followed the Atchison, Topeka and Santa Fe Railroad.

The Arrowhead Trail from Salt Lake City to Los Angeles was an alternate to the Lincoln Highway meant to promote commerce in Utah by keeping motorists in that state longer.

Not all trails were created equal. Some were better maintained than others. Some were paved for one stretch before deteriorating into gravel, dirt or even mud. Still others dead-ended where the funds—or the merchants' motivation—had run out.

Critics accused the highway associations of being more concerned with lining their pockets than maintaining their roads. Some even promoted their roads as federal government projects, even though the government at that point had nothing to do with them. This led the U.S. Bureau of Public Roads to warn that highway groups were guilty of spreading "propaganda" in an attempt to legitimize their projects, which were guided more by their quest for profits than any national interest.

That quest could even prompt an association to change a highway's route if such a move seemed beneficial. The *Reno Evening Gazette* blasted the Pike's Peak Ocean-to-Ocean Highway for changing its western end point from San Francisco to Los Angeles—and in so doing, bypassing northern Nevada. In a 1924 editorial, the newspaper charged that "transcontinental highway associations, with all their clamor, controversy, recriminations and meddlesome interference, build mighty few highways."

Taxpayers in small towns had little say in how the roads were managed, but nonetheless were left to foot the bill for their construction and maintenance, the newspaper said. What did they have to show for it? Noise.

"In nine cases out of ten, these . . . associations are common nuisances and nothing else," the paper concluded. "They are more mischievous than constructive. In many instances, they are organized by clever boomers who are not interested in building roads but in obtaining salaries at the expense of an easily beguiled public."

With all the confusion over which road was which, early road signs supplied a solution—although not a perfect one. Each trail association came up with its own insignia, which it placed wherever it could find a good spot in the motorist's line of sight: on fence posts, rocks, trees, telephone poles, etc. The Lincoln Highway, which ran from New York to San Francisco, used a large capital "L" on a white background sandwiched between narrow red and blue stripes. The William Penn Highway and the Keystone Highway both used the same keystone symbol that still appears on Pennsylvania road signs today. The Horseshoe Trail sign featured a horseshoe (naturally)—although it was depicted facing downward, which couldn't have been reassuring to motorists hoping for a little good luck.

Names, not numbers, denoted the old trails, some of which paved the way for later highways and interstates, while others were neglected and eventually all but forgotten.

The most sophisticated private group that took on the task of posting road signs was AAA in California, where both the northern and southern state auto clubs dove in head first. The Automobile Club of Southern California started posting road signs in 1906, an activity it continued for the next half century. The club erected signs in the state's 13 southernmost counties, but it didn't stop there. It also put up porcelain signs in Arizona, southern Nevada, and Baja California, placing markers on the Old Spanish Trail from San Diego to Texas and the Midland Trail from Los Angeles to Ely, Nevada. In 1914, it undertook perhaps its most ambitious project, placing some 4,000 signs along the western portion of the National Old Trails Road between Los Angeles and Kansas City.

The California State Automobile Association, meanwhile, was doing similar work in the state's 45 northern

A variety of road signs could be seen outside St. Paul's Lutheran Church in Olive, Orange County, in 1967.
Orange County Archives.

counties, putting up its first sign in 1908 at Parkside Boulevard and 19th Avenue in San Francisco. It continued its work through 1969. Among the roads that benefited were U.S. highways 40, 48, 50, 99, 101, and 199 in California, as well as the Lincoln Highway east to Salt Lake City and the Victory Highway as far afield as Kansas City.

The earliest signs were made of wood, but the switch was made to porcelain because it was easier to repair in the field. The durable material, mounted on a redwood post or steel pole, became ubiquitous throughout the Golden State. Glass reflectors were added later to improve nighttime visibility.

Originally, the signs were diamond-shaped with blue lettering against a yellow background, but they eventually gave way to the black-on-white format that became the national standard for informational signs in 1927. Informational signs, featuring directional arrows and distances to towns up ahead, were rectangular and used black lettering on a white background. Signs indicating detours, speed limits, highway junctions, and city limits also fell into this category.

LIST OF TRAILS

Here are some of the 250-plus trails that crisscrossed the United States during the early years of the 20th century. U.S. highways that follow some portion of the old trails are included where available.

TRANSCONTINENTAL TRAILS

Bankhead Highway—Washington, D.C., to San Diego (U.S. 1, 15, 70, 170, 29, 78, 70, 67, 80)

Dixie Overland Highway—Savannah, Georgia, to San Diego (U.S. 28, 80)

Lee Highway—Washington, D.C., to San Diego (U.S. 11, 64, 6)

Lincoln Highway—New York to San Francisco (U.S. 30)

Lone Star Trail—St. Augustine, Florida, to Los Angeles (U.S. 1, 90, 84, 67, 290, 80)

National Old Trails Road—Baltimore to Los Angeles (U.S. 50, 66)

New York National Roosevelt Midland Trail—Oyster Bay to Los Angeles (U.S. 60, 150, 50, 40, 6)

Old Spanish Trail—St. Augustine, Florida, to San Diego (U.S. 70, 80, 90)

Pikes Peak Ocean-to-Ocean Highway—New York to Los Angeles (U.S. 36)

Theodore Roosevelt International Highway—Portland, Maine, to Portland, Oregon (U.S. 2, 302)

Victory Highway—New York to San Francisco (U.S. 1, 40, 83)

Yellowstone Trail—Boston to Seattle (U.S. 20, 12, 10)

NORTH-SOUTH NATIONAL TRAILS

Atlantic Highway—Fort Kent, Maine, to Miami (U.S. 1)

Dixie Highway—Chicago to Miami (U.S. 136, 31, 150, 31W)

Evergreen Highway—Portland, Oregon, to El Paso, Texas (U.S. 99, 10, 97, 410, 30, 30N, 91, 66)

Jackson Highway—Chicago to New Orleans (U.S. 51, 45)

Jefferson Highway—Winnipeg, Manitoba, to New Orleans (U.S. 71)

Jefferson Davis Highway—Washington, D.C., to Mobile, Alabama (U.S. 29, 31)

King of Trails Highway—Winnipeg to Brownsville, Texas (U.S. 75, 73, 73E, 50, 73W, 77, 81, 196)

Meridian Highway—Winnipeg to Houston (U.S. 81)

North-South National Bee-Line Highway—Chicago to New Orleans (U.S. 31, 41)

Ocean Highway—New York to Miami (U.S. 13, 17)

Pacific Highway—Vancouver to San Diego (U.S. 99, 40, 101)

WESTERN REGIONAL TRAILS

Arrowhead Trail—Salt Lake City to Los Angeles (U.S. 91)

California-Banff Bee Line—Cranbrook, B.C., to Los Angeles (U.S. 97)

Colorado Gulf Highway—Denver to Galveston, Texas (U.S. 85, 385, 370, 81, 181)

National Park to Park Highway—Loop (U.S. 99, 40, 2, 66, 50, 85)

New Santa Fe Trail—Kansas City to Los Angeles (U.S. 50, 350, 85, 66)

Caution and warning signs, on the other hand, featured black lettering on a yellow background. Most were diamond-shaped, although railroad crossing signs were circular and stop signs were octagonal. Stop signs originally featured yellow backgrounds, too, sometimes with horizontal lines above and below the injunction to stop. Red was long the standard color for stop signs in California, and the rest of the nation followed suit in 1954, by which time durable red paint became more widely available. (That same year, yield signs in the shape of an inverted triangle were added to the mix, but they were originally yellow, too. It wasn't until 1971 that the design changed to a white triangle inside a thick red border, with the word "yield" spelled out in red lettering at the center.)

The first signs on El Camino Real—where the two auto clubs took over maintenance of the iconic bells in 1921— were yellow-and-blue diamonds that featuring the auto club logo, but these were replaced by the familiar black-and-white shields in 1928. The diamonds disappeared as well, yielding to the standard rectangular shape.

State routes were signed with black lettering on white backgrounds, too, but the markers featured a grizzly bear silhouette and were shaped like a spade in honor of the state's gold rush heritage. The shape endured, but the bear symbol was eliminated and the color scheme changed in 1964 to white lettering on a green background.

Not all signage along the nation's highways is informational. Or cautionary.

The system of standardized signs and markers adopted by the American Association of Highway Officials in November 1925 in Detroit called for the following in its subsequent report, published in January 1927:

SHAPE

"An **octagonal** sign is used to indicate 'Stop,' where for any reason such action is necessary.

"The **diamond** shaped signs, commonly called 'Slow' signs, are used to indicate any condition inherent in the road itself requiring a slow speed and caution on the part of the driver.

"The **circular** sign is used as an advance warning at railroad grade crossings only.

"The **square** shaped signs, commonly called 'Caution' signs, are used to indicate any condition requiring **caution** that is not inherent in the road itself, but which is due to contiguous or adjacent conditions which often are also intermittent.

"**Rectangular** shaped signs of various dimensions are used to carry directions, information and restrictions of use or benefit to the driver.

"The **arrow shaped** direction sign may be substituted for the rectangular direction sign.

"**Route markers**, to carry the designations assigned to various routes, are of various distinctive designs. For United States Highways the standard outline of

the official shield of the United States is used. On State roads that are not U.S. Highways the several States use other appropriate devices, such as the Covered Wagon in Nebraska, the conventional Sunflower in Kansas, the Indian Head in North Dakota, the North Star in Minnesota, the Triangle in Wisconsin, the Keystone in Pennsylvania, etc. Several States including Arkansas, Illinois, Indiana, Ohio and South Dakota, use the State outline as a distinctive marker."

COLOR

"All signs of a **precautionary** character, including the circular railroad sign, the octagon stop sign, the diamond slow sign, and the square caution signs have black designs on a yellow background.

"All **direction**, **information** and **restriction** signs are black on a white background, except the **Rest Station** Sign is white on a green background.

"**Route Markers** have black copy on a white background (A few of the States are exceptions to this.)"

SYMBOLS

"The symbols used on the various signs are those for railroad grade crossings, both for single and multiple tracks, for left and right curves and turns; for reversed curves and turns; the arrow on the directional sign and the arrow which accompanies the route marker."

Most of it is selling something, and you'll see plenty of evidence along U.S. 101 even today. Retail advertising along highways takes a couple of different forms. There are, of course, billboards, which direct motorists to a destination farther down the road or promote something unrelated to the highway—a TV show, a law firm, a religious message. The list is as varied as the number of people who decide to buy that piece of roadside space. Then there are businesses located right along the highway that erect signs letting drivers know they're there.

MEET DR. PIERCE

The first American billboards were *on* the highway rather than beside it. Traveling circuses would affix large posters to the side of horse-drawn vehicles that preceded them into each new town, announcing their arrival.

Even today, some roadside billboards are plastered on existing structures, such as this Martinelli's ad on a silo near Gilroy along U.S. 101.

Just as early route markers were painted on trees and fence posts, some early advertisers used existing structures to convey their message. They had to be big to attract attention, so the most likely candidates were barns and silos. In 2016, a silo next to northbound 101 near Gilroy advertised Martinelli's sparkling cider. There's even an old water tower on Highway 99 in Ripon that has long carried a billboard for a local radio station.

Billboards started out as board specifically reserved for bills—printed notices or advertisements. The word is related to the Latin *bulla*, meaning an official seal on a document (such as a papal bull). Perhaps more familiar are the injunctions to "post no bills" seen in public places where advertisers are wont to affix fliers, stickers, or handbills. In the late 19th century, such activities were so common—especially among theater and circus promoters—that they spawned fierce competition for the limited space available. "Fierce" isn't an overstatement. One promoter would slap his handbill on top of another, and the poster of the first bill would retaliate in kind. If one promoter caught a rival in the act, it often came to blows.

Billboards offered several advantages: If you owned or rented the space, no one could complain about you cluttering up public spaces, and your rivals couldn't (at least legally) paper over your ad with one of their own. Billboards also provided better exposure. They could be made larger and raised higher—some were erected on the top of buildings—to increase visibility.

As time went on, billboards were used less by entertainers such as theater and circus owners, and became increasingly the province of general retailers. *Billboard* magazine, which became the recognized manual of top-40 music in the 20th century, started out as a trade publication for—you guessed it—billboards. As the handbill and entertainment industries drifted apart, the magazine moved toward entertainment until it eventually focused on music charts and trends.

The outdoor advertising industry, meanwhile, was diversifying.

Billboards weren't the only form of advertising to be seen in the open air. As highway travel became more common, advertisers saw an array of opportunities to catch motorists' attention. Some approached property owners and offered them a fee to allow an ad on the side of their barn. It was an easy way to make some extra cash, especially during hard times, and many farm owners took the advertisers up on their offers. Silos made perfect stand-ins for beer or soda cans, and barns could be seen from far off down the road. Even today, one barn ad in Sonoma County on U.S. 101 touts "Dr. Pierce's Medical Discovery," with the additional words "For Your …" painted over with new coat of white paint proclaiming it "A Real Tonic." You can see it as you travel south on 101 near Cloverdale.

That barn was one of several such "barnboards" for Dr. Pierce's cure-all pills and tonics painted in large white lettering on barns across the country—some of which still survive. Out west, they showed up in such locales as Toledo, Washington; Logan, Utah; and Cottage Grove, Oregon. A typical deal, for the barn in Logan, called for the owner to receive $25 the first year and $10 in rent each subsequent year.

But just who was this Dr. Pierce?

Born in 1840, Ray Vaughn Pierce was just one of many opportunists peddling miracle elixirs and cure-all potions in the days before the FDA regulated medical products. In other words: he was your typical snake-oil salesman. Whether he was an actual doctor is open to dispute, although he supposedly obtained a degree from the Eclectic Medical College of Cincinnati around the time of the Civil War. It and other schools like it thrived in the latter half of the 19th century, specializing in the development of herbal medicine, as did Dr. Pierce.

Described by one historian as Buffalo's favorite doctor, Pierce developed a licorice-flavored tonic called "Golden Medical Discovery" that was supposed to give men "an appetite like a cow-boy's and the digestion of an ostrich." It contained, according to one ad, "a very concentrated, vegetable extract," and its ingredients apparently included such things as valerian root, bloodroot, mandrake, goldenseal, and black cherry bark. The good doctor marketed his elixir as a miracle cure for all sorts of ailments, ranging from laryngitis to indigestion, from blood disease to ulcers.

"It does not nauseate or debilitate the stomach or system, as other cough medicines do, but, on the contrary, improves digestion, strengthens the stomach, builds up solid flesh when reduced below a healthy standard by disease, and invigorates and cleanses the entire system," one ad declared. It even addressed the age-old problem of irregularity: "As a remedy for Torpor of the Liver … and for habitual Constipation of the Bowels, it has no equal."

Pierce produced other herbal remedies, including Dr. Pierce's Anuric Tablets, Dr. Pierce's Vaginal Tablets, Dr. Pierce's Pleasant Pellets, and Dr. Pierce's Extract of Smart-Weed. At the height of his success, around the turn of the century, he was sending out some 2 million bottles by mail each year.

Dr. Pierce painted ads for his tonics, elixirs, and miracle cures on barns across the country. Many have disappeared, but this one on a winery off 101 in Cloverdale remains.

**This big red barn off 101 near Prunedale advertises a flea market
and antique mall at that location.**

Some barns he rented for advertising promoted "Dr. Pierce's Favorite Prescription" as a tonic for "weak women"—a potion that supposedly cured conditions caused by "the feminine complaint" and even addressed the problem of infertility. A plaque in Utah proclaims that, "according to the locals, it contained 'a baby in every bottle'" and quotes an ad boasting "there are not three cases in a hundred of women's peculiar diseases that Dr. Pierce's Favorite Prescription will not cure."

Such grandiose claims today would never pass muster with the truth-in-advertising crowd, and they elicited skepticism even during the tonic's heyday. *Collier's Magazine* proclaimed Pierce a quack, and *Ladies' Home Journal* accused him of using opium, alcohol, and digi-

talis in his Favorite Prescription. When lab tests came back negative for each of those alleged ingredients, Pierce sued the magazine for libel and won a $16,000 judgment.

Pierce's other endeavors included serving one term in Congress and running a hotel for invalids whose guests may have included the Sundance Kid and Etta Place.

Pierce himself died in 1914, and his son, Dr. Valentine Mott Pierce, carried on the family business. Despite its successes, however, Pierce's company began to fall out of favor as scrutiny of herbal remedies increased in the 20th century. The era of snake-oil salesman and herbal cure-alls was fading: The Eclectic Medical College in Cincinnati closed its doors in 1939, and the company founded by Dr. Pierce went out of business shortly there-

The following testimonial for Dr. Pierce's Favorite Prescription appeared in a newspaper under the heading "Female Weakness":

Mrs. William Hoover, of Bellville, Richland Co., Ohio, writes, 'I had been a great sufferer from 'female weakness;'

I tried three doctors; they did me no good; I thought I was an invalid forever. But I heard of Dr. Pierce's Favorite Prescription, and then I wrote to him and he told me just how to take it. I took eight bottles. I now feel entirely well. I could stand on my feet only a short time, and now I do all my work for my family of five.

Billboards compete for attention on this hillside along 101 in northern California.

after. Still, many of those old barn ads remain visible to passing motorists in the 21st century. No one's paying rent on them these days, but they endure as a reminder of a simpler time, when Americans were a little more naïve and barn side billboards paid the kind of dividends Super Bowl commercials do today.

BILLBOARDS GALORE

As more miles of roadway were laid down and more cars began to hit the pavement, advertisers were no longer content with renting barns and silos to promote their products. It wasn't long before they began to put up their own signs by the side of the road.

Even then, however, billboard advertising was nothing new. Outdoor advertising dated back to the mid-19th century, and by the 1890s, each state had its own association of "bill posters," as they were known.

The era of the billboard had arrived.

And it wasn't long before billboards were going up everywhere. Only a few months after the Rincon Sea Level Road opened in Ventura County, the breathtaking view of the Pacific Ocean was marred by what one commentator called "bill-board fever."

The *Ventura Free Press* declared that no fewer than 57 varieties of advertising were being put up along the road. "There is nothing quite so disfiguring to the landscape as huge and glaring signboards and each advertiser is anxious that his particular sign should be the biggest," the newspaper complained. "It will only be a matter of time, if the sign-board fiends are allowed to continue, until the mountains on one side of the road are shut out of view. Then no doubt the signs will be placed on buoys in the sea off shore and thus shut out the marine view.

"For goodness sake, stop it."

But California had little recourse. A 1929 report asked what legislation had been enacted to regulate billboards in the state, then answered its own question with two words: Hardly any. Only two limits existed at the time: Signs couldn't be placed on state property "without lawful permission," or on private property without the owner's or lessee's consent. Placing a sign on or over a state highway without a permit was a public nuisance treated as a misdemeanor. But there was no provision, for instance, that would keep billboards from obscuring a driver's line of sight at an intersection.

To their credit, some billboard companies recognized it was in their best interest to put on a good face. Attractive billboards not only addressed complaints about unsightliness, they were more likely to draw motorists' attention.

Foster and Kleiser, a company founded in 1901 that came to dominate the western roadside, was among those to take the lead, forming its own art department in 1917. One of its designs featured white latticework below the display space that looked like something you'd see in an upper-class suburban garden. Narrow, rectangular faux columns on either side appeared to support a top crossbeam. The lattice aprons served a dual function: Not only were they aesthetically pleasing, they hid the posts holding up the sign—and, sometimes, obscured less pleasing roadside sights such as garages, garbage dumps, and scrap yards.

Other billboards featured art deco framing, three-dimensional lettering, and cutout images that rose above the rectangular frame.

Foster and Kleiser even went so far as to design "sign parks," complete with benches, drinking fountains, and flower gardens where "nature's gorgeous colors" supplemented "the work of America's foremost poster artists." Neoclassical goddess-like figures they called "lizzies"—featured on numerous company signs from 1923 to 1931—adorned the columns of these signs, holding floral bouquets that matched the flowers growing in the parks' gardens.

A billboard along Highway 39, near 101 in Orange County, advertises Christmas shopping at Knott's Berry Farm—and 50 acres of free parking—in 1962. *Orange County Archives.*

Despite such nods toward aesthetics, the proliferation of billboards continued to vex drivers who felt as though they were driving through a forest of them on stretches of highway such as U.S. 101 through Orange County.

Finally, in 1958, Congress got around to adopting a law to regulate billboards. The Bonus Act offered states an incentive to limit roadside advertising within 660 feet of the new interstate highway system. It got its name because it offered states a half-percent bonus on construction costs for segments of highway that controlled outdoor advertising.

Then along came Lady Bird Johnson. The first lady considered beautification one of her signature goals, and she began a campaign to pull the nation together through the Vietnam War era: "Ugliness is so grim," she commented. "A little beauty, something that is lovely, I think, can help create harmony which will lessen tensions."

Johnson began a campaign that resulted in thousands of flowers being planted in the nation's capital. She urged schoolchildren to engage in projects to "clean up, fix up and plant up" their communities. Meanwhile, she began lobbying to replace the junkyards, "a solid diet of billboards," and various other eyesores that lined the nation's highways with a tableau of blossoms and green space.

Billboard companies pushed back against the first lady's Highway Beautification Act, forcing a compromise under which billboards were banned "except in those areas of commercial and industrial use." Another amendment required that companies be compensated for removing billboards already in place.

But the act didn't work the way it was supposed to. Loopholes such as the compensation clause allowed some old billboards to remain in place while new signs went up in ever-expanding industrial zones. Another amendment in 1978 required that billboard companies be paid if their signs were taken down for violating state laws or local ordinances—not just for failing to meet the federal standard. As a result, more than 40 years after the Highway Beautification Act became law, there were more billboards along the nation's highways than before—nearly half a million as of 2007—while some 70,000 of those that violated the law had yet to be torn down.

A 1995 *Los Angeles Times* article marking the 30-year anniversary of the act decried the fact that "an island of litter and weed" greeted motorists on the Hollywood Freeway as they entered Los Angeles. Drivers on other freeways found their eyes assaulted by images of "hot-air balloons, high-flying whales and inflatable Godzillas." The writer began the piece by remarking that it had been 30 years since Lady Bird Johnson had declared war on highway ugliness.

He punctuated that introduction with two words: "We lost."

Neon Nights

Neon signs hit the road in North America about the same time the federal highway system came into being. The system of producing a bright glow involved passing voltage through a tube containing neon gas, held there in a state well below atmospheric pressure. The process was first used just before the turn of the 20th century, but it wasn't until 1923 that it made its U.S. debut at a Packard dealership in Los Angeles. Earle C. Anthony bought two

The Noyo in Willits, built in 1939, still lights up its neon sign after dark.

of the signs, with letters spelling out "Packard" (naturally) for $1,250 each.

Three years later—the same year U.S. 101 and the rest of the federal highway system were commissioned—a new technique enabled sign-makers to create lettering in various different colors by coating the inside of the tubes.

Motels loved neon, especially in Las Vegas, where the myriad lights created an otherworldly glow worthy of Area 51 up the road. But all sorts of businesses used it, from burger joints to bars to even sporting goods stores like Bucksport on the west side of 101 in Eureka. There, a glowing fish appears to leap off a sign that proclaims the business has been around since 1948.

That's the era when neon reached its zenith, as signs multiplied into the 1950s before gradually giving way to cheaper signage such as translucent plastic casings that could be lit up from inside. Such signs became typical of gas stations, for example, as well as many other businesses. But neon didn't die. In fact, it enjoyed a renaissance of sorts among merchants seeking to stand out and play upon motorists' nostalgia for a simpler time. Ice cream shops, theaters, and bars in particular continue to make use of it. You can still find the aforementioned cocktail glasses at various points along western highways, which were once headquarters for movie theaters of both the walk-in and drive-in varieties.

Drive along the old "business" alignments of 101 today, and you'll see plenty of theaters still showing first-run movies, their neon names blazing colorful trails across the night sky. Redwood Theatres built both the Noyo in Willits, in 1939, and the Ukiah up the road on Old 101 a few years later. (The Noyo's actually on Commercial Street just a few steps east of U.S. 101.) Each has a distinctive neon sign, with the vertical pylon outside the now-Regal cinema in Ukiah enjoying protected status. The theater itself was built with a single screen in streamline modern style, although the interior was later redesigned as a six-screen multiplex.

The small Garberville Theatre has a vertical neon sign of its own and is noteworthy in that it's still open after more than eight decades on Redwood Drive—the later-bypassed Business 101. Thomas and Margaret Tobin had opened the Garberville Inn on the street in 1923, when it was still just a dirt road and not yet a federal highway. A year later, to heighten the appeal of their establishment, the Tobins built a parking garage for patrons to keep the dust from accumulating on their vehicles. It was a smart move, but it proved unnecessary in the long run: Six years after the garage went up, road workers paved Redwood Drive with oil and gravel. Suddenly, the garage was a luxury the Tobins no longer needed.

As a result, they decided to sell it to a gentleman named William George Cooke Jr., who set about converting the building into a movie hall where first-run motion pictures could be shown. He installed 320 seats with spring cushions and included seating for children near the front, as well as box seats at the rear. Local merchants

such as Piggly Wiggly and the Redwood Inn took out ads in the *Redwood Record* hailing the new theater's grand opening on August 2, 1935, with the Garberville Mercantile anticipating Leonard Nimoy's trademark invocation on *Star Trek* three decades later by declaring: "May It Live Long and Prosper." The Eel River Café across the street added its congratulations, too. (Speaking of neon, the café's sign is one that shouldn't be missed on the old Redwood Highway: Its neon-lit chef can be seen "flipping pancakes" after dark, as the hotcakes flicker on and off in succession above his raised skillet.)

The first feature shown at the Garberville Theatre was a Will Rogers movie called *Life Begins at 40*, a sadly ironic title considering Rogers would die in a plane crash just 13 days after the film's Garberville premier. The theater would be open Friday through Monday nights, with two showings each day, at 7:15 and 9 p.m.

Farther up the highway, the Fortuna Theatre opened in 1938. Like the Ukiah and Noyo cinemas, it was the work of the Redwood Theatres company, and it's also been converted into a multiplex. The vertical neon sign out front went dark for 35 years beginning in 1965, but the theater was restored at the dawn of the new millennium, when 500 feet of new neon tubing was installed and the sign lit up the night once again on Main Street—the business alignment of 101 through town.

The Towne 3 Theatre, a renovated 1920s movie house on an old alignment of 101 called the Alameda, is still open in San Jose, complete with a fancy neon-accented marquee. The road curves westward and becomes Santa Clara Street farther south, and there you'll find another theater promoted by neon—the now-closed Mexico, which opened in 1949 as the Mayfair and featured a space-age spire encircled by a series of neon rings.

If walk-in theaters were common sights along old alignments of the federal highways, drive-ins were even more prominent. You didn't need to build a separate sign to attract drivers' attention: The screens themselves served as their own billboards. All a theater owner had to do was set up a screen so its backside faced the highway, then plaster the face of it with colorful neon and, in some cases, eye-catching scenes such as the neon mural on the now long-gone Valley Drive-in Theatre in Montclair on old Highway 99. Built in 1948, it would have been

Towne Cinemas in San Jose sits along The Alameda, an old alignment of 101.

more appropriate to El Camino Real: The mural showed a Native American watching from a mound as a driver and two passengers in an oxcart cross a stream. In the background, a priest walks out to meet them from the Santa Barbara Mission. The mural featured more than 2,500 feet of neon tubing, and if that wasn't enough of a draw, the owners added a display of primates called Monkeyland for the younger set to enjoy as they entertained themselves in a playground.

Why haven't you seen many of those big screens along California's highways? For one thing, those big screens were built along older alignments before the road builders bypassed the cities. For another, most of them are gone now. In the latter years of the 20th century, the number of drive-ins began to shrink dramatically. Cable TV and increasingly congested highways combined to make watching a movie from the relative discomfort of

one's car—complete with that faraway sounding radio sound—far less attractive as the years wore on. Why take your girlfriend to make out at the drive-in when you could enjoy each other's company in private while taking in a next-to-new release on HBO via your big-screen TV?

The Valley Drive-In was torn down in 1980, and others fell to the wrecking ball, as well. At that point, there were still 2,500 drive-ins across the country; three-and-a-half decades later, fewer than 350 remained. The 101 Drive-In in Ventura, just off the highway on Telephone Road, opened in 1948 and added a third screen in 1969, but it closed before the new millennium after a half century in business and was torn down in 2001.

Still, a couple of drive-ins remained open along the Central Coast segment of U.S. 101 as of this writing. The Hi-Way Drive-In in Santa Maria opened in 1959 between the highway's old (Broadway) and new (freeway) highway alignments on Santa Maria Way. Although the single screen doesn't bear any neon signage, there's a marquee out front that's accented in red-letter neon after the sun goes down. Then, up the highway about 30 minutes in San Luis Obispo, there's the Sunset Drive-In, whose name is emblazoned in large, red letters on the back of a screen that faces the highway and is visible from both directions. Built in 1950, it's still operating 66 years later, but it isn't the most impressive piece of neon on that stretch of highway. That honor belongs to the sign for the Madonna Inn, which is less than a mile away. It features the inn's name, in all-capital white neon, against a pink backdrop that's just below an intricate neon portrayal of a horse-drawn carriage in red, white, and yellow. Also in neon, a third section of the sign advertises the Copper Café's "pastries" and "steak house." Then, of course, there's the standard vacancy sign in red neon.

Some of the neon treasures are vanishing as old motels and retail stores close, giving way to industrial complexes and other businesses that don't have to advertise their presence on the highway. When I drove past the Western Motel on El Camino Real in Santa Clara, its eye-catching cactus sign was still there, but holes were all that remained where the neon lights used to be.

Still, neon continues to be a very real presence along the highway, reminding travelers of a simpler time when bright lights up ahead meant a place to stop for the night, a (sometimes) friendly bartender with a cold beer, or a place to drop in and see the latest Bogart or Marilyn Monroe flick. You don't have to drive off to Vegas to see it; you just have to know where to look.

Muffler Men

Not all roadside markers relied primarily—or even at all—on lettering. Arrows pointing the way to this or that roadside attraction have long been favorites, many of them adorned in dazzling colors. They tell the motorist to "stop here!" without saying it in so many words. One of the most famous arrows among highway buffs is the huge red one that's the focal point of Roy's Motel and Café, a lonely stop in Amboy along old Route 66. But there are plenty of others, as well, on motels, cinemas, and liquor stores (still a frequent sight along old highway alignments, from a time before public service campaigns against drinking and driving). In the 1950s and '60s especially, a standard neon cocktail glass—often tipped to one side and accented with a swizzle stick skewering an olive—adorned many a roadside bar or restaurant.

The holes in the Western Motel's cactus sign in Santa Clara show where its neon used to be.

Then there were the statues: larger-than-life human and animal figures enlisted as mascots for diner chains, auto shops, and golf courses, to name a few. When Bob's Big Boy wanted to attract travelers, the restaurants put up giant signs accented by a circle of neon that appeared to rotate as it blinked on and off around the outer edge. But the chain went further: It began to station statues of a big boy at their front door to welcome guests. A *very* big boy.

The character was originally set to be called "Fat Boy," until a six-year-old youngster named Richard Woodruff walked into Bob's Pantry, a 10-seat coffee counter owned by Bob Wian in

The Big Boy serves up a huge (inedible) burger outside Bob's in Burbank, where the Beatles once stopped for a bite.

The fiberglass big boys came in three sizes: 4-foot statues were used inside restaurants where zoning restrictions didn't allow them outside the front door. There was also a 6-foot model and a big 12-footer, such as the one outside the Burbank location on Riverside Drive, a little over a mile from the 101. That restaurant, the oldest one still operating, was built in 1948, and you can sit in a booth there that's marked with a plaque where the Beatles once enjoyed a meal.

Bob's Big Boy statues were pretty much all the same, with the boy puffing out his chest behind those checkerboard suspenders and hoisting one of those double-deck hamburgers in his right hand. One in Norco, off Interstate 15 in southern California, adds a little extra character to his wardrobe in the form of boots and a cowboy hat.

But the big boys weren't the only statues by the side of the road.

Another burger joint, A&W, commissioned International Fiberglass to create a whole family of burger lovers (known, naturally, as the Burger Family) to serve as mascots for its restaurant chain in 1963. Each member of the "family" corresponded to a similarly sized burger on the menu: the Baby Burger was a bare-bones affair, with a small patty and ketchup on an unseeded bun. The Mama Burger added an onion slice, pickles, and mustard to the recipe, enlarged the beef patty, and added sesame seeds to the bun. The Teen Burger, on top of all that, had bacon and cheese, while the Papa Burger was a Mama Burger with a second patty.

There were other family members, too (an Uncle, Grandpa, and Buddy), but the four "nuclear" family members were the templates for the fiberglass figures, which weren't as big as the Big Boy but struck a similar pose—holding a burger aloft, albeit in their left hand instead of their right. Often, they were placed on top of restaurants for maximum visibility. The Papa Burger, standing over eight feet tall, and the Teen Burger statues each held a mug of root beer in its right hand, but Papa often performed solo: Some locations only wanted to shell out the $600 it cost for the single statue rather than pay the $1,800 price tag for the entire set.

The Burger Family mascots gave way, in 1974, to a "Great Root Bear" promotion, and the chain urged

Glendale. According to legend, Wian greeted the kid, who had arrived to sweep the place, with, "Hey there, big boy." He thought the name was catchy, so he applied it to his signature double-decker burger—reportedly the first of its kind.

The original character, conceived in the late 1930s, was drawn to resemble Woodruff, with checkerboard overalls and no shirt. It was only later, in the mid-1950s, that the cartoon mascot's look was updated by a designer from Warner Brothers' studios, just one town over from that original restaurant, in Burbank. That could explain the wide-eyed look the Big Boy shares with some of the famous Looney Tunes characters. The new big boy was a little more modest, sporting a T-shirt under his overalls, and wore a '50s-style pompadour curl over his forehead.

local operators to put the fiberglass family in moth-balls. Nevertheless, some of the statues survived and can still be seen along highways across the country—often surviving as mascots for independent burger joints rather than A&W. There's a Papa Burger statue atop Winkins' Drive-In off Business 99 in Selma (a former A&W location), and a Teen Burger statue stands guard at the 41 Café off State Route 41 in Lemoore.

Along old Highway 101, a Papa Burger greets customers at one of three Angelo's Burgers locations in Oceanside.

Not all the fiberglass figures were people. Sinclair Oil set up green brontosaurus statues at some of its service stations, some of them made by the same outfit—International Fiberglass—that churned out the Burger Family figures. Indeed, the company kept itself busy throughout the '60s, also creating statues, commonly known as "Muffler Men," that popped up alongside high-ways all across the country.

The fiberglass statues didn't just advertise mufflers at auto shops, although you can still see one doing precisely that at Babe's Lighting and Muffler on the Alameda (Old 101) in San Jose. The blue-shirted statue's head is inclined slightly down and forward, gazing at what's in his hands: a muffler, naturally. But the mold used for the statue was versatile. The muffler could easily be replaced by a golf club, for instance, or an ax that transformed the statue into a good likeness of Paul Bunyan. Just paint on a beard, and voilà! The legendary lumberjack was ready to go. In fact, the first figure created from the mold was designed not as a Muffler Man, but as old Paul himself, for PB Café on Route 66 in Flagstaff, Arizona.

That was in 1962, when Bob Prewitt still owned the company called Prewitt Fiberglass. Steve Dashew bought it from him a year later, changed the name to International Fiberglass, and kept churning out those Muffler Men. They were even more expensive than the Burger Family (they were bigger, after all, at 20 feet tall), costing between $1,800 and $2,800 each, with a discount for bulk purchases.

You could modify them as needed for whatever sort of business you wanted to promote. One of the giants was created for a burger/ice cream stop called Frostie Freeze (home of the Hickory Burger) along the Pacific

A Muffler Man serves as the mascot for Babe's Lighting and Muffler on the Alameda in San Jose.

Coast Highway in Malibu. The building was built in 1949, the highway was signed as the 101 Alternate, and the statue was added later. He was decked out in a white outfit and a chef's hat, holding—instead of a golf club, ax, or muffler—a gigantic hamburger in his outstretched hands.

Time passed, though, and the shop eventually changed hands to become a burrito place known as La Salsa. No need for a 20-foot-tall burger chef looming over the business? No problem. Just add a sombrero, a stylish mustache, and a colorful blanket over the shoulder, and you've got a "taco guy" mascot for your restaurant instead. (The hamburger, of course, had to go, and was replaced by an empty platter equipped with spotlights shining up on the now-much-darker-skinned face of our transformed burgermeister.)

The Muffler Man mold was also used as the basis for pirates, a gold miner, and even a clown. The arms were adjusted for a Native American statue, and a different head was added for some that took on the look of *Mad Magazine* mascot Alfred E. Neuman. A separate mold was used for the statue's feminine counterpart, known as Miss Uniroyal because it was used to promote the tire company. She looked a little like Jackie Kennedy, her left hand raised in a mirror of Lady Liberty and holding anything from a torch to a sandwich platter to beach ball. She might have worn a waitress's outfit, a cheerleader uniform, or a bikini.

While the Muffler Men and Women were ubiquitous roadside fixtures in the 1960s, their heyday was relatively short. Demand started falling in the early '70s, with more and more freeway bypasses going in. Dershaw got married, and his priorities changed: He refocused his attention on the construction business. He tried to sell the Muffler Man molds, but found no takers, so they languished in a construction equipment yard. The last statues were made around the beginning of 1976, and when the yard was sold in the middle of that year, the molds were destroyed.

It was the end of an era to which scattered Muffler Men like Babe in San Jose remain as a testament along highways such as Old 101.

This Muffler Man once served up burgers but was later converted into a sombrero-wearing mascot for a Mexican restaurant on State Route 1 (formerly U.S. 101 Alternate) in Malibu.

3
WORKING ROAD

A pea picker uses his vehicle as a makeshift home in February 1936 off Highway 101 at Nipomo.
Dorothea Lange, Library of Congress.

U.S. 101 wasn't the conveyor belt for migrant labor that 66 and 99 were, but that doesn't diminish its role as an artery for farmworkers who plied their trade on either side of the asphalt. In places like the Salinas Valley, known as "America's Salad Bowl," and the Nipomo Mesa farther south, laborers still work harvesting crops like lettuce, tomatoes, spinach, and strawberries.

Take a detour from the modern freeway up the old alignment of 101 known as Cattlemen Road between San Ardo and San Lucas, and you might notice an abandoned farm labor camp toward the northern end of this now lightly traveled road. There's a chain-link fence around it now, but peer beyond it, and you'll see a collection of one- and two-room wooden structures with peeling red paint, no glass in the windows, and woodstove chimneys.

I asked the owners of the property how long it had been there, but they couldn't tell me. From the look of it, it had been abandoned for years.

Travel north on the highway toward Chualar, and you'll reach a placed called the Bracero Memorial Highway, site of what the highway patrol described at the time as "the biggest single fatal vehicle accident of any kind in the history of California." The National Safety Council said it was the worst bus-train accident in U.S. history.

**An abandoned migrant camp sits along Cattlemen Road (old U.S. 101)
in the Salinas Valley, south of San Lucas.**

The collision in September 1963 took the lives of 32 celery pickers aboard the bus, which was carrying them home to a Salinas-area labor camp following a day in the fields. It was coming up on 4:30 in the afternoon, and the workers' day had concluded just less than 10 minutes earlier. The man behind the wheel, Francisco Espinoza, was driving toward 101 along a private road owned by Merrill Farms when he came to an unguarded railroad crossing.

He stopped.

But when he looked right to check the tracks, all he could see was the man in the passenger seat: the foreman, Arturo Galindo, who was busy filling out timecards.

Meanwhile, a Southern Pacific freight train hauling 71 open-top cars of sugar beets was barreling northward at 65 mph. It had left Gonzales at 4:15 p.m., and engineer Robert E. Cripe sounded his whistle as the bus came into view. He didn't reduce speed, though, seeing that the driver had what appeared to be a clear view of the tracks. Surely, he would see the train coming.

But he didn't.

And when Espinoza pulled the bus out onto the tracks, there was no way the engineer could stop in time.

"Bodies just flew all over the place," said Tony Vasquez, 29, who saw the accident from a lettuce field near the crossing. "Two of the men died in my arms."

The train continued for a full mile before Cripe could bring it to a stop.

"The entire front of the northbound locomotive was covered in sheet metal," said Bob McVay, a local radio station owner who arrived just as the first of 15 ambulances got there. "The metal formerly was the side of the bus."

Bits of clothing, Mexican straw hats and shoes, were embedded in the metal.

"One body was hooked under the engine," Monterey Coroner Christopher Hill Jr. said. "Shoes, hats and cutting knives were all around. Everywhere, you could hear the injured moaning."

Twenty-two occupants of the shattered bus died right there by the rail lines; the rest perished after being rushed by ambulance to Salinas hospitals. Bodies and clothes were so badly tangled in the wreckage that the coroner had a hard time identifying any of them in the crash's immediate aftermath.

"We found some passports in the wreckage, but I couldn't in good conscience say we've made any positive identification," he said. "The clothing was all mixed up. It was a hodgepodge, and you can't tell much from the faces."

Espinoza, the only man not hurt, was charged with manslaughter but later acquitted.

At the time, farm labor camps in California housed an estimated 49,000 migrants toiling for wages of $1 to $2.50 an hour.

"They don't fit the picture of the lazy Mexican sitting in a village with a hat on his head," said John Murray of the Federal Bureau of Employment Security. "They're dedicated and willing to work."

But far too many died in accidents similar to the one that claimed those 32 lives near Chualar. According to Don Miller's book *They Saved the Crops*, more than 1,200 farm transportation crashes claimed 169 lives in 1962 and 1963 alone. The year after the Chualar accident, the bracero program was discontinued.

An itinerant worker walks along U.S. 101 near San Luis Obispo in 1939. *Dorothea Lange, Library of Congress, public domain.*

LETTUCE STRIKE

It was far from the first time farm laborers had encountered hardship in the Salinas Valley.

Not long before he completed perhaps his best-known work, *The Grapes of Wrath*, John Steinbeck took aim at the Salinas lettuce industry—and its treatment of farmworkers—in a book titled *L'Affaire Lettuceburg*.

Although a work of fiction, it was based on a real event: the Salinas lettuce strike of 1936. And it hit close to home. Steinbeck was born in Salinas, and his experiences there helped shape his outlook, despite what might be described as an acerbity toward the town.

"Salinas was never a pretty town," he wrote in the 1955 piece for *Holiday* magazine. "It took a darkness from the swamps. The high gray fog hung over it and the ceaseless wind blew up the valley, cold and with a kind of desolate monotony. The mountains on both sides of the valley were beautiful, but Salinas was not and we knew it."

Whatever Steinbeck's bias against his hometown, there was no denying that it got really ugly in September of 1936, when the events that inspired *L'Affaire Lettuceburg* took place.

Tensions between growers and packing shed workers in Salinas had grown during the summer of that year, with the Fruit and Vegetable Workers' Union demanding that growers give preference in hiring to union members.

The growers refused.

Instead, they offered to meet the union's demand for a raise of five cents an hour, while making minor concessions to the union's demands concerning working periods, holiday schedules, and shed conveniences.

The union balked.

On September 5, 3,500 lettuce trimmers and packers in the Salinas-Watsonville area walked off the job and set up picket lines around 70 packing sheds in the area. The growers called it a strike; the union said it was a lockout. Whatever it was, while it proceeded peacefully at first, losses to the $10 million industry began to mount at a rate of $75,000 a day, and box makers made matters worse by joining the walkout.

The growers couldn't continue to absorb those losses for long, but they weren't about to capitulate to union demands for a closed shop, either.

As the pressure built on both sides, State Highway Patrol Chief E. Raymond Cato sent officers with radio cars to Salinas to keep U.S. 101 open in the strike area.

"We are not interested in the strike," he declared, "but there have been numerous instances of motorists being stopped to determine if they were strikebreakers, and one farmer, driving one truck was assaulted. We continue to keep the highway open and assure the free movement of traffic. If more men are needed to do this, they will be sent to Salinas. We have no other interest in the situation."

Whether that statement was true or not, the highway patrol would soon find itself in the thick of one of the nastiest strike conflicts of the era.

On September 12, the sheriffs swore in 20 special deputies to build a barbed-wire barricade around the Salinas Ice Company. One report called them deputies; another referred to them as "vigilante cowboys dressed in wild west regalia and armed with guns and lariats." Eighteen policemen and some of those highway patrol officers stood watch nearby as they went about their business. They'd be doing more than watching soon enough.

Women joined the picket line and jeered as non-union workers were brought in to work the packing sheds.

"We are going to pack lettuce and we are going to do it soon," declared Charles Brooks, secretary of the grower-shipper association, responding to fears that nearly 1,000 carloads of lettuce would mature in the week ahead and go to waste if it weren't promptly harvested. By this time, about 50 state highway patrol officers were in the area.

The union wasn't about to be intimidated, even if the hastily deputized cowboy vigilantes were prowling around like they wanted blood.

Two decades later, in an article for *Holiday* magazine titled "Always Something to Do in Salinas," Steinbeck would recall these vigilantes being under the direction of a "general" who was orchestrating their response to the pickets. This general, he wrote, "installed direct telephone lines to various stations, even had one group of telephones that were not connected to anything. He set armed guards over his suite and he put Salinas in a state of siege. He organized Vigilantes. Service-station operators, owners of small stores, clerks, bank tellers got out sporting rifles, shotguns, all the hundreds of weapons owned by small-town Americans who in the West at least, I guess, are the most heavily armed people in the world…. In addition to the riflemen, squads drilled in the streets with baseball bats. Everyone was having a good time. Stores were closed and to move about town was to be challenged every block or so by viciously weaponed people one had gone to school with."

A group of longshoremen, he said, were marching toward Salinas to join the strike, along a route marked

Hauling a trailer along U.S. 101 near King City in 1936. *Dorothea Lange, Library of Congress, public domain.*

by red flags—the color of communism. It later turned out that the flags weren't communist banners at all, but merely survey flags that had been put out by the Department of Highways. Nonetheless, Steinbeck said, the "general" had them removed and burned on Main Street for everyone to see.

The lines were squarely drawn. On the one side, Joseph Casey of the American Federation of Labor called for a national boycott on lettuce handled by the non-union workers during the strike. "Everyone is on the side of property rights and privileges," he proclaimed. "The poor devils who work in the field have no rights at all."

On the other side, Gov. Frank Merriam said he had irrefutable evidence that the strike organizers were, in fact, communists seeking to subvert the lettuce trade.

On September 15, the powder keg finally blew.

As the growers brought strikebreakers in, state highway patrol officers armed with rifles lined the roadway, warning strikers that unless they cleared a lane to the plant, they would open fire with machine guns. The growers tried to ship out truckloads of lettuce but the protesters blocked their path, cutting the ropes on one of the trucks and dumping the lettuce into the street.

It wasn't long before officers were unleashing a barrage of tear gas and "dysentery gas" over a six-block area, all the way from the business district to the packinghouses. The onslaught was so severe and the gas so pervasive that children playing in yards near the demonstration were overcome, and some of them had to be treated by physicians.

The workers responded by stoning trucks and attacking strikebreakers with rocks and hot pepper. Some accounts reported hand-to-hand conflict between strikers and authorities in the street.

The situation became so bad that sporting goods stores put padlocks on their firearms and ammunition sales areas for fear that the crowd would break in and seize their weapons.

"It looks like war to me," Chief Cato said, as Sheriff Carl Abbott rode through the streets and broadcast a call via loudspeaker for all able-bodied citizens to help bring order to the chaos. Within an hour, 400 to 500 men arrived at the county jail to volunteer. The police chief brought in uniformed reinforcements from San Jose and San Luis Obispo, while sending an urgent message to San Francisco for more tear gas bombs.

In the end, the growers and their allies triumphed. The strike was broken, and the incident gradually faded from the memories of many in the region.

But not from Steinbeck's.

Long before he wrote his biting account of "the general" waging his Battle of Salinas against the striking lettuce workers, he completed an entire book on the subject: the aforementioned *L'Affaire Lettuceburg*.

His publisher was all set to print it up when he received a letter from Steinbeck telling him to scrap it.

"This is going to be a hard letter to write," Steinbeck wrote. "This book is finished and it is a bad book and I must get rid of it. It can't be printed. It is bad because it isn't honest. Oh! these incidents all happened but — I'm not telling as much of the truth about them as I know. In satire you have to restrict the picture and I just can't do satire."

Of course, he was wrong about that. The incident continued to gnaw at him, and reasserted itself in print when he wrote "Always Something to Do in Salinas." And even as he put aside the manuscript to *L'Affaire Lettuceburg*, Steinbeck didn't give up on writing about the plight of American farm laborers: The very next year, he produced *The Grapes of Wrath*.

The Photographer and the Migrant

If Steinbeck helped define the Great Depression with his writing, Dorothea Lange did the same with her photos. And like Steinbeck, Lange's work was closely tied to the ribbon of road known as U.S. 101.

Born in 1895, Lange endured her share of hardship as a child growing up in Hoboken, New Jersey. A bout of polio in 1902 left her right leg weakened, and she walked with a limp for the rest of her life.

"I think it perhaps was the most important thing that happened to me," she would say. "It formed me, guided me, instructed me, helped me and humiliated me—all those things at once. I've never gotten over it, and I am aware of the force and power of it."

The scars weren't only physical: Throughout the rest of her childhood, her classmates teased her and called her "limpy." Then, five years after her illness, Lange's father left; he never attempted to contact her again.

After graduating from high school, Lange set herself on the course that would forge her reputation, working with Arnold Genthe, who was known for his photos of the 1906 earthquake that devastated San Francisco. And it was San Francisco that became her destination when

Dorothea Lange shot her iconic "Migrant Mother" photo of Florence Owens Thompson at a Nipomo pea pickers' camp in 1936. *Library of Congress, public domain.*

she decided to move west in 1918 after taking just a single photography class at Columbia University. She had just $140 to her name when she made the trip, but her determination and natural eye soon paid off: She found a job as a department store photofinisher and, within a year, had left to open her own portrait studio.

Her dedication to her craft was deep and unwavering.

"Pick a theme and work it to exhaustion," she once said. "The subject must be something you truly love or truly hate."

Lange found that theme on the streets, on the highways, and in the fields during the Great Depression. She found it in breadlines in the cities; among the Dust Bowl refugees who flooded into California, their cars piled high with mattresses, clothes, and whatever else would fit; in the cotton fields of the San Joaquin Valley and the fields of the Central Coast.

It was a visit to one of those fields, at a farm labor camp for pea-pickers off Highway 101 in Nipomo, that produced what would become her defining image: that of a woman named Florence Owens Thompson, the 32-year-old mother of five children, looking out wearily on the world from inside the shelter of a tent. Her still-young face is already lined with the wrinkles of worry and hardship as she gazes out on the camp, flanked by two of her children—Katherine and Ruby—clinging to each of her shoulders and hiding their faces from the camera.

Thompson and her family weren't actually residents of the camp: Their car had broken down on U.S. 101 as they headed north from Los Angeles to Watsonville, and it had been towed as far as the pea-pickers' camp in Nipomo. (Thompson's two oldest boys had headed into town to see about having it repaired.) The Thompsons weren't exactly Dust Bowl refugees, either, although she and her husband Cleo Leroy Owens, were both from Oklahoma, where they married in 1921 before moving to Oroville in California. It was there that they became victims of a different kind of tragedy: Thompson's husband died of an asthma attack in 1931 and was buried in a paupers' cemetery there.

His widow and children had become migrants in order to survive.

The work was familiar to them: She had picked cotton in Porterville and Shafter, while her husband had worked in sawmills before he died.

Lange happened to arrive at the camp just after Thompson's car had broken down. She had seen a sign on the highway, between raindrops and windshield wipers, as she headed home on a rainy day: "PEA-PICKERS CAMP." Her camera was already packed, and she was eager to get home: It would take her seven hours at 65 mph, and she had no interest in stopping to take more photos in the rain.

Or did she?

She had driven 20 miles farther down the road when she decided to turn around and go back.

"Almost without realizing what I was doing, I made a U-turn on the empty highway. I went back those 20 miles and turned off the highway at that sign, PEA-PICKERS CAMP," she said. "I was following instinct, not reason; I drove into that wet and soggy camp and parked my car like a homing pigeon.

"I saw and approached the hungry and desperate mother, as if drawn by a magnet. I do not remember how I explained my presence or my camera to her, but I do remember she asked me no questions. I made five exposures, working closer and closer from the same direction.

"I did not ask her name or her history. She told me her age, that she was 32. She said that they had been living on frozen vegetables from the surrounding fields, and birds that the children killed. She had just sold the tires from her car to buy food. There she sat in that lean-to tent with her children huddled around her, and seemed to know that my pictures might help her, and so she helped me. There was a sort of equality about it."

Lange's encounter with the Migrant Mother, as she came to be known, came a year after she had closed her portrait studio and begun working for the federal Farm Security Administration, documenting the plight of the nation's poor and destitute.

Lange's other photos of Thompson showed her with a baby cradled under one arm; in two of them, a wild-haired youngster is seen peering out from over her left shoulder. The photos told the story not only of Thompson, but of a generation uprooted by drought and economic disaster. A generation forced to leave fore-closed homes and barren farms that yielded nothing but loose earth raised up by the wind to be as fierce and thick as the locusts from a biblical plague. New wanderers in a different wilderness.

More than half a million Americans were left home-less by the Dust Bowl disaster, and the vast majority of them—Okies and Arkies, families from Texas and Kansas and Nebraska—journeyed west to pursue promises of a better life in California. What they found was more poverty, strife, and disillusionment. California didn't want them, and Los Angeles Police Chief James "Two-Gun" Davis even set up a "bum blockade" at the state line in an effort to keep them out. He sent 136 officers to

Another of Dorothea Lange's photos shows Florence Thompson's camp in 1936. *Library of Congress, public domain.*

crossing points in Arizona, Nevada, and even Oregon to turn back what he called "thieves and thugs."

Davis bragged that his officers turned back more than 11,000 before their efforts were ruled unconstitutional and the state ordered him to rein in his forces. But countless others made it through, only to face nearly as much hardship as they'd endured in the shattered homes they'd left behind. They knew how to farm, so when they reached California, they found the kind of work they knew—not on their own land, but working for starvation wages in labor camps up and down California's high-ways. Conditions were often abysmal, with poor sanita-tion bringing disease and, often, death.

I'd rather drink muddy water
Sleep out in a hollow log
Than be in California
Treated like a dirty dog.
—Lyrics to a song sung by Dust Bowl refugees

The road was long and tortuous, but some of the migrants made it out of poverty. Unfortunately, Florence Thompson wasn't one of them. She remarried, had five more children, and did a little bit of everything to take care of them—everything from tending bar to working the fields. She moved to Modesto in 1945, where she worked in a hospital. Still, she struggled to make ends meet and disappeared from public view until a reporter with *The Modesto Bee* tracked her down living in a trailer in 1978.

There's no indication she was told about Lange's quote—her statement that there was "a sort of equality about it" when the two women had met briefly at that pea-pickers' camp nearly four decades earlier. If she had been, it's doubtful she would have agreed. The photo of Thompson and her children had helped cement Lange's legacy as a photographer, but the subject of that photo was still just trying to make ends meet.

"I didn't get anything out of it. I wish she hadn't taken my picture," Thompson said in 1978. "She didn't ask my name. She said she wouldn't sell the pictures. She said she'd send me a copy. She never did."

The Library of Congress, meanwhile, sold prints of her iconic image for $120 apiece.

Five years later, as Thompson was dying of cancer, her children had to ask for donations just to help pay for her medical bills.

All those years later, and she was still struggling to survive.

Through everything, however, she never lost hope. "If I'da lost hope," she said in a 1979 interview, "this country would never have made it."

Dorothea Lange holds her camera while seated on top of her automobile in 1936. *Library of Congress, public domain.*

4

OIL'S WELL

A bird soars over the coastline at Gaviota, where U.S. 101 switches from an east-west to a north-south direction.

These days, the state of California is all about protecting its coastline—all 1,100 miles of it. The state founded its Coastal Commission to do just that. If you're wondering why some sections of coast look like one big city and others don't, chances are those "urban beaches" date back to before 1972, when the commission came into being.

Californians don't care much for offshore oil drilling, either. A blowout on an oil platform in 1969 sent 3 million gallons of crude oil pouring into the Pacific off Santa Barbara, creating a 35-mile-long spill that killed birds, fish, and marine mammals by the thousands.

The oil slick extended its tentacles as far as the Channel Islands in the nation's worst oil disaster until the Exxon Valdez spill in Alaska 20 years later.

Reacting to the devastation caused by the spill, California placed a moratorium on all new oil drilling off its coastline—a moratorium that was later extended and continues to the date of this writing. Arnold Schwarzenegger proposed lifting the ban as governor in 2009 but terminated the idea after seeing the devastation caused the Deepwater Horizon spill in the Gulf of Mexico. Schwarzenegger, an Austrian immigrant, had arrived in the United States just a year before the 1969 spill and, presumably, was paying more attention to his bodybuilding career than the environment at that point.

Other people, however, were suddenly paying very close attention—and not just to the California coastline. Images of sea mammals caked in black gunk and birds unable to fly because their feathers were steeped in oil found their way into American living rooms on the evening news. Interior Secretary Bruce Babbitt would later call the Santa Barbara oil spill "the event that galvanized public awareness of the environment and support for a decade of profound change."

Membership in the Sierra Club doubled, the first Earth Day was celebrated just over a year later, and before the spill's first anniversary, President Nixon signed the National Environmental Policy Act (which requires environmental impact reports). California added its own Environmental Quality Act shortly afterward.

The state shortly began to develop a reputation as a national leader in protecting the environment, so it's easy to forget that, for years before the Santa Barbara spill, it was a leader in oil production. In fact, the world's first offshore oil wells were built in 1896 not far from the area where that 1969 spill occurred in Santa Barbara County.

But it hasn't always been that way. Oil companies once pumped massive amounts of oil from fields on the continental shelf, just off the coastline, not to mention millions of barrels from land-based wells. Many of both were long visible from U.S. 101 and other highways, in places such as Huntington Beach and Santa Barbara. A few still remain today, supplying the myriad service stations along the highway with gasoline for cars and other vehicles that travel up and down the coastline every day.

THE STORY OF SUMMERLAND

The name "Summerland" is likely to evoke images of sunshine sparkling off whitecaps and endless stretches of golden sand; of sunglasses, beach towels, and palm trees. But for years, the only "trees" in the Summerland area were oil derricks rising up from piers that jutted out over the water.

Summerland didn't start out as an oil community. In fact, the name makes a lot more sense considering its founder's vision was to establish a 150-acre Spiritualist community. Henry Williams bought the land for that purpose in 1883 and subdivided it for sale five years later.

This structure on Business 101 in Pismo Beach was a Union Oil station in the 1950s and a Wilshire Gas stop a decade later. Most recently, it has served as an auto detailing shop.

The Spiritualists responded, founding a church (complete with a séance room) as the town's focal point. The church endured until a new alignment of U.S. 101 was built in the 1950s, but the character of the town as a Spiritualist haven didn't last nearly as long. Unfortunately for Williams, he wasn't able to find enough buyers to make a profit on that concept: Indeed, the parcels were selling too slowly to satisfy the demands of his mortgage company, and Williams feared the land might be repossessed.

The first clue to Summerland's future direction came in 1890, when someone digging a well struck a pocket of natural gas. As it turned out, gas was so common in the area that kids playing the newly popular pastime of baseball got a head start on the pros in playing past nightfall by sticking pipes in the ground until they hit a pocket of gas, then lighting a match over the top of them. Even today, passing motorists can look to the inland side of the freeway and see a large pipe sticking up, topped by a flame fueled by the same natural gas.

A resulting gas boomlet led to the discovery of oil in 1894, when a resident digging for gas to heat his home struck oil by mistake. Soon, the opportunistic Williams was drilling a pair of wells along the beach and marketing his unsold property to oil speculators.

Over the course of the following year, two dozen oil wells had been drilled, and the most extravagant project yet came in 1898, when a railroad mining engineer named J. B. Treadwell went to the county board of supervisors with a request to build a "wharf." Treadwell had managed to claim ownership of lands below the high-water mark along the coast by using false names to procure a number of fictitious placer mining claims.

The board approved the project, much to the chagrin of some community residents (including Williams, who had hoped to build his own wharf but had yet to secure the funds to do so); all Treadwell had to do was make a single payment of $101 to Santa Barbara County for the right to build the pier. The project was supposed to

The Summerland oil field in its heyday during the early 20th century.
Public domain.

be similar to the Stearns Wharf project in Santa Monica, "but in sober fact," the *Los Angeles Herald* reported, "it was more intended as a platform from which to bore for oil beneath the waves."

Meanwhile, another enterprising resident, one W. M. S. Moore, had purchased a plot of land along the coast with the intention of drilling more wells. He chose the site because other people had already drilled wells on the land behind him, and he figured no one would touch the land in front of him: It was, after all, underwater, and as part of the continental shelf, it was government property. What he hadn't counted on was Treadwell's initiative in building his pier, the wooden piles of which were being built directly in front of Moore's wells.

This might not have been a problem except for the fact that the underground oil reservoir was tilted in such a way that the oil all wound up where Treadwell was drilling. In effect, his wells would tap into the same source as theirs—draining them dry before the oil could be extracted. So, while Treadwell was bragging about a new oil gusher about 200 feet from shore in Summerland, there was considerable debate as to whether the oil was rightfully his.

As the *Los Angeles Herald* explained in an editorial, "The whole oil-bearing strata form a reservoir, tilted at a sharp angle, and Treadwell's 'gusher' had merely tapped into the sources of supply." This, the newspaper continued "made other well owners uneasy [because] they foresaw ruin by the draining of their wells."

Moore and the other landowners were livid—and their mood didn't improve when Treadwell started boasting that he was a paid agent of the railroad, which had enlisted him to build the wharf as a place to run a straighter section of track. The piles, he reportedly declared, were merely the first step in the process of making this happen.

Clearly, the piles had to go.

Treadwell had hired a group of armed men to guard the unfinished project, but one of the landowners, Thomas B. Wood (whom the newspaper described as "a large Summerland oil man") went out and confronted them. Then, daring the men to stand in his way, he proceeded to hack down each of the piles that had been erected in front of his own beach claims. Treadwell, for his part, was away in San Francisco, where he was seeking support from the attorney general.

Both sides dug in their heels in what one newspaper called "a little civil war." There was talk, the newspaper said, of building two wharves out on either side of the oil field, then connecting them with a lateral wharf out at sea—thereby cordoning off the precious site. Whether this was the intention of Treadwell or his opponents is unclear from a news report, but apparently it came to naught.

Instead, a truce was arranged between the warring sides, and more wharves were built by various parties: A dozen in all were constructed over the next two years. By 1900, the Treadwell wharf alone boasted 19 wells and had grown to more than 1,200 feet in length. Altogether, oil prospectors drilled more than 400 sea wells between 1898 and 1902, and a forest of derricks seemed to rise from the sea.

A blight on the seascape?

Not according to the Southern Pacific, which made Summerland a refueling stop along a rail line that was still under construction (it didn't reach San Francisco until 1901). Once in place, the railroad touted Summerland's oil field by inviting riders to "See the Oil Wells by the Sea." The railroad depicted a ride up the coast that featured a view of orange groves from one side of the train and the derricks from the other. Beauty was truly in the eye of the beholder—or, in this case, the marketer.

But the oil operations weren't particularly sturdy. In January 1903, one of them fell victim to a seven-year-old boy, who set fire to a large oil tank just to see "the thing go off."

It did.

According to the *San Francisco Chronicle*, the boy used a large spike to make a hole in the side of the tank, then stuck a piece of cloth in the hole, and lit it aflame. The result was that "the tank blew up and burning oil and scrap iron were scattered over a large territory."

That same year, a severe winter storm knocked down many of the derricks, and those that remained had stopped producing much oil by 1906. After that, some were removed, but many were simply abandoned, their skeletal frames littering the coastline for decades as silent testimony to a brief black gold rush along California's Central Coast.

The Ellwood Strike

But that wasn't the end of oil drilling in the region.

A few miles west of Summerland, on the other side of Santa Barbara, an even bigger find was made in 1928. If you drive along Hollister Avenue, an old alignment of U.S. 101 in Goleta, you'll come across a three-story tower near the western end of the road that's surmounted by a cupola and inscribed with the words "Barnsdall Oil Co." over "Rio Grande Oil Co." in faded blue letters on the front and both sides. A chain-link fence, topped with barbed wire, surrounds it, and a small sign on the premises proclaims it to be "the first gas station of the Barnsdall-Rio Grande Oil Co., which drilled the Ellwood Oil Field discovery well in 1928."

Rio Grande was founded in 1915 by a store owner in El Paso, Texas, who had the good fortune of opening his doors at the same time Pancho Villa was conducting a series of raids across the border. The U.S. Army's supply trucks needed fuel to pursue Villa and his men into Mexico, and the Rio Grande store happened to be in the right place at the right time. With some 600 Army trucks involved in the operation, Rio Grande did a booming business.

In the 1920s, the company relocated to California, and it soon became a familiar name to travelers of California highways. Rio Grande boasted that more police and fire vehicles in California and Arizona used its high-performance "cracked" gasoline than any other formula. It sponsored the popular radio program *Calling All Cars*, a crime re-enactment series that ran from 1933 to 1939 and was a forerunner of such TV shows as *Dragnet* and *Cops*.

Rio Grande gasoline was sold across California, including at several stations in the Santa Barbara area, as well as at World's Largest Redwood Tree Service Station in Ukiah, on the Redwood Highway. But even that impressive building was hard-pressed to surpass the one in Goleta, which was built at the entrance to the Ellwood field that helped make Rio Grande a major player in the oil business when it struck black gold there.

It was Katherine "Kate" Den Bell who owned the property adjacent to the field, having inherited 519 acres along the coast from her father, Goleta pioneer Nicholas Den. In 1920, Bell and her extended family came together to celebrate her 76th birthday on the dunes at the mouth of Las Armas Canyon—which would later be renamed Bell Canyon in honor of her husband, John Stewart Bell. It was there, just west of where the Sandpiper Golf Course is today, that she made a birthday speech predicting that oil would be found.

Pointing to a prickly pear cactus—the only one growing in the area—she declared, "If you drill an oil well where that cactus is, you will strike a gusher. Mark my words well, for it will make you rich someday."

Bell didn't allow anyone to drill for oil there during her lifetime, but when she died six years later, her daughter decided to test her mother's prediction. In 1927, a year after her mother's death, she and her husband granted Frank Morgan, a geologist from the Rio Grande Company, permission to drill a test well on the property; the spot he chose was right beside the still-growing cactus. Rio Grande partnered with Barnsdall Oil Company on the project, striking a deal to drill to 3,000 feet—if they hadn't struck oil by then, they'd call it quits.

It's a good thing they didn't.

The crew pushed on a bit past 3,000, down to 3,160 feet, without any luck, and the supervisor suggested calling off their efforts. Other oil companies had drilled in the general vicinity before and had come up dry; this appeared to be another dead end. Barnsdall's president called Rio Grande's offices and said he wanted to pull out of the partnership: If Rio Grande wanted to keep drilling, it could rent Barnsdall's equipment for $100 a day.

Rio Grande didn't want to make any final decisions before having one last look at the site, so it sent Morgan back out to do one more assessment. When he got there, he asked to examine the most recent coring sample extracted from the well, and what he found there changed everything: There were unmistakable traces of petroleum in the sample.

That was all Rio Grande needed to dissolve its partnership with Barnsdall, which had already given up on the well.

Or had it?

In the meantime, Barnsdall's own geologist decided he wanted to be sure of things, too, and ordered his own company to take another coring sample. Workers drilled 10 feet farther down and hit a pocket of natural gas. Thirty feet beyond that, they struck oil—and not just a little oil, but a *Beverly Hillbillies*-style gusher that started spewing out 3,000 barrels a day of high-grade crude.

Needless to say, Barnsdall pulled its offer off the table, and the partnership remained intact.

The well, Luton-Bell No. 1, paid for itself in just two weeks. Shortly after the strike, Barnsdall refused an offer of $15 million for its share of what an *Oxnard Press-Courier* report described as "California's greatest prospective oil field."

Standard Oil and a concern called Texas Company did manage to purchase some of the land on the Ellwood field, and long piers surmounted by oil derricks were being built out over the ocean along the continental shelf, where much of the oil turned out to be.

Nearly overnight, Barnsdall-Rio Grande became the nation's biggest taxpayer, and it seemed only fitting that the company should create a monument to its success. What better place than along U.S. 101 at the gateway to the Ellwood oil field? And what better monument than a gas station? But not just any gas station. This would be the Taj Mahal of filling stations: a three-story square tower with a 2,000-gallon water storage tank on the third

The Barnsdall-Rio Grande gas station in Goleta still stands on Hollister Avenue, an old alignment of U.S. 101.

floor, a pump island out front, and restrooms in the back. It was designed by Morgan, Walls & Clements, which had designed several Los Angeles movie palaces in the mid-'20s. About the same time as it drew up plans for the Barnsdall-Rio Grande station, the firm designed another iconic homage to petroleum, the art deco Richfield Tower with its distinctive faux oil derrick rising high above the city.

The Ellwood station had a decorative steel derrick of its own outside the company headquarters, which was built beside the station. To the west, an eatery called Spud Inn—named for the process of "spudding," a term for digging an oil well—opened shortly afterward, catering to oil workers and passing motorists alike. Briefly renamed the El Bar Rio Café (using elements of the names Ellwood, Barnsdall, and Rio Grande), it became Wheeler's Inn after Laurence and Hilda Wheeler took over in the early '30s. The addition of a liquor store after the repeal of Prohibition two years later added another layer to the clientele.

But Ellwood was famous for more than just the oil strike, a fancy service station, and a restaurant. In February of 1942, it became the target of a Japanese military attack on American soil.

First some background. Flash back to three years earlier.

According to a 1982 story in *Parade* magazine, that's when a Japanese tanker captained by a man named Kozo Nishino docked at Ellwood to take on a shipment of oil. There was nothing unusual about this, as tankers from Japan and other foreign ports of call were frequent visitors to the site in those days. What *was* unusual was what supposedly happened to Nishino when he went on a stroll as he waited for his ship to take on its supplies. The path he chose took him up the bluffs, where he stumbled—literally—upon the cactus that had been the object of Katherine Den Bell's prophecy nearly two decades earlier.

The story goes that he wanted to take a cutting from the plant back to Japan to plant in his garden, but when he tried to climb the fence that surrounded it, he stumbled and fell into the prickly plant—eliciting a round of laughter from American oil workers who happened to witness his plight.

Nishino reportedly vowed revenge—and he got it when the Japanese I-17 submarine he commanded set out on a mission to attack oil installations along the California coast, none of which was more famous than the Ellwood site. When he was in range, at 7:15 p.m. on February 23—on Washington's birthday and right in the middle of President Franklin Roosevelt's "fireside chats"—he gave the order to start firing at the oil fields.

Nothing much happened.

The first shot came up short, falling harmlessly into the water. The second hit the beach, and others landed inland, one of them slamming into a hillside. One of the shells did minor damage to the Ellwood Pier, destroying a derrick and a pump house. Another sailed over Wheeler's Inn, prompting Laurence Wheeler to call the sheriff and brace for an aerial bombardment that never came.

"We saw the shells tearing up the ground as they landed," Hilda Wheeler recalled. "We couldn't see the submarine because the sunset was very brilliant."

Laurence Wheeler added that "the third shot shook the building." The rest, he said, "whined overhead and dropped across the highway: their marksmanship was rotten."

But although the attack ended after 20 minutes and did little physical damage to the oil field or its assets, it did inflict a measure of psychological damage.

A waitress at Wheeler's, Estelle Staniff, said she initially thought it was just target practice, "and then we looked out back and saw the earth spurting up, and we were scared to death."

So were other Americans. The idea that the Japanese could get that close to American soil once fueled worries that it could happen again—with much more frightful consequences the next time around. In response, the lighted globes that surmounted gas pumps up and down the coast became a thing of the past. The possibility that they might serve as targets for enemy fire made them simply too great a risk.

Two days after the attack at Ellwood, air-raid sirens screamed across Los Angeles and anti-aircraft guns started firing. At 2:25 a.m., the Fourth Interceptor Command ordered a blackout of the L.A. area after receiving reports of unidentified aircraft in the area. Some residents reported seeing as many as 200 planes over the area, and others got so caught up in the frenzy that they reported seeing UFOs. Even though it was the middle of the night, the chaos led to what one report called the worst traffic jam in Southern California history (a record that has doubtless been long since eclipsed).

The third-floor tower of the Barnsdall-Rio Grande held a 2,000-gallon water tank.

The *Los Angeles Times* reported that "scores of searchlights built a wigwam of light beaming over Los Angeles." Anti-aircraft batteries launched more than 1,300 rounds of fire into the skies over the Southland, many of them falling back again to damage commercial and residential properties. In Santa Monica, a bomb squad was called out to deal with an unexploded anti-aircraft shell that wound up in a driveway. "There were no planes over Los Angeles last night—at least that's our understanding," Navy Secretary Frank Knox said afterward, calling it a "false alarm."

A year later, a war-bond drive carried the theme "Avenge Ellwood"—ironic given the tale that the Japanese sub captain's own attack was an act of revenge. (Incidentally, the legend likely has no truth to it: There's no record of Nishino ever serving as a tanker captain, and his record indicates he trained specifically to work on submarines, on which he'd served since 1923.)

PALACE SERVICE STATIONS

The Barnsdall-Rio Grande station wasn't the only example of a "palace" service station during the era. The Sherman Oaks service station on Ventura Boulevard (Old 101) featured a similar design, with a sturdy canopy supported by a pair of thick columns out front and a tower surmounting the station's ground floor. In this case, however, the tower appears to have been modeled after the Los Angeles City Hall building. Affixed to the side of the tower were the words "Blu-Green Gas," indicating it sold Gilmore brand fuel.

A General Petroleum Violet Ray station on Cahuenga Boulevard in Hollywood featured a smaller tower off to one side that evoked a mission bell tower, appropriate for El Camino Real. A gently gabled canopy fronted by twin adobe arches shielded customers from the sun in twin fueling lanes with two pumps each. (In 1926, General Petroleum was purchased by Socony Oil, which later acquired Vacuum Oil Co. to form what would become Mobil Oil.)

In the mid-1930s, a series of tall, matching towers could be seen rising in succession along Westwood Boulevard, each one topped with the symbol of a different oil company: Richfield, Associated, 76, and Chevron.

Other stations in the Los Angeles area featured such designs as a Moorish-style dome and a Fokker F-32 airplane that shaded pumps on Wilshire Boulevard.

On Santa Rosa Street (State Route 1) just northwest of U.S. 101 in San Luis Obispo, a ConservFuel station with a small domed tower evokes the feel of the Barnsdall-Rio Grande station, including the checkerboard tile on the side.

Wheeler's Inn, meanwhile, saw a significant decline in the number of motorists stopping in for a bite to eat. Who wanted to risk coming under enemy fire during a stopover for a cup of coffee? The Wheelers boarded the place up not long after the attack and moved their restaurant a safer distance inland, to Victoria Street in downtown Santa Barbara.

A few years later, in 1947, the highway was rerouted away from Hollister Avenue, causing a further decline in traffic, and the station itself closed in the 1950s and was converted into a bulk plant for fuel storage. Sometime later, the local Rio Grande distributor reactivated the pumps and reopened the station part-time as a fuel dispensary, giving his preferred customers a key so they could gas up at night, when the plant was closed. That era ended when the distributor went out of business in 1972, and the building was never used as a gas station again—with one very brief and notable exception: In 1981, the station experienced a brief revival—at least on the silver screen—when scenes from the movie *The Postman Always Rings Twice*, starring Jack Nicholson and Jessica Lange, were filmed there.

As for its architecture, the Barnsdall-Rio Grande Station was something of a trendsetter. Drive east on Hollister Avenue just a short distance, and you'll notice the entryway to a building on the north side of the road adorned with the same blue-and-white-tile checkerboard pattern used on the Ellwood service station. It's the entrance to Ellwood Elementary School, which was built in 1929—the same year the service station went up. (The school's original nickname was the Drillers, in honor of the oil drilling done in the Ellwood Field.)

There's even a building at the Santa Barbara Zoo that not only includes the same tile pattern but emulates the service station's tower design, as well.

What ever happened to Barnsdall-Rio Grande?

In 1940, Barnsdall Refining took on a new name, Bareco Oil, and shortly after the end of World War II, it stopped refining oil altogether.

Rio Grande, meanwhile, merged with Sinclair Oil in 1931, and then took over what was left of Richfield Oil when it emerged from receivership in 1936, assuming the Richfield name but continuing to sell Rio Grande-branded gasoline.

TANK FARM TORNADOES

Other sites along U.S. 101 had—and still have—ties to the oil industry.

Just as the Summerland wells were starting to run dry, California Petroleum Refineries began an ambitious project to the north known as Oilport. In 1907, the company opened a half-mile-long pier and refinery, together with an electric railroad that ran through the 1,000-acre property just north of what's now Shell Beach.

It had its own general store, post office and power plant, together with dining halls and cottages to feed and house some 500 employees. Eight massive storage tanks could contain as much as 55,000 gallons apiece, and the company planned to ship oil all over the world. The entire plant, which brought oil in from a site near Santa Maria, took two years to build.

Plans called for the refinery to ship oil all over the world. One contract called for 2 million barrels a year to be shipped out of Oilport for delivery to Japan.

But it all came crashing down in December, a mere two weeks after the project's completion, thanks to a severe storm described in at least one publication as a "tidal wave." There's no mention of a tsunami in other contemporary news reports, but there's also no debating the fact that exceptionally high seas and savage surf were the culprits. Add winds that were "blowing at a furious gale" to the mix, and the pier was no match for Mother Nature. According to the *Santa Cruz Evening News*, 800 to 1,000 feet of the structure was washed away, along with a pile driver and a steam engine that were being used to make repairs on the structure.

Up the coast in Avila, the *Daily Telegram* in San Luis Obispo reported, many of the pilings on the People's Wharf were uprooted, and the structure was said to be in bad shape.

The Oilport wharf was damaged beyond repair, but the Avila pier was salvaged. This was a good thing for the refinery, which continued to operate sporadically for a few years, sending its oil up to Avila via pipeline for distribution. There, Union Oil had built a tank farm for storage in 1906, adding a second four years later in nearby San Luis Obispo. But it apparently had so much oil that even this wasn't enough, so the company leased the Oilport tanks to use as extra storage for a few years. The Oilport refinery ultimately shut down, and most of the equipment was sold during World War I, leaving only the brick walls from the power plant and the concrete foundations that had supported the steam engines as testimony to its existence. Eventually, these too were removed, giving way to residential development.

Union Oil might appear to have been the beneficiary of Oilport's bad luck, but as things turned out, its luck was even worse. Both the tank farms it opened in the region wound up at the center of major catastrophes—in fact, they were the two biggest environmental disasters in the history of San Luis Obispo County, and both of them were within shouting distance of U.S. 101.

The first took place in 1926 at the San Luis Obispo site, the largest tank farm in the world at the time with 21 steel storage tanks and six underground reservoirs. As with the destruction of the Oilport pier, Mother Nature was the cause. This time, her wrath came not from the sea, but from the air: Around midmorning on April 7 of that year, a bolt of lightning shot down out of a stormy sky and struck the ground between two of the underground reservoirs. Four tanks exploded, one after another, and what one report described as "huge geysers of fire" soared to a height of 75 feet quickly spread across the entire site.

"I saw two balls of lightning strike reservoirs No. 5 and No. 7," an oil company employee said. "A clap of thunder and an explosion followed immediately, and the tanks burst into flames. At the same time, the earth rocked so violently under my feet that I was almost thrown down."

Another reservoir exploded 15 minutes later, possibly from another lightning strike and perhaps ignited by burning timbers from the roof of another reservoir, thrown aloft by one of the first two blasts.

A Civil War veteran named A. H. Seeber and his son were killed instantly when the explosion leveled their house 300 yards away—one of six homes to be destroyed along with a dozen other structures that suffered damage from the blasts. Windows shattered for miles around, and the 250 residents of Edna, just south of San Luis Obispo, were sent into a panic, fearing further explosions might flatten the town. Whirlwinds eerily similar to tornadoes formed over the site, and a column of blue-black smoke three-quarters of a mile in diameter rose upward into the atmosphere.

One Union Oil employee named Berry reported seeing a "funnel" leave the fire and move toward Edna Valley Road. A San Luis Obispo-based Weather Bureau employee recorded his account in that month's official monthly review:

"Near the mushroom-shaped top of the funnel, about 200 feet in the air, a small shed or chicken coop was floating around in a counterclockwise direction," J. E. Hissong wrote. "Looking back occasionally as he fled, Mr. Berry says he saw at least 20 'spouts' between the Seeber house and the fire, some of them very small. He reports that a brisk northwest wind was blowing at that time, and that the roar from the whirlwinds was terrific."

A flaming chunk of wood 8 inches wide by 16 inches long fell out of the sky and skewered the earth like an overdone shishkebab stick near a home two miles from the tank farm. Other debris was found on the slopes of the Santa Lucia Range, about three miles to the northeast. And while none of the tornadoes was thought to have traveled farther than that, soot from the conflagration ultimately fell to earth again in "black rain" as far away as Fresno, more than 110 miles away. It was cruelly ironic that, after much of the fuel had been brought over from Kern County to be stored in San Luis Obispo, it was now returning there via the wind.

One news report called San Luis Creek "a flaming ribbon of light" filled with burning oil that was easily visible from the highway, which ran alongside it. According to witnesses, the oil made it all the way to the ocean at Avila, and "skeletons of burned trees lined the creek."

Adding to the oil company's woes, lightning from the same storm struck a second Union refinery in Brea, north of Anaheim, a day later. Damage from that strike

was less severe but also in the millions of dollars. When all was said and done, more than 8 million barrels of oil were lost in San Luis Obispo, and firefighters had to sit by and watch helplessly for days before the fire burned itself out. The good news for Union Oil was that insurance covered all its losses for both the San Luis Obispo and Brea fires, with a record payout of $9 million. The bad news for the county was the resulting devastation. The trees would grow back, and the creek would purge

The site of the largest oil tank fire in the world when it ignited in 1926 was still being cleaned up nearly a century later along Tank Farm Road in San Luis Obispo.

itself of impurities soon enough, and even the tank farm itself was rebuilt in the 1930s.

Oil storage at the site finally ended in the 1980s, with most of the tanks being removed in the following decade, leaving newcomers turning off old Highway 101 (Higuera Street) onto Tank Farm Road to wonder about the source of the name. But the land itself remained a toxic waste site into the 21st century. Oil from the disaster had collected in low spots, where it seeped into the earth and disappeared beneath hardened sediment … only to bubble to the surface again on hot days.

In the meantime, some low-lying portions of the site have become seasonal wetlands, attracting waterfowl that may be at risk of contamination. Chevron, which purchased Union Oil in 2005, began pursuing cleanup of the site, and plans called for a mixture of open space and commercial development in the future. The San Luis Obispo City Council approved an environmental study on the site in September 2014.

AVILA ANGST

Union Oil's other tank farm disaster took place just down the road, a couple miles west of the highway at Avila. In this case, however, natural forces didn't have a hand in the calamity—the company made a mess of things all by itself. And what a mess it was. The tank farm there was the commodity's last stop before heading overseas: By the time World War II rolled around, a whopping 2 million gallons of crude a day was being funneled from the massive hillside containers into tanker ships waiting to convey it overseas.

Not all of the oil, however, wound up on distant shores. Some of it was seeping into the ground.

A lot of it, actually.

In 1989, one of about 400 residents of Avila Beach, was puttering around in his basement when he struck oil. But the oil hadn't been deposited there millions of years ago; it had leaked into the soil from the oil tanks around town, forming a huge underground reservoir: 400,000 gallons of gasoline, diesel fuel, crude oil, and who knew what else. The company had known about the leak as far back as 1977, but it had been going on longer than that. The company's tank farm had been there since 1906, and a Unocal spokesman acknowledged in 1994 that the pipes under Front Street had been leaking "for some time—no one knows for sure how long."

The company first learned of the problem when petroleum fumes built up in the basement of a building along Front Street, a roughly half-mile-long road paralleling the ocean in the sleepy little town. Unocal thought it had solved the problem by fixing the source of that leak

Sunbathers and swimmers enjoy Avila Beach on a recent summer day. It's hard to imagine that the entire community had to be torn down and rebuilt after an underground oil leak was discovered there.

and putting up an underground barrier to hold back any further seepage. But either the barrier didn't hold or there were other leaks the company didn't know about. Whatever the case, the true extent of the contamination didn't become clear until the 1990s.

County Supervisor Peg Pinard called it "a bomb that dropped on Avila."

Mike Rudd, the owner of a swimwear shop in Avila, ran into the oil when he was doing preliminary work on opening a second business downtown. He threatened to sue before accepting Unocal's offer of $500,000 for his property instead. But he bitterly proclaimed in an interview: "I wouldn't buy a gallon of Union Oil gasoline if I was dying. I don't think anyone who comes to Avila Beach should ever buy another gallon of Union Oil gasoline."

The reborn and revitalized town of Avila Beach draws throngs of locals and out-of-town visitors for beachside festivals, music, and other events.

Rudd wasn't the only resident who had to give up his business. Eventually, the company agreed to rip up almost the entire business district to clean out the contamination underneath it. Such drastic measures were unprecedented, and Unocal had initially proposed injecting air into the earth to give bacteria a boost in consuming the toxins from the spill. But townsfolk, understandably, didn't want to wait the decade or more it would take that process to play out, so they demanded a more drastic solution.

Bulldozers would remove 300,000 cubic yards of dirt, digging as deep as 15 feet into the ground at some places, to remove the pollutants. This meant razing or moving some of the historic structures along Front Street and, in essence, rebuilding the town from the ground up. The business district was shut down and evacuated during this process; the toxic soil was carted off to a landfill in Bakersfield and replaced with sand from the Guadalupe

Dunes to the south. When all was said and done, the process took two years and cost Unocal in excess of $100 million. Forty-six homes and commercial buildings were razed, while just two of the original buildings survived: the grocery store and yacht club.

Front Street was repaved, and a new beach walk inlaid with seashells was added.

The community, once an old hippie town that showed its age, was reborn as a shiny and trendy new seaside village with beachside bars, souvenir shops, and candy stores.

When the project was completed, Unocal project manager Richard Walloch was philosophical but realistic: "The town will never be identical to what it was."

Whether that's a good thing or a bad thing depends a lot on one's perspective.

SAN ARDO

Oil treated other towns better.

San Ardo, a small, unincorporated town off 101 in the Salinas Valley, struck it rich in 1947. A glance eastward from the highway 70 years later reveals scores of dinosaur-shaped pumps nodding their heads in metronomic cadence as they extract heavy crude from beneath the soil.

As of 2015, it was the 13th-largest oil field in California, but unlike other gushers, the San Ardo strike didn't result in a horde of new residents putting down roots nearby. In fact, with a population of just over 500, San Ardo's human population is far less conspicuous than those steel "dinosaurs." The old highway ran straight through downtown along Cattlemen Road until 1971, when it was bypassed by the new freeway alignment—after which the old Richfield, Shell, and Norwalk stations closed up shop. Sure, they were right next door to an oil field, but they were no longer next door to the highway, and motorists were unwilling to take a mile-long detour to fill 'er up.

Many towns along the highway are named for Catholic saints, but don't be surprised that you've never heard of a "Saint Ardo." There isn't one. The name on the town post office was San Bernardo when it opened in 1886, but it was shortened a year later to avoid confusion with San Bernardino.

An old Texaco service station, later converted into a retail store, sits on the bend of old Highway 101 (Cattlemen Road), where it curves north in the Salinas Valley town of San Ardo.

HUNTINGTON BEACH

Far more famous than the San Ardo oil field is the one down the coast in Huntington Beach.

The surfers and sun worshippers who flocked to "Surf City" once shared this 9.5-mile stretch of white-sand beach with dozens of towering oil derricks pumping black gold.

The city, ironically, was named for a pioneer in a different form of transportation: Henry Huntington, whose "Red Line" trolleys were seemingly everywhere in the Southland before the age of freeways. The city was originally called Shell Beach (not to be confused with the section of Pismo Beach) and, later, Pacific City before it became Huntington Beach.

A few who got there before the boom struck it rich quite by accident … by buying a set of encyclopedias. Sometime during the 1910s, a company called Encyclopedia Americana hit on the idea of buying up a bunch of land in Huntington Beach and giving it away as a bonus to anyone who bought its product. The company shelled out $7,000 for 35 acres of land that it promptly subdivided into 420 lots offered as a special "bonus" to anyone who bought its product.

The encyclopedias weren't cheap—a full set sold for $126, the equivalent of about $3,000 in 2016—but the land was. It consisted mostly of swampland, hills, gullies, and other locations that were anything but prime. Most of them weren't suited for any kind of construction at all, and the plots even looked like encyclopedias lined up next to one another, exaggerated rectangles 112 feet long and just 25 feet wide.

They were roughly the same width and about half again longer than a tennis court, much too small to build anything on—except maybe an outhouse.

Still, the company marketed it as "beachfront" land, and its customers had no way of knowing any different. Ads in New England newspapers painted the following exaggerated picture: "For a payment of a small sum down and a

Oil derricks rose in Huntington Beach near U.S. 101 in the 1920s and '30s. *Orange County Archives.*

mortgage on the future, secure that 'fount' of all knowledge … a modern encyclopedia, together with a city lot in the booming town of Huntington Beach, California, overlooking the blue Pacific and [within] shooting distance of the orange groves."

What wasn't to love?

Huntington Beach itself, a newly incorporated city in 1909, was only too eager to make a buck by selling the property to the company, which then unloaded the worthless land on its customers.

A massive oil strike in 1920, however, changed everything. On May 20, 1920, a derrick drilled about a mile inland struck black gold, hitting 70 barrels of crude. Within a month, the sleepy beach town of 1,500 became a bustling hub of 5,000 people—and that was just the beginning. On November 6, a big gusher farther inland sent 2,000 barrels rocketing skyward. Suddenly, the encyclopedia lots weren't worthless at all, and speculators were all too eager to snatch them up from the book buyers who'd taken possession of them just a few years earlier.

Tom Talbert, a county supervisor and real estate investor, organized a syndicate that sent letters out to all the encyclopedia lot owners and bought 33 of the lots

for prices ranging from $5 to $15. It was literally a steal. Other groups approached encyclopedia buyers in the Midwest and offered to lease the land from them: Globe Petroleum and Reliance Oil each managed to obtain leases for about 15 acres.

Most of the encyclopedia buyers hadn't done anything with the deeds after they'd received them. By and large, they'd stayed back east, either by design or out of necessity, being unable to afford a cross-country move.

The land was of secondary concern to Ezra Hapfield, a farmer who bought the encyclopedia to help with his daughter Hattie's education and set the deed to the Huntington Beach land aside, depositing it in an old trunk for safekeeping. He didn't think anything more about it, and life went on as it always had: His daughter completed finishing school, got married, and gave birth do a son—then returned home when her husband died unexpectedly.

Then, one day, a letter arrived from a California law firm checking the status of that land in Huntington Beach. It jogged Hapfield's memory, and he retrieved the deed from the trunk where he'd deposited it years earlier. Curious, he responded to the law firm's letter, and eventually, an offer was made on the land: The firm was willing to pay $300 for it, nearly two-and-a-half times what he'd spent on the encyclopedias.

Hapfield knew something was afoot, and a little investigation revealed that his land was smack-dab in the middle of a huge underground oil reservoir. He headed west, secured some royalty payments from the oil, and used them to buy a bungalow with some orange trees and an ocean view. For him, the encyclopedia company's promise of orange groves and land "overlooking the blue Pacific" came true—just not in a way the company itself could ever have envisioned.

The speculators who succeeded in buying or leasing land from the encyclopedia customers got rich, too. By 1923, the lots were selling for $2,000 apiece, and the owners were getting royalty checks of $60 to $150 a month. The Talbert syndicate earned a quarter of a million dollars between 1922 and 1952, a huge return on an investment of just $100 by each of the five men involved in the venture.

For decades, the Pacific Coast Highway—then known as the 101 Alternate—through Huntington Beach was lined with oil derricks.

Long after the oil boom had subsided, however, Huntington Beach was reaping its karmic reward for the part it played in pawning off "worthless" land on unsuspecting buyers. As the city grew, it found the lots it had sold to Encyclopedia Americana stood in the way of some planned construction projects. Finding the owners of these parcels was hard enough; getting them to sell was an additional challenge.

Barbara Harmon, for instance, didn't want to part with her lot, one of seven the city needed to acquire for a street-widening project. "My grandfather was a Russian immigrant who lived in Bisbee, Arizona," she told the *Los Angeles Times* in 1990. "He bought the encyclopedias to educate himself, and he always told us to hold on to the land that came with the encyclopedias. He was sure the land would one day be valuable."

The city had offered her $10,000 for the land, but she said it wasn't enough. Other landowners agreed and protested when the city declared its intention to purchase the property using eminent domain so the street project could move forward. One of the landowners said a similar

A gyroscope-type city sign on the Pacific Coast Highway (U.S. 101 Alternate) stands in the foreground, with Huntington Beach oil derricks in the background. *Orange County Archives.*

plot had sold for $62,500, and another put up a cyclone fence around his property to keep the city from confiscating it. The issue went to court, with the process being dragged out over the next several years.

In the midst of all this, ads popped up in the *Los Angeles Times* offering "contiguous encyclopedia lots in area of million dollar homes" to "builders, investors, and contractors" for $50,000.

Twenty-five years later, the city was still trying to buy back 38 remaining parcels, and continued to face roadblocks in even finding the owners. Who knows? Maybe some of those old deeds are still locked up in a forgotten trunk somewhere in New England. Meanwhile, the land sits vacant, no longer suitable for an oil well—or even a tennis court.

⑤
ROADSIDE DINING

When I was a child, shortly after the autumn leaves began to fall, Mom would start serving me soup for lunch. The thin tendrils of steam rising up from the bowl were a comforting sight amid the foggy and sometimes frosty Fresno winters. I tolerated the tomato soup and enjoyed the Campbell's vegetable, but it was the pea soup that really tickled my taste buds. Somewhere along the line, Mom decided to add a dollop of sour cream to the bowl, which made it even yummier. I'm not sure where she got the idea, but every time I have a bowl of pea soup today—with or without ham—I add that spoonful of sour cream to the mix.

Imagine my excitement when I learned that an entire restaurant built around my favorite soup dish not only existed, but was just a few hours up the highway from my home. When I was nine, my parents moved from Fresno to Woodland Hills, at the east end of the San Fernando Valley. Topanga Canyon Boulevard was our gateway to U.S. 101, which could take us east to a game at Dodger Stadium or west toward Ventura and points beyond.

One of those points was a place called Solvang, a town settled largely by Danish immigrants in the late 19th and

Pea Soup Andersen's has been a popular roadside stop in Buellton since the 1920s.

early 20th centuries. Like the Swedish village of Kingsburg along U.S. 99, it had a distinctive Scandinavian flavor, complete with steeply gabled roofs, half-timbered fachwerk facades, and even four windmills. The big attraction for my parents—actually, for my grandmother, who lived with us nearly half of each year—was the selection of shops in the town. Franny (as she liked to be called) loved to shop at the boutiques, gift shops and sweet shops in town.

Solvang straddles State Route 246, a couple of miles east of Highway 101 and the town of Buellton, which was my favorite stop during the trip. It was there that we'd typically grab lunch at Pea Soup Andersen's, which featured the same half-timbered style you'd see up the road in Solvang and a windmill of its own. (The name Andersen was a dead give-away that the Danish settlers had populated the entire Santa Ynez Valley region, not just the town of Solvang.)

It was, and is, impossible to miss the restaurant. Its owners have stationed billboards up and down the highway, from a few yards to hundreds of miles away, each featuring their familiar cartoon mascots, Hap-Pea and Pea-Wee. The rotund, smiling Hap-Pea always appears with a formidable mallet raised over his head as he prepares to bring it down on a chisel-shaped tool held over a pea by his nervous companion, Pea-Wee. A bandage on the side of Pea-Wee's face implies that Hap-Pea's aim hasn't always been true; hence the look of trepidation on the much smaller chef's face as he eyes the mallet.

Hap-Pea and Pea-Wee, the mascots for Pea Soup Andersen's, adorn the front of the restaurant on U.S. 101 in Buellton.

The idea came from a comic strip by Charles Forbell that appeared in *Judge* magazine during the 1930s titled "Little Known Occupations." One of these showed several craftsmen out in the woods, listening to a bird's song as they tried to tune their cuckoo clocks. Another depicted a pair of chefs standing at a table, splitting peas one by one as they descended from a chute. It was this second cartoon that caught the eye of Robert Andersen, who received permission to use the characters in his advertising. He hired Disney-trained illustrator Milt Neil to put his distinctive stamp on them, and the result was the iconic pair of mascots that continue to adorn the restaurant's soup cans, merchandise, and billboards.

The business, however, wasn't always known primarily for its pea soup. Founded in 1924 by Anton and Juliette Andersen, its biggest selling point was the new electric stove the couple had purchased to cook their meals. The sign outside Andersen's Electrical Café featured a pair of lightning bolts and advertised sodas, cigars, and candy—nary a word about split pea soup.

It was a modest endeavor at the outset: just three booths and a counter with six stools, but the business grew quickly. Perhaps the biggest advantage it enjoyed was location: Andersen's Electrical Café opened about the time the coastal highway was diverted through Buellton, and was the first stop along the road after a lengthy stretch of countryside that extends nearly 40 miles heading north from Goleta. By the time travelers heading for Cambria, Monterey, San Luis Obispo, or Salinas made it there in their Model T's, they were more than ready for a break. Those heading south had to endure a similar distance (more than 30 miles) of rural highway between Santa Maria and Buellton, nearly an hour's trek in a Model T—if it didn't break down.

(One destination then, as now, was Hearst Castle in San Simeon. Publishing magnate William Randolph Hearst often withdrew to the retreat he called La Cuesta Encantada—"The Enchanted Hill"—where he would throw lavish parties for movie stars like Charlie Chaplin and Clark Gable, statesmen like FDR and Calvin Coolidge, and American icons including Charles Lindbergh. Journalists who worked for Hearst Newspapers also made the trip—and stopped for sandwich or a bowl of soup at Andersen's. Among them: O. O. McIntyre and Arthur Brisbane. McIntyre wrote a column titled "New York Day By Day," and Hearst reportedly paid Brisbane a staggering $260,000 a year for his column "Today," which at one point boasted 20 million daily readers.)

The Andersens' restaurant became so popular that a hotel with a full dining room was added in 1928, called "Buelltmore" in a play on the Los Angeles Biltmore, which Anton Andersen had helped open a few years earlier.

Although pea soup wasn't on the Electrical Café menu at first, Juliette's family recipe was added three months after it opened; its fame spread rapidly up and down the highway. A mere three years later, the Andersens found they had to order, literally, a ton of peas to keep up with the demands. They stacked them up in the window of the café, which they declared to be "The Home of Split Pea Soup."

By the 1980s, the restaurant was trucking in 55 tons of peas a year in 100-pound sacks from Moscow, Idaho, and attracting celebrities such as John Travolta and comedian Flip Wilson. Its evolution from Electrical Café to pea soup mecca, however, didn't happen all at once. The definitive step in that transformation took place courtesy of the founders' son, Robert Andersen, after World War II. The restaurant had closed during the war, when the hotel was used to house service members stationed locally, but it reopened after the Axis forces surrendered and, in 1947, changed its name to Pea Soup Andersen's.

In that same year, the postwar construction boom brought significant change to Buellton in the form of a new highway alignment through the center of town. The expressway was completed two years later, and Robert Andersen was so enthusiastic he wrote a letter to the state Division of Highways commending it for the changes.

Before the new expressway, it had been, in the words of one merchant, "a small crossroads, strip developed, traffic-bottlenecking village."

But now, all that had changed.

In his August 1949 letter to the state highways agency, Andersen wrote: "We believe that, due to the new outer highway arrangement, the future highway business life of Buellton as a service town, and Andersen's as a roadside restaurant and hotel, is well assured."

The use of the term "service town" in Andersen's letter proved to be prescient. The next month, California Highways and Public Works magazine writer J. F. Powell bestowed upon Buellton the title of Service Town, U.S.A. Its location at the intersection of U.S. 101 and State Route 150, roughly halfway between Santa Barbara and Santa Maria, made it "a logical stopping point," Powell wrote. Now, it had a road built to accommodate the traffic: According to Andersen's letter, more than 250,000 motorists a year stopped to eat at Andersen's.

So many people used the road, in fact, that Buellton became not just a service town, but a service *station* town.

Powell wrote in 1949 that "Buellton, despite a population of only 250, today boasts on its outer highways alone no less than eight service stations." And old postcards show Chevron, Shell, Seaside, and Associated gas stops, among others, along the short segment of gently curving highway.

The expressway was itself bypassed by the new freeway alignment in 1965—the same year Robert Andersen sold the restaurant to Vince Evans—but the road remained a community focal point as the Avenue of Flags, a mile-long section featuring eight large American flags atop flagpoles forged by a local blacksmith. These were dedicated by then-Governor Ronald Reagan in September 1968.

As for Andersen's, Evans expanded the business with a second location in Santa Nella, on Interstate 5 not far from Los Banos. Other restaurants opened during the 1980s in Mammoth Lakes, Carlsbad, and along Highway 99 in Selma. None of them lasted, although the Selma location—complete with a windmill—survived as the Spike N Rail Steakhouse, still serving pea soup and still located on a street called Pea Soup Andersen Boulevard.

Avenue of the Flags, old U.S. 101, entering Buellton from the north.

The Andersens' restaurants in Buellton and Santa Nella, together with their roadside hotels and gift shops, remain open as well. In 2012, they reported serving 500 to 600 gallons of their specialty a day, much of it through orders of their all-you-can-eat pea soup Traveller's Special. You can add bacon bits, chives, cheese, or croutons to your order.

And, of course, sour cream.

History on a Clamshell

If Andersen's is a couple of years older than the highway's formal designation as U.S. 101, there's another eatery that dates back more than half a century earlier: the Old Clam House in San Francisco.

Of course, it wasn't called "old" at the beginning. Its original name was the Oakdale Bar & Clam House.

It sits in an industrial district on Bayshore Boulevard—an old alignment of 101—and was there when the "boulevard"—or its predecessor—was a wood-plank road and the name "bayshore" could have been taken literally. Back when the restaurant opened in 1861 (yes, that's 18, not 19), the planks were necessary to carry horses and buggies across the marshy swampland that bled out into the ocean. The restaurant itself sat on Islais Creek, a freshwater stream that emptied into San Francisco Bay.

Nowadays, the road is about a mile from the actual shoreline. Over the years, enterprising businessmen used earth and debris to create an ever-growing gap between the highway and the eatery. Ten years after the marsh was filled, 100 buildings had gone up there, many of them belonging to butchers who established their own district in what had once been an area dedicated to the fishing trade.

Debris from the catastrophic 1906 earthquake was later added to the growing landfill, removing the restaurant and its clams even farther from shore.

A trolley crosses a freeway overpass near the Los Angeles Civic Center in 1954. © *California Department of Transportation, all rights reserved. Used with permission.*

But the eatery itself remained, even as a McDonald's went in around the corner.

Today, the city's oldest restaurant to operate continuously in the same location still serves up mussels, shrimp, roast Dungeness crab "in our secret garlic butter sauce," and, of course, clam chowder (in a bread bowl or a cup, if you prefer).

RIDING THE RAILS

Small as Buellton was, Andersen's wasn't the only game in town when it came to roadside dining. Ed Mullen had a place—and a gimmick—of his own, in the form of two old streetcars, which he converted into stationary dining cars.

Mullen opened the café a mile and a half north of town just after World War II, in 1946. According to one account, he had worked as a steward on actual dining cars and managed to get his hands on a pair of Type-B Huntington standard models, built in St. Louis in 1911 and used on the Los Angeles Railway's Yellow Line.

The line had been developed by Henry Huntington, for whom the Huntington Library near Pasadena is named (before it became a library and an art museum, it was his residence). In 1898, Huntington had purchased the Los Angeles Railway lines, three years before he formed the larger Pacific Electric Railway system in the area. The former was known as the "Yellow Car" line, while the latter was known as the "Red Car" system.

Huntington died in 1927, and his estate continued to operate the rail lines until they were sold in 1944. With the end of the war, ridership began to decline as a new era of automotive travel got underway. Once hostilities ceased, Americans quickly turned their attention from rationing rubber and gasoline for the war effort, taking to the highways in record numbers. It was here that Mullen saw an opportunity: More motorists than ever would be whizzing up and down U.S. 101 between Los Angeles and San Francisco, and the dining cars would be an eye-catching way to lure them in for a midday meal.

The two railcars he would use for his diner were decommissioned in 1944, and Mullen trucked them up the road from Los Angeles. Customers entered the establishment through the main building in the center, and they could enjoy a meal in one of the dining cars, which were situated on either side. Mullen attired his waitstaff in special uniforms that featured conductors' caps, and left in place the old streetcar signs that declared, "Passengers will have fares ready." At some point, he even installed gas pumps to boost business.

Unfortunately, the same renewed fervor for automotive travel that made the café seem like a good idea proved to be its undoing. Shortly after the business opened, the Department of Highways announced its plan to bypass the section of road where the business had opened in favor of a sleek, new section of highway. The old highway became a mere frontage road called Jonata Park Road.

As business began to decline, Mullen sought to draw customers with a different sort of attraction. When members of the Lompoc Model T Club approached him with an offer to lease his land for use as an oval racetrack, he took them up on the idea. The "T" Club Speedway, as it was called, offered fans admission to the races for a dime in the summer of 1950, and they could watch the action from a grandstand built on a hillside behind the track.

The new attraction, however, failed to stem the loss of business as cars continued to roar past the diner on the new highway. In 1955, a new owner named Jack Chester took over the business and added a Seaside Service Station, but more plans for expansion of U.S. 101 led the Department of Highways to erect a barrier across the roadway, blocking access to the restaurant and effectively putting it out of business.

It closed for good in 1958 and remained vacant for many years until the early 2000s, when the land was rezoned for residential use even as the then-owners worked to restore and reopen the diner. With those efforts stymied, they tried to sell the streetcars or even donate them to the city of Buellton … which expressed no interest in assuming ownership. A retired contractor from Cayucos finally came along in 2012 with plans to move them onto a vacant lot he owned at Highway 41 and Main Street in Morro Bay—a feat he managed, only to run into permitting problems with the city of Morro Bay.

The following year, they were moved again: this time up the coast to Arroyo Grande, where they became part of a display at the site of the Bitter Creek Western Railroad. The site, operated by Karl Hovanitz "for the benefit of

Carney's features railcar dining along Ventura Boulevard in Studio City.

all his friends who like to play with trains," includes a 7.5-inch gauge railroad with more than a mile of mainline track, a number of sidings, and two rail yards.

After all those years, the dining cars were right back where they started: on the rails.

(For those who still want a railcar dining experience on the Old 101, you can grab a bite at Carney's Restaurant on Ventura Boulevard in Studio City. The restaurant, which brags that it serves "probably the best hamburgers and hot dogs … in the world," consists of a kitchen car built in 1938 and a dining room car from four years later, both once used by the Southern Pacific.)

Fjord's

Another distinctive shape in highway dining was Fjord's, a chain of budget buffet restaurants with a slanted, peaked-roof design that made each one look like the bow of some angular land-bound ship rising out of the waves.

The building was hard to miss on State Street, the former 101 alignment, at the northern end of Ukiah, and its billboard-type sign was sure to attract travelers who stopped there for the nearly quarter century it was in business. Featuring a menu of cold salads, chicken, cheeses, and other standard buffet fare, it attracted travelers, athletic teams, and a host of others during its heyday. According to one newspaper account, it wasn't unusual for teams from Humboldt State, Chico State, and other colleges or high schools in the region to stop in after games for a visit to the buffet.

Founded by owner of a Sno-White Drive-In franchise, the Ukiah Fjord's was part of a chain of "Smorg-ettes," buffet restaurants that operated for a couple of decades starting in the mid-1960s. You could find them in places like Chico, Bakersfield, Fresno, and a couple of blocks off the Cabrillo Highway south of Santa Cruz—where the building was later converted into an IHOP. There were even locations in Portland, Oregon, and Guam (yes, Guam).

(As a Fresno native, I looked up the location there and found it at the northwest corner of Blackstone and Dakota, where it opened its doors in 1967 but was out of

Fjord's in Ukiah has gone by the wayside since this photo was taken in 2016; an In-N-Out Burger took its place.

business by 1972, having been replaced by Sun Stereo. The building, which is still there today, was built in 1962—predating Fjord's—so it doesn't have the distinctive slanted/peaked roof.)

Fjord's offered both a smorgasbord and a full menu. All-you-can-eat lunches were $1 there when it opened, with dinners and Sunday meals that cost a little more, and discounted prices for children. Desserts were extra.

The owners in Ukiah, Lyle and Zera Hobby, were avid bowlers who sponsored two teams at Yokayo Bowl—which, conveniently, was right next to the restaurant. Their son Ted later took over as manager, but he died at the age of 42 in 1973. New owners took over the next year.

The Ukiah restaurant, which also featured a gift shop, stayed in business until 1988, housing a bagel house briefly after that but then remaining vacant for the next couple of decades. By mid-2016, it had been purchased by the Southern California-based In-N-Out Burger chain. The building was torn down in August of that year.

6
OVERNIGHT SENSATIONS

As highway traffic grew, so did the dreams of businessmen looking to cash in on the burgeoning travel industry.

One of the ways they did so was the motel, or motor hotel.

It was an innovation that crossed the camping craze of the late teens and early 1920s with the established hotel industry. The first step in the evolution of these roadside fixtures was so-called "auto camps," which began as little more than parcels of land set aside on the outskirts of town where travelers could pitch a tent and stay the night. It was easier (and cheaper) than driving all the way into the city center and spending the night at a hotel, and it was that sort of convenience that gave birth to a new industry.

Tent camping wasn't all that convenient, when it came right down to it, and it wasn't long before owners of the camps began finding ways to make things more comfortable for the highway traveler. They built small cabins to save weary motorists the trouble of setting up a tent at the end of a long day on the road, and to offer more protection from the elements. These could be constructed cheaply and quickly, and the earliest examples were little more than four walls: You could pay extra for such niceties as a mattress, blankets,

The Motel Inn in San Luis Obispo was the first inn to call itself a "motel" when it opened in 1925.

and pillows, and you might get a bucket of water on the house.

It was still camping, but it was better than getting stuck inside a sopping-wet tent during a sudden rainstorm.

Further innovations weren't far behind. Auto camps slowly gave way to more permanent motor courts—with cabins often arranged in a U shape around a central courtyard (hence the name). Additional amenities such as

The Motel Inn was closed for years, and only a small portion of the original complex remained when this photo was taken in 2016, but plans were in the works to rebuild and reopen it under new ownership.

indoor plumbing and electricity were added, and owners began installing carports or even single-car garages alongside each of the cabins—which were often referred to by the more welcoming, civilized term "cottages."

These establishments gave the traveler a middle ground between hotel and auto camp—a Goldilocks zone between the luxury of a high-rise hotel and the economy of a tent, all right by the side of the road. It was left to Arthur S. Heineman to coin the obvious term for such a business, merging the terms "motor court" and "hotel" into a new label for a new age: "Mo-tel."

"The motel plan eliminates a long walk through dark streets in a strange town between a garage and a hotel," the *Los Angeles Times* explained in 1926. "The motorist's car is where he is, ready for the road for an early morning start."

That was Heineman's vision. A Chicago native from a family of six children, he had moved west with his parents as a teenager in 1894 and, a decade later, got involved in real estate. Over a period of five years, he designed a series of bungalows in Pasadena and, in 1909, launched an architectural firm with his brother Alfred—a partnership that would endure for nearly three decades.

Heineman referred to the motel as an innovation "destined to democratize the highways," but in reality, he had the opposite goal in mind: to monopolize them.

A few years later, the Richfield Oil Corporation would launch an ambitious program with a similar idea in mind: Richfield Beacon stations would be set up at regular intervals along major highways such as 99 and 101, with an eye toward giving motorists a place to stop whenever they needed gas. The initial plan called

This plaque at the site of the Motel Inn was dedicated in 1988.

for these stations to serve as hubs for small highway communities in rural areas outside of town. They were to include a small grocery store (anticipating the convenience stores associated with many gas stations today), a café, and a "Beacon Tavern," which wasn't really a tavern at all, but an inn.

Had Richfield been able to realize its vision, it would have effectively locked up the highway, freezing out the competition by offering the best service facilities at every important stopping point between the Mexican and Canadian borders. That was the idea, anyway. But the timing was all wrong: The first Beacon stations opened just before the Wall Street crash of 1929, and the Richfield Corporation only managed to complete one of its "taverns" (along Route 66 in Barstow) before the economy grounded the project and the company was forced into bankruptcy.

Richfield's idea, however, wasn't new. It had been tried before, by none other than Heineman, who had envisioned a similar series of inns placed strategically along the highway up and down the coast of California. The concept, hatched during a 1924 meeting at Heineman's Los Angeles office, involved building 18 motor courts between Seattle and San Diego, spacing them 150 to 200 miles apart to serve as "milestones" where motorists could pull over and spend the night after a day on the road. This was the era of the Model T, which topped out at about 40 mph and didn't go nearly that fast around the myriad twists and turns in the West's early highways. A 200-mile drive might take eight hours—if your car didn't break down in the meantime, which was always a danger.

The milestone concept gave the company its name: the Milestone Corporation. And Heineman's company lost no time in buying up land in such places as Sacramento, Salinas, San Jose, and Santa Barbara as the first step toward realizing its goal. The first motor court to be built would be at the north end of San Luis Obispo on El Camino Real, which was on the verge of being designated a federal highway as part of a new nationwide network of major thoroughfares. The site was chosen because it was roughly halfway between Los Angeles and San Francisco, with four other Milestones planned farther south, and the rest of the chain stretching northward.

Heineman bought a little more than four acres of land from a local rancher for $6,000 and announced plans to rent rooms at $1.25 a night—a price he planned to standardize at all his Milestones up and down the coast. The San Luis Obispo inn would include a public dining room, a lobby with a fireplace and a small store, a free laundry, playgrounds, and full-service garage facilities out back. Some of the units would be single rooms, but the standard was a four-room setup, and six-room apartments were available to be shared by couples traveling together.

A premium was placed on comfort—and service. At the outset, travelers didn't even have to leave their cars to check in: The supervisor on duty would come out and register them for the night "without leaving the car at all," then provide an escort to show them their rooms.

The cabins were to contain more amenities than could be found at most motor courts, promising the traveler "not only the scenic beauties of the open road, but all the comforts of his own home, while away from home." There would be electricity, and indoor plumbing (with hot and cold running water) would be provided in private baths and kitchenettes. Telephones, refrigerators, easy chairs, couches, walnut furnishings, and gas ranges were among the features planned for the rooms at what Heineman announced on a roadside billboard would be called the "Milestone Motel."

The term was so new, however, that it confused passing motorists, who called the sign maker to insist that the word "hotel" had been misspelled on the billboard. So Heineman had it changed to read "Mō-tel," with a hyphen and a long accent over the "o," to avoid any further confusion.

The architecture was Mission Revival style, a fitting choice for its location along El Camino Real (and one that the Richfield Corporation would likewise adopt for the southern half of its Beacon chain). The San Luis Obispo location featured curved archways, sloping tiled roofs, and even a replica bell tower—patterned after the one at the Santa Barbara Mission—as its centerpiece.

Indeed, a 1925 piece in *Pacific Travel* magazine painted the chain as a successor to the fabled Spanish missions: "If Junipero Serra is looking down today on the California he loved so well, he is noting the fact that the King's Highway, with its old missions a day's horseback ride apart … there is now being established a chain of remarkable hotels for motorists, which has been given the names 'Milestone Mo-tels.'"

The *San Luis Obispo Daily Telegram* effused that the new motel was "assured of success" and that it would "soon be known up and down the coast as a unit of a series of the most comfortable, economical and hospitable inns that can be found anywhere in the country."

Like the Beacon Tavern in Barstow, however, the San Luis Obispo Milestone Mo-tel turned out to be the only one of its kind ever built. Plans for an expansive chain up and down the highway never materialized. Heineman's failure to realize his vision ultimately doomed the architectural firm that bore his name, which closed its doors in 1933. He later created designs

for other projects that owed something to his motel design: Plans for a new Los Angeles Public Library and a Hollywood movie museum both featured updated Mission Revival buildings and U-shaped courtyards, but neither ever came to fruition.

Later owners changed the name of the Milestone Mo-tel to "Motel Inn," capitalizing on the word Heineman had created. Joe DiMaggio and Marilyn Monroe stopped there on their honeymoon in 1954, and Ronald Reagan delivered a speech there during his tenure as California's governor in the 1960s.

The business remained open until it finally closed in 1991. The garages and bungalows were torn down in 2010, leaving only the office, bell tower, and the front of the restaurant still standing.

But plans to rebuild the inn as a 28,000-square-foot facility—complete with a restaurant, RV parking, and a reflecting pool—were announced in 2015. And, of course, the word "motel" became part of the popular lexicon: It was added to the dictionary in 1950.

THE MAN WHO INVENTED JAZZ

Up and down the highway, you'll see remnants of an earlier time, when motor courts and early motels seemed to be everywhere. Most of the early ones were built on a shoestring and weren't designed to last more than a decade or two; the owners either made improvements or sold them, or left them to become rundown "seedy" motels. In places where the old highway was bypassed by a new alignment, new developers often tore them down to make way for new retail or industrial businesses.

A few motel rows remain, such as the one on Monterey Street (Old 101) on the north end of San Luis Obispo, and other old alignments—Broadway in Santa Maria and Spring Street in Paso Robles are examples—contain scattered remnants of that earlier time. The Shady Rest Motel still stands at the north end of San Miguel; it probably dates back to the Great Depression, and it looks pretty depressed today, having been converted into (very) small apartments that serve as home to low-income workers.

Farther south, across the beach at the mouth of Topanga Canyon, is the Topanga Ranch Motel, which still stands on State Route 1—formerly the 101 Alternate.

**The Shady Rest Motel on old 101 in San Miguel
is a remnant of an earlier era.**

No one stays there now, but the 30 red-and-white bunga-lows were still standing, silent sentinels alongside the busy highway, as of 2016.

The motel, once known as the Topanga Beach Auto Court, has an interesting history. For one thing, it might be the oldest motel on the Pacific Coast Highway. Newspaper baron William Randolph Hearst bought up much of the coastal land in the area during the late teens and early 1920s, and according to one account, he built the cottages as beach houses for his friends who wanted a quick getaway to the scenic Malibu coastline. He and his mistress, actress Marion Davies, would hold costume parties there, dressing the part of cowboys and Old West pioneers as they set out on horseback on the trails in the surrounding hills.

Just across the highway was La Esperanza, Greta Garbo's 5,300-square-foot mansion, and celebrities who stayed at Topanga Ranch over the years included Errol Flynn, Peter Lawford, and Marilyn Monroe. But Hearst sold his Topanga properties to the Los Angeles Athletic Club—which already owned a minority stake—in 1943, and it wasn't long afterward that it became associated with another famous name from the entertainment industry.

Sometime in the 1940s, the motel came into the possession of Anita Ford and her husband, Jack. They were a mixed-race couple, something unusual for the time: Jack was of Irish descent, and Anita was a Creole from the South who could, none-theless, pass for white or Mexican. (At some point, she even took on the name Gonzales.) Mrs. Ford was in her late 50s by the time she and her husband bought the Topanga Beach Auto Court, as it was still known at the time, the latest in a series of business ventures she'd pursued in an eventful life.

Born Bessie Julia Johnson back in 1883 in Montgomery, Alabama, she had moved with her family to New Orleans at the age of 5 and had grown up fast. At 17, she became the common-law wife of one Fred Seymour, a relationship that produced a daughter, Hattie, but doesn't seem to have lasted. A couple of years later, she turned up working as a "sporting lady" (a.k.a., prostitute) in New Orleans's red-light district, and it was during this time that she seems to have met pioneering jazz legend Ferdinand "Jelly Roll" Morton.

Anita—or Juanita, as she sometimes called herself—came from a family of jazz players herself: brothers Bill and Ollie "Dink" Johnson were both accomplished musi-cians. Bill, who lived to be 100, is credited with inventing the slap style of double bass playing.

Morton fell in love with Anita and married her, fulfilling his own words of a couple of years earlier: "When I get married, gonna marry a whore." But Anita's past didn't dim his esteem for her: "Personally," he would say later, "I don't believe there ever was one born any finer than Anita." Despite his obvious affection for her, though, Morton and Anita went their separate ways in 1909, when she bought a ticket to Las Vegas and opened the Arcade Saloon.

The next few years were a blur. Morton kept himself occupied on the jazz circuit, playing in Memphis, St. Louis, Detroit, New York, Chicago, and even in Europe for a couple of months.

Jelly Roll Morton, third from left, stands with bandmates outside the Cadillac Café in 1918. *Public domain.*

Anita's saloon was a success, and in 1913, Bill Johnson wrote his sister a letter asking her to help pay for a trip to California. When he got there, he was a hit with audiences, and it wasn't long before his brother wound up in Los Angeles, too. Morton joined them there in 1917 and hoped to be reunited with Anita, but Bill wouldn't tell him where she was. Eventually, though, he found her mother, who got word to Anita that Morton was in L.A. She sold the saloon and traveled west to be reunited with her husband, and the two of them spent the next four or five years together. Anita bought a hotel in Los Angeles and named it (fittingly) the Anita.

Eventually, though, they broke up again. "I think that I have missed an awful lot by leaving her," Morton would say. " 'Course, it was all a mistake, but nevertheless it happened."

The Anita Hotel didn't pan out, and eventually, Anita left for Jerome, Arizona, where she renamed herself Annie Johnson and opened a billiard hall/bordello called the Cuban Queen. It was there that her life took an even stranger turn. One of Anita's borders was a man named Jack Ford, with whom she soon developed

a relationship. She also befriended the mayor of Jerome, a saloon keeper named Francisco Villalpando, and his wife, Guadalupe, who gave birth to a son named Enrique in 1923. Only a year later, his father died in a saloon fight, and after that, Guadalupe went to work as a prostitute in Anita's bordello.

In 1927, Guadalupe was found dead in her own bed, killed by a gunshot.

Shortly after that, Anita fled with Ford—whom she later married—and the pair took the young child with them, telling the boy he was their natural son, and resettling in Canyonville, Oregon. (Ford eventually found out the truth in the 1990s, thanks to a phone call from his big sister by blood, Angelina Parra.)

But Jelly Roll Morton wasn't out of Anita's life for good. In fact, it was Morton who brought Anita back to Los Angeles. In failing health, suffering from asthma and a heart condition, Morton had fallen on hard times during the Depression. Even though swing-era jazz artists had started to cover the tunes he'd written, he wasn't receiving the bulk of the royalties. A lawsuit and letter-writing campaigns went nowhere, so Morton went back to L.A. with the idea of producing a new recording.

The Topanga Ranch Motel has been closed down but had yet to be demolished as of 2016.

Sadly, however, he was too ill to play at the sessions, and he died before the recording could be completed.

Anita was with him when he died. Even though she hadn't seen him in years—and was married to another man—she identified herself as his wife at the hospital where he passed away. Morton himself had since remarried, having wed Mabel Bertrand in 1929. Less than two weeks before he died, she handed him a document to sign, a will that stated, "I hereby devise and bequeath all the rest and residue of my estate, whether real or personal property or mixed to my beloved Anita Gonzales, who has been my beloved comforter, companion and helpmate for many years, and whose tender care I sincerely appreciate. This shall include all Ascap royalties, and Southern Music Co., Melrose Music Co., and all property of every kind personal and otherwise wherever located."

There can be little doubt that Morton loved Anita, having composed at least two songs (*Mama 'Nita* and *Sweet Anita Mine*) in her honor. But he was also sending $5 to $15 back to his wife, Mabel, from Los Angeles before he died. Did he willingly leave his estate to Anita, or did she trick him into signing that will? There's no definitive answer, but the circumstances were certainly suspicious. For one thing, the text above Morton's signature on the "will" was written by a different hand. For another, Anita's brother hired the lawyer who crafted the language.

The question is, why would Anita go to so much trouble, considering Morton's financial state when he died? At the peak of his popularity in the roaring twenties, he'd worn Chesterfield jackets, carried a wad of $1,000 bills in his pocket, and had a penchant for diamonds, with a half-carat stone embedded in his front tooth. But when he died at just 50 years of age, he was destitute. The tax man assessed his estate's worth at a paltry $7,500, his "wealth" amounting to little more than that diamond, a Cadillac—on which he still owed $295—and his clothes.

The sign outside still marks the site of the Topanga Ranch Motel, but you can't stay the night anymore: The land was purchased by the California State Parks in 2001.

His income over the last few years of his life had consisted of a few meager payments from ASCAP that topped out at $185 a year. (This was at a time when people like Cole Porter and Irving Berlin averaged more than $15,000.)

Chicago Tribune writers Howard Reich and William Gaines called Morton "the victim of the first great swindle in American recorded music." His music publisher, they wrote "was picking Morton's pockets at the very moment the musician believed he had hit the jackpot." The Melrose Brothers Music Company once sent him a check for $87 … to cover a decade's worth of work—this for a man who bragged that he had invented jazz and whose music had become a hit all over again for the likes of Benny Goodman and Tommy Dorsey.

Lots of people were profiting from Morton's work, and others continued to do so after he died. The executor for his estate drew up a new contract to get more money from the Melrose brothers, who paid Anita nearly $3,000 in 1947. That was the same year Anita and Jack Ford put Henry in charge of their business in Oregon, presumably to take possession of the Topanga Beach Auto Court.

Jack Ford even ended up with the diamond that had been embedded in Morton's tooth: Some accounts say it was pried loose by someone who had broken into the funeral parlor after his death. Who that person may have been and how the diamond ended up in Ford's possession aren't clear.

Neither of the Fords lived long enough to see the lion's share of Morton's estate, though. The royalties really started rolling in after they both died—she in 1952 and he in 1956. Four years after Jack's death, a court ordered ASCAP to restructure its payment system based on how often a song was played commercially rather than on an arbitrary system of "categories." Henry Ford and Anita's daughter, Hattie Holloway Eysaman, continued to collect those royalties—royalties that kept on growing—for decades after Morton's death. By the turn of the 21st century, his estate had earned $1.1 million.

The Topanga Beach Auto Court, meanwhile, would be the scene of one more important event connected to Jelly Roll Morton.

After his passing, the jazz legend's gravesite at Calvary Cemetery in east Los Angeles lay unmarked and neglected, so in 1950, members of the Southern California Hot Jazz Society decided to do something about it. They planned a benefit concert to raise money for a marble plaque and maintenance on the site, advertising the event on an FM radio station in the area. One of those ads reached the ears of none other than Anita Ford, who promptly called the station manager and protested: If anyone was going to buy a marker for Morton's grave, it would be her.

Whether she didn't like the idea of being embarrassed—having not pursued the matter herself in the nine years since his death—or merely felt a sense of responsibility is hard to say. But the radio hosts who were organizing and promoting the fundraiser, Bob Kirstein and Floyd Levin, suggested they meet with her to discuss the matter. The place of this meeting? The Topanga Beach Auto Court.

Anita cooked them up some fried chicken, served them each a bottle of beer, and reminisced about her days with Morton. But when they brought up the subject of the grave marker, her mood soured. She would not, under any circumstances, allow strangers to purchase a grave marker for Morton. In fact, she said, she planned to visit the cemetery the very next day and purchase it.

She made good on her word and did, indeed, purchase a plaque for Morton's gravesite. A year and a half later, she was buried in the same cemetery.

The Topanga Beach Auto Court, meanwhile, went into decline. Sometime before the 1980s, it was renamed the Topanga Beach Motel and, a few years later, the Topanga Ranch Motel. Jack Ford owned it until he died, then it passed to a succession of owners: Charles and Blanche Gaskins moved in in 1965 and took over management nine years later, eventually buying the place.

"A lot of people think this is a bad neighborhood, but it isn't," Blanche Gaskins said in 1982. "The guys that run around, they have long, wild hair. Most of the people around here, a lot of them are surfers. A lot of them don't work a lot, but most of them, they're not bad people. They're just casual. They just don't like to work too hard."

In 1985, you could still get a room for the night for $30. It also offered monthly rates, as it had at least since '51, back when the Fords still owned the business. That's when Aneta Siegel moved in, although at the time, she payed $30 for an entire month, not just a day. She still lived there in 2004, at which point half of the people staying at the motel were permanent residents. By then, though, its days were numbered.

California State Parks had bought the land from the L.A. Athletic Club three years earlier and had begun plans to evict the motel's residents. Siegel didn't want to leave the motel, her home for 53 years, and it must have seemed callous to be served an eviction notice at the convalescent home where she was recuperating from surgery. A veteran of the Women's Army Corps and former secretary at the U.S. Embassy in London, Siegel said she had nowhere to go and told a reporter that, at the age of 86, she felt like she'd just been eighty-sixed.

The evictions came even though a State Parks official admitted the agency had no specific plans for the property, but added that it wouldn't be bulldozed because it was eligible for inclusion on the National Register of Historic Places.

Thirteen years later, the buildings remained, empty of occupants except for a single state park ranger.

Sadly, Aneta Siegel never got to go home again. She died in June of 2004, just four months after receiving her eviction notice.

The Log Cabin

Movie stars didn't just flock to Malibu during Hollywood's golden age, they ventured farther south, as well. San Diego County was a popular destination, with its beaches, sunshine, and of course Del Mar Racetrack, which opened in 1937. Many celebrities stayed at ritzy hotels such as the Hotel Del Coronado out on Coronado island, but others opted for more modest accommodations such as the Log Cabin Apartments on Highway 101 in Leucadia.

Built as an auto court in 1935, the site was refurbished by new owners in 1962 and served as host to the likes of Desi Arnaz Jr., who reportedly spent a honeymoon night in room 7, and flamboyant pianist Liberace. Owner Jeanne Fuller told the *San Diego Union-Tribune* that Bette Davis once stopped in at the flower shop she opened alongside the motel, adding that she impolitely refused requests for an autograph.

Sammy Davis, the vaudeville dancer and father of Sammy Davis Jr., was a regular visitor to the Log Cabin during horse racing season, and Fuller told the *Union-Tribune* that Davis used to park his gold Lincoln Continental out behind room 5, his favorite room at the motel. Fuller said the elder Davis would cook macaroni and cheese for the local surfers, and his son would call up to ask how he was doing.

The Log Cabin in Leucadia, San Diego County, has hosted the likes of Desi Arnaz Jr. and Sammy Davis Sr.

The Log Cabin is still there today, unlike another popular 101 overnight stop, Jimmie Thompson's Beacon Inn. Branded as a hotel and featuring an illuminated lighthouse tower, it was a little more upscale than the Log Cabin and attracted the likes of Betty Grable, Peter Lorre, Jimmy Durante, and Henry James. Built in 1928, it closed in 1962 after its final New Year's Eve party.

Candyland in Pepto-Bismol Pink

In its obituary for Alex Madonna, the *New York Times* described the Madonna Inn as "a fantasy-theme hotel of outrageous excess and enduring California charm."

According to legend, he designed it on a napkin.

Madonna was used to starting things from scratch. While in high school, he started his own construction company in 1938 with nothing more than a pick, a shovel, a wheelbarrow, and a Model T Ford truck.

Long after he was using sophisticated equipment to pave long sections of highway, Madonna still "liked to talk about the pick and the shovel and the wheelbarrow," said Clint Pearce, who worked his way up from laborer to project foreman to superintendent and, as of 2016, served as the company president. "Modern equipment could do all kinds of things, but that didn't mean it made sense. He liked to ask if you were only using a pick and a shovel and a wheelbarrow, how would you do the job? He really brought it back to basics."

That's how Madonna started out.

"He would go down to the Santa Maria River and load up sand from the river into his Model T," said Pearce, adding that, when he started out, Madonna also used red rock, a rocky clay substance found in the region, to do small-scale jobs such as paving driveways.

Then, when he was 18, he got a job with Pacific Gas & Electric to erect three power poles on San Luis Mountain (a.k.a. Cerro San Luis), a nearly 1,300-foot peak in San Luis Obispo that came to be so closely connected with Madonna that

The Madonna Inn off Highway 101 at French Street in San Luis Obispo in 1962, before that stretch of road was converted into a freeway and French Street got a new name: Madonna Road. © *California Department of Transportation, all rights reserved. Used with permission.*

many referred to it as Madonna Mountain. There's even a giant "M" stenciled into the hillside, although it's in honor of Mission Prep High School, not Madonna.

Belying his later fame, Madonna's first professional trip up its slopes didn't go so well: A hardware store loaned him a new tractor to do the job, but it "somersaulted down the mountain and rolled, doing considerable damage to the machine," his wife, Phyllis Madonna, wrote in her 2002 book, *Madonna Inn: My Point of View.* Madonna broke his arm in three places but managed to finish the job anyway.

It was the first of many construction projects for Madonna, who got his first job with the state Division of Highways in 1947 and won three more contracts on the Central Coast the following year. In the years that followed, he not only built the inn that bears his name but also the San Luis Obispo County Regional Airport, also doing work on U.S. 101 itself. His projects included five bridges and pedestrian undercrossings in the Atascadero area, along with significant highway construction on 202 miles of road from Buellton in Santa Barbara County all the way north to Salinas.

"He was really proud of the road he built through San Luis Obispo," Pearce said, referring to a segment of 101 that ran past the land on which his inn would later sit. "It was his hometown, and everybody was watching him"— some of them expecting him to fail. There was a reason for that: Madonna had won the state contract by submitting the low bid, but it was *so* low, even the state doubted that he could complete the project.

The state offered to let him out of the contract, but Madonna wouldn't hear of it.

"He just found ways to get creative," Pearce said. "He still built it with the right materials and the right specifications, but he just got really creative on how he did his work. He was a risk taker. He would look at any project and he wouldn't get scared off because it was complex."

To get a leg up on the competition, Madonna used his connections with suppliers of the raw materials he needed to do his jobs. Even when it seemed as if he might be biting off more than he could chew, he found a way to make it work. Once, for instance, he assigned one crew to work on repaving about 10 miles of U.S. 101 from Greenfield to King City, while another crew worked on a segment of the same highway between Atascadero and Paso Robles.

"We had a little hot plant up in Bradley," he said, referring to a now nearly deserted town along the old alignment of 101 about 20 miles north of Paso Robles. "The

From left: Connie Madonna, Alex Madonna, Karen Madonna,
John Madonna, and Louis Bassi (Alex's uncle) at a ribbon-cutting
in San Ardo after Madonna Construction completed the San Ardo-to-
San Lucas section of U.S. 101. *Collection of Clint Pearce.*

Then, in the 1970s, Madonna's company completed the final segment of Interstate 5.

"I think his crowning achievement was when he completed I-5," Pearce said. "He had a 12-mile stretch of I-5 up in Thornton (between Stockton and Sacramento), and when he finished it, they cut the ribbon on the interstate from Mexico to Canada."

Madonna had come a long way since the hardware store loaned him the tractor to do that job on San Luis Mountain. What ever happened to that store? Well, Madonna visited the place years later and, according to his wife, became irritated when they didn't have bolts in the size he needed. When the owner asked him if he thought he could do any better, Madonna responded by buying the store.

Such was Alex Madonna's influence and so familiar was the iconic inn he had created, that in 2006, the state assembly adopted a resolution declaring a stretch of U.S. 101 from Atascadero south to the inn itself the Alex Madonna Memorial Highway.

equipment was maybe 1950s vintage, and it was held together by haywire. Our competitor at the time, which was Union Asphalt, was really upset that we had gobbled up all this work and were being kind of gluttonous. They didn't think we could get it all done. They even had a big banner that they held from their plant in Paso that said (sarcastically), 'Good luck, Alex.' "

Madonna managed to get both jobs done.

"Alex knew where all the rock quarries were, and he'd just set up a rock-crushing operation right there," Pearce said.

In all, Pearce estimated that Madonna worked on hundreds—perhaps as many as a thousand—bridges. He also did pavement and/or bridge work on State Routes 1, 41, 46, 58, and 166, including a long, gently curving bridge high over a canyon on 166 that at one time was named the nation's most beautiful span, Pearce said.

U.S. 101 today runs just east of the Madonna Inn property.

The Madonna Inn sign features a neon horse and carriage.

But for all his work on highways and other projects, the inn remained by far his most visible achievement. the *New York Times* writer described it as "reminiscent of the board game Candyland" and noted that it was "doused in Pepto-Bismol pink." It's an apt description, but the inn is, in fact a whole lot more.

Many of the themed rooms have rock walls, matching the inn's rock foundation, and more than a dozen come equipped with waterfalls. Yes, waterfalls. Others have fireplaces or balconies. Some of the rocks used in construction weighed as much as 200 tons.

Themes for the guest rooms range from international (Swiss Chalet, Irish Hills, Oriental Fantasy) to historical (Old Mexico, Sir Walter Raleigh, Ren); from regional (Yosemite Rock, San Francisco) to—of course—romantic (Old Fashioned Honeymoon, Mountain Cabin, Anniversary Room). And that's just the tip of the iceberg:

As of 2015, the inn had 110 guest rooms in all, not to mention a wine cellar, gift shops for men and women, a bakery, cocktail lounge, gourmet shop, coffee shop, and dining room. The last of these features a carved marble balustrade from Hearst Castle, just across the coast mountain range in San Simeon.

"He was the antithesis of cookie-cutter," Pearce said, recalling Madonna's rationale in giving each room its own distinct character. "He said, 'At least this way, I'm only going to make every mistake once.' I think it was the first theme motel."

Madonna bought the land on which the inn sits from the city of San Luis Obispo in 1954.

"The ten acres the inn was originally built on, he just bought at a city auction," Pearce said. "He had his secretary go place the bid. I think he bid $10,000 or $15,000, and he was disappointed because he thought that was so much more than it was probably worth."

It turned out to be a bargain after Madonna hit on an inspiration of how to use it.

"He'd travel up and down the state doing his highway work," Pearce said. "In his mind, San Luis really lacked a great place to stay and a great restaurant, and he wanted to build something that was really one of a kind between L.A. and San Francisco."

The inn began with a dozen rooms—and the first guests got to spend the night free of charge on Christmas Eve, 1958 (the normal rate was $7).

"Together, Alex and I decided on how we wanted to decorate and furnish the rooms," Phyllis Madonna wrote in her book. "We had so many thoughts and ideas, it was difficult to make one choice for all 12 units. So, we decided that rather than number each room, we would name them and proceeded to decorate each room according to the name."

Twenty-eight other rooms were soon added: 14 on each side of the original 12.

"It quickly became known far and wide," Pearce said. "Within a few years, his occupancy [percent] was right up there in the 90s all the time."

One thing Madonna apparently neglected to include in his grand creation, however, was a system of fire sprinklers—an oversight that would prove costly less than eight years after the uber-motel's grand opening. The

The Madonna Inn entrance and office.

inn's location on relatively open land, far from city fire hydrants, made matters worse when, in May 1966, some newlyweds staying at the opulent inn decided to pile some bedclothes against a wall heater. What they were doing without their bedclothes can be left to the imagination, but considering it was their honeymoon, one can safely conclude they were having a hot time. They could not, however, have predicted how hot it would get.

At 2 in the morning, those bedclothes caught fire, and the flames quickly spread to a dozen units, forcing a full-scale evacuation. No one was hurt, but a number of guests found themselves without bedclothes, dress clothes, or any other kind of clothes when their belongings went up in smoke during the fire.

With the only available source of water a three-inch pipe in front of the inn, firefighters found themselves badly outgunned. One fireman lamented that, had they had access to a hydrant, the fire would have been contained to at most three units. But even so, firefighters managed to keep the blaze from spreading to the dining room, the lobby, and other sections of rooms.

Alex Madonna showed his own determination by picking up a loose fire hose and aiming it at the burning structure. Then, when it was all over, he displayed it once again in rebuilding what had been destroyed and adding to it with a pool and expo center—where his wife, Phyllis, continued to stage her annual fashion show a decade after his death in 2004. (Phyllis Madonna herself has performed regularly at the event, which began in 1987 and benefits those affected by child abuse and domestic violence.)

The company Madonna had founded stopped building roads shortly after he died, turning its attention to real estate and running the inn, but Alex Madonna's imprint remains indelible on both the inn and the highway that now bears his name in San Luis Obispo County.

"He was very creative; he was very headstrong and persistent," Pearce said. "He was highly intelligent, and he had a great sense of humor, and he kind of mixed those things together. … He was just one of a kind, and he was a pleasure to work for. I'll never forget it."

A STEP BACK IN TIME ... SORT OF

If the Madonna Inn set the standard for themed motels, it certainly wasn't the last. Drive south about 48 miles on 101 and you'll find another in the Victorian Mansion at Los Alamos.

The Mansion is like a miniature version of the Madonna Inn, minus the pink décor. It's got six themed rooms: A Gypsy Suite and '50s Suite at ground level, Roman and Egyptian suites on the second floor, and French and Pirate suites up top. There's also a boat out back that was hauled to the site three decades ago by the former owner, who had the notion of converting it into suite 7. The boat, which belonged to the king of Denmark, was shipwrecked and remains a gutted hull—but the idea of someday using it as a guest room (despite its odd shape) remains alive.

The mansion is one of several buildings along the old alignment of U.S. 101, now signed as State Route 135 from the north end of Santa Maria south to Los Alamos, where it rejoins the modern freeway. But appearances can be deceiving: The mansion and a vintage gas station next door aren't native to Los Alamos: They were both brought in from elsewhere in the 1980s by then-owner Dick Langdon, who wanted to make the town more of a tourist destination.

The two buildings were meant to complement his other property, which is very much a part of Los Alamos's history. The 1880 Union Hotel next to the gas station got its name because it was, naturally, built in 1880 as a Wells Fargo stage stop.

Sort of.

Actually, the structure that stands there now isn't quite that old. The original burned down in 1893, and a new building went up on the site in 1915. That's the one that's there today, hotel general manager Pearl Chavez explains. The hotel originally had 21 rooms, just two of

The original Union Hotel in Los Alamos opened in 1880, but the present building, seen here, dates to 1915.

which had private baths; today things are a little more private: nine of the 14 rooms currently operating have their own bathrooms.

Everything in the front desk area looks vintage, from the antique telephone to the old switchboard. If the place looks a little familiar, it may be because Paul McCartney and Michael Jackson filmed the music video for their 1983 collaboration *Say, Say, Say* there. And the two colorful chandeliers in the bar? They were used in *Gone With the Wind*. Actor Kurt Russell has been among its famous visitors.

A few doors down is a building occupied, as of 2016, by a tasting room operated by Malibu-based Casa Dumetz Wines. The building itself is a lot older, though, and was originally used as a general store.

"It had a big sign up front saying, 'Coffins,'" said manager Emily Phenicie, who added that the store carried just about anything Los Alamos residents might want. "It was a general store, and it just happened to be a need that needed to be met in the community."

ATTRACTIONS AND DISTRACTIONS

Mention the words "amusement park" these days, and you're likely to conjure up images of mega-roller coasters and other wild rides in worlds populated by fictional figures brought to life: Mickey Mouse, the Seven Dwarfs, Bugs Bunny, and now, more recently, the boy wizard Harry Potter.

But there was a time when the amusements were simpler—if sometimes stranger and even more dangerous: a time when zoos and circuses set the standard with bizarre "freaks of nature," feats of derring-do, and of course those amazing animals. Instead of riding down gleaming rails at the speed of a car on the Hollywood Freeway (probably a lot faster, when rush hour traffic is considered), you sat in wooden stands and watched swordswallowers, knife-throwers, acrobats, and, of course, lion tamers.

During the first half of the twentieth century and for a couple of decades after that, animals were the star attractions at circuses and zoos, both public and private, across the country. In Lincoln Park just off U.S. Highway 99 in southern California, filmmaker William Selig opened an amusement park in the second decade of the 20th century whose carousel attracted 150,000 riders a year, who paid

The entrance to Jungleland in Thousand Oaks welcomes visitors in 1959. *Collection of David Eppen.*

a nickel a head for the privilege of riding. The park also featured an ice-skating rink and dance pavilion, and Selig had grand plans for an expansion that would include even more marvelous rides and attractions.

But the main attraction, as with other amusement parks of the era, was the animals. The Selig Zoo had the largest wild animal collection in the United States, including elephants, lions, monkeys, and a chimpanzee named Mary who was insured for $100,000. Many of the animals were used in Selig's movies or rented out to other movie studios in the burgeoning Hollywood film scene. But when they weren't "acting," they were performing for visitors to the zoo, which was a major—if brief—southern California sensation (Selig, who opened the zoo in 1911, ran into financial difficulties that forced him to sell the place more than a decade later).

Selig wasn't alone in seeing dollar signs dancing on four paws in gilded cages. Other southern California attractions included a couple of ostrich farms, an alligator farm, and not one but two lion farms.

When I was researching my previous work on U.S. Highway 99, I learned of a place in El Monte called Gay's Lion Farm. It flourished from the 1920s through the early '40s as a home for movie-star felines of epic proportion, while doubling as a roadside attraction that served up an eyeful of Africa's kings of the jungle. What I didn't know is that a similar and more enduring lion farm existed along U.S. Highway 101 in Thousand Oaks.

Louis Goebel created Goebel's Lion Farm there in 1926, just a year after Charles and Muriel Gay founded their similarly named big-cat showcase in El Monte. Although the Gays' facility closed for good in 1942, Goebel's remained open until 1969—by which time it had expanded and changed its name to Jungleland USA.

The two "farms," however, had an uncanny number of things in common. Both opened around the same time and fronted highways that ran east and west, even though, for most of their length, they ran north and south. Both at one time housed Slats, the original MGM lion. Each served as the inspiration for a high school mascot. And both experienced tragedies that damaged their respective reputations.

Goebel actually got his start in the business with the Gays, who started working with lions in Hollywood before moving to El Monte. Despite its original location,

The first fire truck in the Conejo Valley area, which Louis Goebel purchased after a fire at the lion farm, which later became Jungleland. *Public domain.*

Goebel's job there wasn't glamorous: He was responsible for cutting up animal carcasses that would serve as food for the lions. Being the son of a New York butcher, he knew the work, but when the Gays moved their operations eastward, he stayed behind, working as a meat cutter and groundskeeper at Universal Studios—which had its own zoo—until 1926.

That year, the studio decided it didn't need its own zoo any longer, and Goebel suddenly found himself without a job—but with a new opportunity. When the owner of Universal started selling off the animals, he bought six of them: all lions, named Andy, Bill, Little Caesar, Min, Momma, and Poppa. Caesar was a highway cat of the first order: The young lion enjoyed car rides so much he ran to Goebel's Chevrolet the moment it was driven to his enclosure for a trip to some location shoot. Then, once he had arrived, he refused to get out of the car again.

Another lion, named Humpy, was added shortly afterward and served as an able sentinel. The 25-year-old veteran of numerous comedy films built a reputation for his genial disposition, but that didn't stop him from being an intimidating presence: According to one newspaper account, Goebel never needed to lock his car "as long as Humpy is napping in the neighborhood."

Goebel originally wanted to open his business closer to L.A., in Agoura, but he couldn't get a permit, so he trekked farther down Ventura Boulevard (old U.S. 101) to Thousand Oaks, a community some 32 miles from Los Angeles that wasn't much more than a bunch of fields and a few scattered homes at that point. Apparently, even the Ventura County sheriff wasn't quite sure where it was. He finally recognized it as a "godforsaken place" after Goebel said you could get there by "driving up a crooked road to the top of the hill."

He got his permit when officials decided Thousand Oaks was so far out in the boondocks the animals weren't likely to be a nuisance to much of anyone.

Goebel purchased five lots there for $10 each.

By 1928, the park's leonine population had grown to ten, and a year later, it was up to fifteen. Before long, Goebel was adding other animals to rent out to the studios. By the 1930s, he had 101 other wild animals at the park in addition to the lions, and a census in 1935 found the farm now home to six camels, four leopards and a tiger in addition to forty-three lions. A souvenir guide from the 1950s described the attraction—by then renamed the World Jungle Compound—as the "home of the motion picture animal actors—birds, beasts and reptiles from the jungles of the world."

You could ride in a chariot pulled not by horses, but zebras. You could visit water buffalo, llamas, kangaroos, bison, and deer, and as many as six kids at once could ride an elephant (no solo rides, please). Cheetah—not a big cat, but a chimpanzee who played Tarzan's simian sidekick on the big screen—could be found there. Camels from the farm were used in a variety of movies like *King Richard and the Crusaders*, a 1954 film featuring Rex Harrison and Virginia Mayo.

Scenes from several movies were filmed on the property itself, as well, including *Tarzan* and *The Adventures of Robin Hood*.

As years went by, the park expanded, adding such attractions as a safari tram bus and a monorail. Water fountains shaped like lions and hippos opened their mouths to young guests. There were ostrich rides and camel rides, a reindeer corral and a snake pit, a seal bowl and a petting zoo, as well as intriguingly named

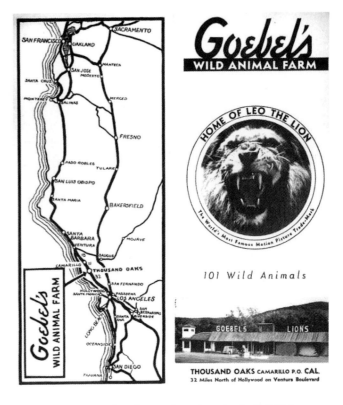

A pre-1940 brochure advertises Goebel's Wild Animal Farm and locates it on the map for prospective visitors. *Public domain.*

attractions such as the Garden of the Gods, Temple Ruins, and Thieves Market.

Lefty Hymes, outdoor writer for the *Winona (Minnesota) Daily News*, described Jungleland in January 1969, just months before it closed: "The grounds are green with thick vegetation that has been allowed to flourish for decades. Centuries-old oaks shade the grounds, and stands of bamboo and other tropic growth provide natural borders for various areas. Ivy entwines bridge railings and crawls up the sides of bamboo buildings."

When the new freeway bypass for U.S. 101 was built, Jungleland found itself on the old and new alignments of the highway, giving it maximum visibility from both sides. But that didn't guarantee its success.

For starters, things didn't always go smoothly at the park.

In 1940, a fire started in a hay barn and spread through the elephant barn, camel barn, hay shed, and machine shop. Among the victims were Sally and Queenie, a pair of elephants who were just getting ready to work with actress Dorothy Lamour in Paramount's production of *Moon Over Burma*. Sally burned to death, and Queenie was so badly hurt she had to be put down. Seven tigers and three camels also perished as a result of the blaze.

"The camels were killed when the roof caved in on them," Goebel said.

Five lions, including MGM's reigning mascot, were more fortunate: They were locked in rolling cages that could be quickly removed from the burning buildings.

A panther escaped from the compound in 1963 but was found a couple of days later hiding under a warehouse. The incident reportedly inspired Newbury Park High School to choose the panther as its mascot.

No harm was done on that occasion, but the story was sadly different in another incident a few years earlier. In December 1949, May Kovar Schafer's three children watched as a four-year-old lion named Sultan mauled their mother in a cage. Her 18-year-old son, Michael Kovar, ran into the enclosure and tried to drive the lion away with a chair and stick, and the children's cries for help reached the ears of an elephant trainer named Rudy Muller.

"I grabbed up a pitchfork and an eight-foot length of pipe," Muller said, recalling that he stabbed Sultan with the pitchfork and used his other hand to bring the pipe down on the animal's head. "That made the lion drop her and back up—must have stunned him for a second, because he sagged back on his haunches. But I didn't have much time—just enough time to pick up Mrs. Schaefer. Then the lion started for me and the children."

He backed up slowly, inching his way out of the cage as Schaefer's 14-year-old daughter, May, held the door.

Unfortunately, they got Schaefer out of the cage too late. Muller said he saw her move her arm as he picked her up but she was apparently dead by the time he got her out of the cage. The lion had clamped down on her neck with his jaws, severing her spine.

One of the park's biggest attractions was another female animal trainer named Mabel Stark, who once

WITH A LONG, TIRING DRIVE ON MEMORIAL DAY WEEKEND . . .

BRING THE FAMILY AND CELEBRATE

The 40th ANNIVERSARY YEAR of NEARBY

Jungleland

The Home of Famous Movie & TV Animal Stars at 2034 Thousand Oaks Blvd., THOUSAND OAKS

MINUTES AWAY ON THE VENTURA FREEWAY

A 1966 newspaper ad touts the 40th anniversary year of Jungleland.

described herself as "the only woman in the world crazy enough to fool around with tigers."

Stark's fascination with animals began when she was studying nursing in Louisville, Kentucky: "On my afternoons off, I always went to the zoo while the other girls had dates," she would later recall. "I loved to watch the lions and tigers pace up and down the cage."

After completing a nursing degree, she traveled to Los Angeles and ran into a fellow named Al Sands who managed the Al G. Barnes Circus.

"He asked me how I liked Los Angeles. I told him I hadn't seen the city but the zoo was great. He was surprised to learn that I liked animals. One of my friends spoke up and told Al my ambition was to become an animal trainer. He was interested and asked me if I'd like a job in the circus."

Stark gave him her answer the next morning, after taking a look at herself in the mirror wearing her nurse's uniform.

"Then I took it off and wrapped it up carefully," she said. "I knew I would never wear it again."

Her gig at the Barnes Circus turned out to be a letdown: Instead of putting her in with the big cats, Sands assigned her to ride around on a horse. When the circus folded its tent for the season in Venice, Stark found herself with nowhere to go and nothing better to do than watch the trainers work with the animals. The man who ran the circus, Al Barnes, asked her if she wanted to sign up for another year, and she told him she would on one condition: if he would give her an animal act. He agreed and assigned trainer Louis Roth (to whom she was later briefly married) to work with her.

There happened to be an opening for a tiger trainer at the time: Stark's predecessor, Marguerite Haupt, had been killed by one of the animals.

That didn't faze Stark, who worked with big cats for the next half century, earning a reputation as the most accomplished female animal trainer of her day. At one point, she performed with as many as 16 tigers in one cage.

"A tiger is strictly an individual," she explained. "He fights his own fights—and usually with other tigers. They are all like children, with all of them having different personalities."

"Usually" was the operative word. There were times when some of her "children" chose to pick a fight with Stark. During a 1935 show in Phoenix, some 20,000 people watched as she tripped over a stool and one of the animals sprang at her. She managed to fend it off with a flash gun, but the incident still earned her a trip to the hospital. By that time, she'd already been scratched by 18 other tigers.

The most serious incident occurred in 1928. The circus train was running late as it headed for Bangor, Maine, in a rainstorm, and there was no time to feed the big cats before the show. Two of them, Zoo and Sheik, hungry and wet from the rain, took their frustrations out on Stark.

"Sheik was right behind me and caught me in the left thigh, tearing a two-inch gash that cut through to the bone and almost severed my left leg just above the knee," she later recalled. "I could feel blood pouring into both my boots, but I was determined to go through with the act."

Then Zoo "jumped from his pedestal and seized my right leg, jerking me to the ground. As I fell, Sheik struck out with one paw, catching the side of my head, almost scalping me."

Sheik continued, "I wondered into how many pieces I would be torn," but added that her biggest concern was for the audience: "I knew it would be a horrible sight if my body was torn apart before their eyes. And all my tigers would be branded as murderers and sentenced to spend the rest of their lives in narrow cages instead of being allowed the freedom of the big arena and the pleasure of working. That thought gave me strength to fight."

Stark got out of the cage alive, but barely. She took 378 stitches after the mauling, and the doctors who worked to repair her torn muscles doubted she'd pull through. But not only did she survive, she returned to work within a few weeks—although further trips to the hospital were necessary over the next two years for additional muscle repair.

By the time of her mauling, Stark had left the Barnes circus for Ringling Brothers and Barnum & Bailey, and had moved on to the John Robinson Circus. Although she preferred to work with tigers, she also served as Mae West's stunt double for the lion-taming scenes in the 1933 film *I'm No Angel*.

It was five years later, in 1938, that she came to Goebel's lion farm, and she worked there for the next three decades, starting full-time in 1957—by which time the attraction had been renamed the Jungle Compound. Four years later, she appeared as a mystery guest on the game show *What's My Line?*—in which a panel of four celebrities (including Jerry Lewis) tried to guess her occupation. They were unable to do so.

Stark was 79 years old in 1968, when the property came under new management, and the new owner fired her. Not long afterward, one of the tigers she'd been working with escaped and was shot. In despair over the loss of her career and the death of one of her animals, she took her

The interior of the brochure pictured earlier proclaims that "Leo, the famous lion, known to screen patrons everywhere as 'The World's Most Famous Motion-Picture Trade-Mark,' lives on the Farm and is on view to visitors."

own life with an overdose of barbiturates. The following year, Jungleland itself closed.

The attraction fell victim to increased competition from ride- and character-based theme parks such as Disneyland and Knott's Berry Farm, as well as its own bad publicity.

The most widely reported incident occurred in November 1966, when actress Jayne Mansfield took three of her children—Miklos, eight; Zoltan, six; and Mariska, two (who would grow up to star in TV's *Law and Order: SVU*)—to Jungleland for a photo shoot with one of the lions there. According to press accounts, the lion was allowed to roam freely around the compound during the session. A friend, May Mann, described what happened next:

Jayne was adjusting Miklos' tie when Zoltan was grabbed by a big lion. I grabbed Jayne and held her. She screamed and screamed and screamed. The owners rushed over and pried open the lion's mouth and took the child out.

But not before severe damage had been done. Zoltan was unconscious by the time Jungleland manager Roy

Kabat and an animal trainer managed to extricate him from the animal's maw. The boy's skull was fractured and his spleen punctured in the attack, requiring two operations—the first a six-hour procedure to sew up a gash on his cheek and relieve pressure caused by a fracture on the back of his skull. A third operation was performed later to ease pressure on his spinal cord.

Zoltan's condition was initially described as guarded, but he ultimately survived and was released from the hospital on Christmas day, just under a month after the incident occurred. Mansfield stayed at his bedside throughout the ordeal and ultimately had to be hospitalized herself with a case of pneumonia.

In January 1967, Mansfield filed a $1.6 million lawsuit against the park, seeking $500,000 in general damages and $1 million in punitive damages for Zoltan and an additional $100,000 in damages for herself resulting from "severe shock to her nervous system." The lawsuit wasn't settled until more than five years later, by which time Jungleland was out of business and Jayne Mansfield was dead, having

Two Jungleland elephants engage in a friendly tug-of-war with their trunks in this 1959 photo.
Collection of David Eppen.

A young girl rides an elephant statue at Jungleland in 1958. *Collection of David Eppen.*

been killed in a car crash six months after the lawsuit was filed.

The value of the eventual settlement to Zoltan Hargitay was $10,000.

As for the Jungleland site, its 1,800 animals were sold at auction as nearly 25,000 people arrived at the park for the bidding. Among them was a 1,700-pound hippo named Sam, who went to a 24-year-old unemployed construction worker for just $480. Ronnie Hochleutner had visions of exhibiting Sam for a profit but found the amount of money needed to feed and house the animal was three times what he'd paid for it.

At one point, Hochleutner convinced an Orange County horse rancher to house Sam until he could find a permanent home: "A hippos is known in Africa as a river

horse," he said. "He waddles and the horses gallop, but they get along wonderfully."

That beautiful relationship ended abruptly, however, when Sam spooked the horses and broke out of his corral. It took four hours for catch Sam and load him into Hochleutner's truck and—after a zoo turned him down—off to a nearby dog pound of all places. Hochleutner eventually wound up selling Sam to an auto dealer, who in turn donated the hippo to the Kern County Zoo Society.

Other animals brought various prices at the Jungleland auction. The Brownsville Zoo paid $20,000 for a couple of orangutans, but a female lion went for $150, an untrained gibbon for $137.50, and a red fox who'd appeared in the movie *Doctor Dolittle* just $75.

"Thus the animals went their ways—separately and together," Frank Anderson reported for the *Long Beach Independent*, "and the Ark that was Jungleland lay foundering on the reefs in a sea of red ink."

LAND OF THE GIANTS

The elephants at Jungleland were impressive, but the biggest living tourist attractions along Highway 101 lie to the north, in the region known as the Redwood Empire, home to the tallest trees on Earth.

A section of old U.S. 101 runs directly through the heart of it, where it's known as the Avenue of the Giants. The 31-mile stretch of road was bypassed in 1964, but it's still there; running parallel to the new highway starting just north of Garberville, it's now signed as State Route 254. Redwoods hundreds of years old tower above the ribbon of asphalt that runs through Humboldt Redwoods State Park. Among them is a 950-year-old redwood called the Immortal Tree that stands 250 feet tall. It's not the oldest tree in the forest, but it's perhaps the most tenacious, having survived a direct lightning strike that shaved 45 feet off its crown, an attempt by loggers to cut it down in 1908, and a major flood in 1964.

Then there's the Founders Tree, which was dedicated to those who formed the Save the Redwoods League in 1919 with the intent of preserving thousands of acres of redwood forest in Humboldt County from the threat of timber concerns. Nine years later, they had succeeded in placing 3,500 acres of the county's forested land in the hands of the state, shielding more than 15 miles along the Avenue of the Giants from being cut down by lumber companies. By 1952, the state park's acreage had grown to 22,000.

One of the trees saved in the endeavor was the massive Dyerville Giant, which at nearly 370 feet was more than twice the height of Niagara Falls. Perhaps dating from the time of Christ, it measured 52 feet around and weighed more than a million pounds when it came crashing to earth in 1991. Though fallen, it lies in state for visitors to see along the Dyerville Loop Road, just off the Avenue of the Giants.

As if the grandeur of the redwoods alone weren't enough to attract the attention of motorists navigating Old 101, enterprising men and women found ways to "enhance" the experience during the early and middle years of the 20th century.

The trees are so wide that, if there's a hole in the trunk, you can actually drive through them.

And people do.

The Shrine Drive-thru Tree in Myers Flat on the Avenue of the Giants is one of three such trees in the region. Unlike the other two tree tunnels, which were created artificially, its opening is natural, with a gabled peak, and just wide enough to let average-sized cars go through. Early travelers delighted in traveling through it on wagons before the automobile became the dominant form of transport.

The Chandelier Tree in Leggett, the southernmost of the three tunnel trees, lies along a different section of Old 101, which was bypassed in the early 1970s and redesignated as State Route 271. At 315 feet tall and 21 feet across, it's been dated to 500 BCE. It's called the Chandelier Tree in honor of the large branches that rise on either side of the trunk, creating an image similar to a three-armed candelabra. It's on private land that's been in the Underwood family since 1922, and you can drive through it today for a $5 fee.

The tree tunnel was cut in 1934.

Then there's the Klamath Tour-thru Tree far to the north, beyond Eureka and heading toward the Oregon border. It's the most recent of the bunch, with its tunnel dating to 1976.

If you don't want to merely look at or drive through the trees, you can go one better and live inside them.

Well not quite.

But a few hollowed-out trees were so big they were converted into pseudo-houses to serve as tourist attractions.

Way back in 1933, *Ripley's Believe It or Not* declared the World Famous Tree House in Piercy to be "the tallest one-room tree abode on earth." The tree itself is 250 feet high, and a fire centuries ago hollowed out a cavity 50 feet tall.

"It was a cozy place, the inside of that tree, finished, of course, in very natural redwood," one visitor remarked. "It would make the perfect home for a Hobbit. Or for Winnie-the-Pooh."

Drive about 20 miles north on the Avenue of the Giants, and you'll see a similar attraction: the Eternal Tree House in Redcrest, which likewise was carved out by fire long ago. A wood splitter named Harry McLeod used an ax and adze to improve on nature in the early 20th century, and in 1950, the hollowed-out but still-living stump became home to a gift shop—one of many that line this section of highway.

The One-Log House in Garberville is a little different. It was hollowed out in 1946 from a section of redwood tree weighing 42 tons. Two men worked eight months to hollow out a 32-foot-long room with a ceiling high enough to accommodate Shaquille O'Neal or Wilt Chamberlain.

"Enough chips came out of here to build about five houses," the owner, Bill Butrica, estimated, adding that the house toured the country for three years after it was built "just to show how big redwoods are." It eventually wound up in Leggett, where it spent 25 years before moving to Phillipsville for 23 and, from there, to Garberville.

One of the most extensive attractions on the highway lies to the north: the Trees of Mystery, less than 40 miles from the Oregon state line. The trees themselves are massive and, in some cases, bizarre. Take the Cathedral Tree for instance: It's actually nine trees growing together in a semicircle that resemble (naturally) a cathedral. You can walk the trails or take a sky tram that allows you to look the giant trees in the eye, so to speak.

But perhaps even more eye-catching are the huge statues of Paul Bunyan and Babe, the Blue Ox, in the attraction's parking lot. Paul measures just over 49 feet tall and weighs in at a hefty 30,000 pounds—the same weight as Babe, who stands 35 feet tall and has actually been there even longer, since 1952.

The present Bunyan statue was installed in 1961, but he isn't the original. The first of the Bunyan lineage was built in 1946 but didn't prove as durable as his legend—not by a long shot. Heavy rains destroyed the statue within a year when his papier-mâché head buckled and caved in beneath the winter rains. A second Bunyan, half as tall as the current statue at just 24 feet, was apparently in place during the 1950s.

Babe, for his part, was once even more fearsome than he now appears: His head nodded, he rolled his eyes, and his nostrils expelled smoke. But the head had to be fixed in place when the statue was moved to the other side of the parking lot, and the smoke was extinguished because it frightened small children.

And for all the natural wonders in the Redwood Empire, some folks couldn't resist the temptation to add a little unnatural fun to the mix.

That's where Confusion Hill comes in, a manmade tourist attraction that has nothing to do with supernatural phenomena and everything to do with sleight-of-hand on a scale befitting the redwoods. In its Gravity House, one ad boasts, water runs uphill, people grow (and shrink), and you can lean at a sharp angle without falling down. Other attractions on the site 18 miles south of Garberville include a redwood "shoehouse" used as a float in a 1947 parade and brought to Confusion Hill when it opened two years later, and a 40-foot-tall totem pole advertised as the worlds's largest freestanding redwood chain saw carving. Other wood carvings include a giant panda and make-believe horned chipmunks dubbed "chipalopes." A mountain train ride completes the list of attractions.

A sign points the way to the Avenue of the Giants.

Repeated mud slides in the area spurred work on a highway bypass around Confusion Hill that was completed in 2009, so the attraction itself is no longer directly on the highway.

SANTA CLAUS LANE

Sometimes, street names outlast their inspiration. Take, for instance, Pea Soup Andersen Boulevard off Highway 99 in Selma, which was named for a restaurant in the Buellton-based chain that later changed hands. The distinctive windmill is still there, but the eatery changed its name to the Spike N Rail.

Even stranger is Santa Claus Lane, a short segment of Old 101 in Carpinteria. If you need a little Christmas, right this very minute, you'll be disappointed when you exit the freeway to find nothing in the nature of decorated evergreens and multicolored lights. But this wasn't always the case. There was a time, back in the day, when Santa Claus Lane was about as close as you could get to the North Pole in California.

Santa Claus Lane got its start in 1948, when Patrick McKean built a five-stool juice stand in what used to be a lima bean field. The featured attraction was McKean's date shakes—a beverage popular with travelers down in Indio County, but not typically found in Santa's Arctic Circle abode (at least, not as far as I know). Still, the shakes were *cold*, and that may have helped spawn the idea of connecting the place to Saint Nick.

Or maybe not.

According to one account, McKean chose the name because it matched all the other "Santas" in the area: Santa Barbara, Santa Maria, Santa Paula. …

But two years later, the story goes, a traveler hard up for cash pulled into the juice stand and offered to build a Santa statue for $500. McKean agreed, and the result was an 18-foot-tall Santa made of concrete and chicken wire, which was hoisted onto the roof of the juice shop. A loudspeaker was hooked up and blared a greeting across the highway: "Welcome to Santa Claus!" Travelers took note, and the Christmas theme was born.

As time passed, the concept grew into a block-long Christmas extravaganza. There was Candy Kitchen and a Toyland store, where you could have your cards postmarked "Santa Claus, CA." And kids could hop on the merry-go-round or bug their parents for the 50 cents needed to ride the miniature train. They could toss coins into a wishing well, and their parents could wet their whistles at a bar called the Reindeer Room.

The highway moved inland, bypassing Santa Claus Lane in 1954, threatening to kill the attraction. But a businessman from New York named Hap Shargas took over in 1956 and launched a campaign to "save Santa Claus." He succeeded—at least in the short term.

A 1950s-era postcard shows Santa popping out of a chimney atop a gabled roof in a row of roadside buildings that epitomized the Christmas spirit. Santa raised a black-gloved hand and appeared to be waving at (or saluting) travelers as they passed the area. He presided over the highway stop's original business, McKean's juice shop, which stood just a few doors down from St. Nick's Bar-B-Q. Between the two stood a giant, pipe-smoking Frosty the Snowman statue atop (naturally) an ice cream eatery. At one time, Frosty's eyes lit up and smoke wafted up out of his pipe.

Toward the end of the century, however, Santa Claus Lane's popularity started to wane. Shargas sold the lane and retired in 1976, moving to Acapulco. After that, businesses came and went. One diner adopted the name Santa Claus Chinese Deli, which is about as bizarre an example of crossing the streams as you're likely to find.

The miniature train stopped running around '84, Frosty was taken down in the 1980s, and by 1999, more than two-thirds of the retail space along the Santa Claus Strip was vacant. Santa himself left for good shortly after the dawn of the new millennium.

The buildings from the old Santa Claus strip are still there, but these days the place has a seafood theme.

AND … THEY'RE OFF!

Bing Crosby was famous for a number of very good reasons, his singing voice foremost among them. A close second were his movies, including a series of satirical "road pictures" filmed with Bob Hope: *Road to Zanzibar, Road to Morocco, Road to Rio.* … The duo made seven of them in all. But if you found yourself taking a road trip with Crosby in real life, there was a good chance you'd end up in Del Mar. That's where the Del Mar Racetrack was located, at the new fairgrounds built to house the county fair.

The fairgrounds cost $1 million to build, and the racetrack was built under the Works Progress Administration. It was the Depression, after all. But the irony would still have been hard to miss: Here was a facility built with public money at which more public money would be wagered—and one that would be run by Hollywood stars, no less.

First, a little background.

The fair had come a long way from its humble beginnings.

There'd been a fair in San Diego County since the 1880s, and it had moved around several times. The *Los Angeles Herald* referred to a San Diego fair in 1880 and plans for a "citrus fair" to be staged by the National Ranch Grange in 1881. Formally known as the San Diego County Horticultural and Agricultural Display, it took place under a canvas tent just east of modern Interstate 5. (A modern park on the site is named for Frank Kimball, first board chairman of the county's agricultural society, which was formed at the citrus fair.)

No fair was held for the next few years, but what some regard as the first true fair enjoyed a three-day run at the Armory Hall in 1885, with exhibitors traveling from as far away as Julian. The event returned to the same site the following year for what the *San Francisco Chronicle* referred to as a "second San Diego County Fair." Like the citrus fair, it was still largely focused on fruit exhibits, featuring no fewer than 49 displays of apples and 32 more of peaches.

From there, the nomadic fair hopscotched across the county, moving to Oceanside in 1888 and Escondido the following year and later back to San Diego. The 1912 fair in Escondido featured horse racing—the attraction that would help give the fair its permanent home a quarter century later. But the fair wouldn't stay in Escondido. Instead, it returned to San Diego after World War I, this time in buildings constructed for a 1915 expo that celebrated the opening of the Panama Canal (the buildings, in San Diego's Balboa Park, are still there today).

Meanwhile, south of the border, the Agua Caliente racetrack in Tijuana was pulling in large crowds from Southern California to play the ponies and consume vast quantities of alcohol—which was illegal in the U.S. under Prohibition. It was a gold mine for Mexico, even after Prohibition ended in 1933, and California wanted to get in on the act.

The state, which was in the throes of the Depression, realized it could raise a lot of money by making it legal to play the ponies. Legislation passed in 1933 allowed pari-mutuel betting at both private and fairground racetracks, and the state would, of course, tax those bets, with the funds going to support county fairs.

Demand spiked even further when Mexico went in the opposite direction: In 1935, the incoming Mexican president launched a series of reforms that ended gambling, evicted foreign companies, and, most notably, closed the Agua Caliente track. With business suddenly booming at Santa Anita and Hollywood Park, there was plenty of room on the scene for a third major track in southern California, and what better place for it than a new fairground in Del Mar?

That's where Crosby and the Hollywood crowd came into the picture. The crooner, a shareholder in Santa Anita since it opened in 1933, was approached by stockbroker William Quigley about the prospect of opening a track in Del Mar. Not long afterward, the pair founded the Del Mar Turf Club and assembled a collection of Hollywood stars to help run it. Crosby would serve as

president, with actor Pat O'Brien and comedian Oliver Hardy as officers; the executive committee would include such luminaries as Gary Cooper and Joe E. Brown.

Under a 10-year lease negotiated with the state, the turf club would be responsible for building a grandstand, offices, and facilities to house both the horses and jockeys. They lost no time in constructing a lavish facility in Spanish Colonial Revival style and marketing it in the media as "the playground of the stars." It lived up to that name, with stars such as Red Skelton, W. C. Fields, Dorothy Lamour, Edward G. Robinson, and Ava Gardner visiting the track.

Crosby courted the press by putting reporters up at the Del Mar Hotel and arranging for them to share trains from Los Angeles with celebrities who provided entertainment during the trip. Crosby even persuaded NBC to run a half-hour radio program on Saturday mornings that originated in Del Mar, featuring horse racing trivia and (of course) a few tunes sung by Bing himself.

The Crosby tune most closely linked to Del Mar was—as anyone who's visited the track will know—"Where the Turf Meets the Surf," which is still played before the first and last races at the track every day of the racing season. Crosby came up with the catchphrase and wrote the tune with Midge Polesie.

In terms of horse racing, the track's breakthrough event was a 1938 match race between Seabiscuit and Crosby's horse Ligaroti in front of 20,000 fans. The $25,000 winner-take-all race took place in August, two months before Seabiscuit's legendary upset of War Admiral at Pimlico, but the 6-year-old Ligaroti—who had won 13 of his 21 starts—gave as good as he got. He had an advantage, as he was carrying 15 pounds less than his rival, and he stayed with Seabiscuit the entire way. As the race heated up, the horses started crowding one another, with Seabiscuit on the rail, and the jockeys stopped using their riding crops on the horses—and turned them on each other. According to Ligaroti's jockey, Spec Richardson, rival George "Iceman" Woolf whipped Ligaroti five or six times before Richardson reached out and tried to grab Woolf's wrist. Then, he said, Woolf grabbed Ligaroti's bridle near the bit just before the finish line.

A protest was lodged, but Seabiscuit's victory was upheld. The Del Mar stewards wanted to suspend both jockeys but were powerless to do so because the race was an exhibition. Regardless, Del Mar was now on the horse racing map, destined to attract not only celebrities but top horses and jockeys such as Johnny Longden, Laffit Pincay, and Bill Shoemaker.

Crosby sold his share of the turf club in 1946, but the track continues to host horse racing each year. It's impossible to miss it: The fairgrounds are visible from both old U.S. 101 and Interstate 5.

Pier Wars

No survey of roadside attractions would be complete without at least a brief look at the Santa Monica Pier, which stands at the westernmost end of old Route 66 (current Interstate 10), where it meets the Pacific Coast Highway—the former 101 Alternate.

Santa Monica actually has two piers next to each other. The municipal pier was built in 1909 to carry sewer pipes out beyond the breakers; the fun was to be had just to the south on the Newcomb Pier, as you can tell by its other name: the Pleasure Pier. It was built in 1916 by Charles Looff, who had built the first carousel at Coney Island four decades earlier. Now he sought to duplicate that success out west.

And so, he did.

Looff had started off as a wood-carver, and he'd parlayed his fascination with carving carousel animals into a thriving business. Having established amusement resorts over the years in New York, Dallas, Providence, Seattle, and San Francisco, he moved from Rhode Island to California in 1910. There he took up residence in Long Beach, where he set up a factory and built a carousel for the Pike—a waterfront amusement area that he founded in 1902 (it finally closed in 1979).

But Looff had bigger plans. He considered Santa Monica, north on the coast route, the perfect place for his latest venture, a mammoth undertaking described in a *Los Angeles Times* report published in March 1916: "Persistent rumors of a gigantic amusement pier to be constructed on the old North Beach of Santa Monica ceased to be rumors the past few days, when carloads of creosoted piling and heavy lumber began to appear on the ocean front just south of the Santa Monica municipal pier."

The pier was to be 700 feet long and 247 feet wide, and the cost of the enterprise was put in the neighborhood of $400,000.

Once the pier itself was built, Looff created a carousel building using a hodgepodge of architectural styles, ranging from Byzantine arches to Spanish Colonial turrets. The carousel itself—which featured goats, camels, and giraffes as well as horses—was on the ground floor of the two-story structure. Upstairs were apartments that, at various times, housed such notables as William Saroyan and Joan Baez. Spectators could take their leisure in rocking chairs surrounding the carousel as they waited their turn in line. That original carousel was removed long ago, but the building still houses a merry-go-round, built in 1954 and moved to Santa Monica from the Venice Pier.

There were other attractions at the Looff pier, as well: Looff brought in a racing roller coaster called the Blue Streak from San Diego, employing 50 men to dismantle it and then reassemble it on the pier, out over the water. Other attractions included the Whip and Aeroscope, a circular swing that featured "flying boats." Looff also built a bowling and billiards building and set up picnic grounds.

Unfortunately, Looff died in the summer of 1918, putting any further plans on hold. A new owner took over five years later and installed a new 80-foot-tall Whirlwind Dipper roller coaster in 1924, opening the massive La Monica Ballroom a few months later. The indoor hall, with its 10 majestic towers looking like something you might find in India or the Middle East, had enough room for 5,000 dancers to share its maple wood floor.

Why such a huge dance floor?

To say dancing was a popular pastime would be an understatement. These were the Roaring Twenties, after all, and young adults were ready to roar. Dance contests sprang up, and within a decade would morph into the marathon dances that served as a sort of spectator sport during the Great Depression. One major obstacle to the dance craze was the city of Los Angeles, where elected officials considered dances a corrupting influence and virtually banned them within their jurisdiction.

That didn't stop piers outside the city limits from building giant monuments to the trend, and the Santa Monica Pier was no exception.

Unfortunately, a storm nearly destroyed the pier in 1926, washing away two-thirds of the pilings that were supporting the La Monica. Money that had been earmarked for further improvements on the pier was used instead for the repairs that were needed to save it. Then the Depression ended its golden age, with many of the rides being sold off during the 1930s, and the pier found a new purpose: as a launching pad for boats ferrying high rollers to offshore gambling ships. The biggest of these, the S.S. *Rex*, was a 24-hour-a-day operation that could accommodate as many as 3,000 gamblers at once. The ships continued to operate until California attorney general Earl Warren (later a Supreme Court justice) shut them down.

The iconic neon sign at the entrance to the pier was added in 1940, celebrating a "yacht harbor" that no longer exists there.

The ballroom, meanwhile, survived and served as a staging ground for radio and TV broadcasts. Western swing music star Space Cooley's television show, the first ever to be broadcast live, originated at the ballroom in 1948, and it was converted into a roller-skating rink ten years later. It was eventually demolished in 1962.

By then, there was a new pier in town: Pacific Ocean Park (or P.O.P.), just about a mile down the road in Venice.

The park was "new," but the pier itself wasn't. Ocean Park Pier had been a longtime rival of Santa Monica Pier as a seaside destination.

Tobacco tycoon Abbot Kinney had gotten the ball rolling with his Pacific Ocean Casino in the last decade of the 19th century. Kinney persuaded the Santa Fe Railroad to extend one of its lines north to his nascent resort, and it quickly grew into a full-fledged country club featuring a golf course, tennis courts, horse racing track, and swimming pool.

It might be argued that Kinney was the father of the southern California amusement park, and he was determined to do things on a grand scale. His Venice of America development, which opened on Independence Day 1905, was built on marshland he'd won from four former business partners in the flip of a coin. (One of those partners, a man named A. F. Fraser, will re-enter our story shortly.)

Kinney had drained the marshes and diverted the water into several miles of canals he'd dug out of the earth, then invited tourists to see the sites by climbing aboard one of his Italian-style gondolas—each piloted by one of more than twenty gondoliers he'd hired from the *original* Venice. If they preferred, they could take in some sun on the beach, dine in a floating restaurant, or have some fun at the pier.

Yes, there was a pier. And there were amusements, ranging from the "finest ballroom on the Pacific Coast" to the Crystal Tangle fun house to speed boats that went up to (gasp) 15 mph! Kinney also enlisted Frederick Ingersoll to build one of his roller coasters extending out over the water. Ingersoll was to the roller coaster what Looff was to the carousel. He built 277 of them, including his $30,000 Toboggan Railroad at the Ocean Park Pier, a maple-and-pine structure that ran in a figure 8, with one of its loops rising 75 feet over the surf. Completed in 1904, it lasted until 1910 and was the first of several such attractions on the site.

The problem with building amusements on a wooden pier, as Kinney and others would learn and relearn time and again, is that they're exposed to the elements. A storm can wreck a pier, and a fire can burn it.

An electrical fire at the Abbot Kinney Pier in 1908 was contained before it could do more than $6,000 worth of damage, but his old partner would not be so lucky four years later.

In the interim, Kinney's former partner, A. F. Fraser, had constructed what the *Arizona Daily Star* proclaimed it to be the best "pleasure pier" in the world: "No feature of pleasurable seaside life is overlooked at Ocean Park," the publication crowed. "Money has been expended with a lavish hand in securing the cream of attractions," such as the Grand Canyon Electric Railway, which cost $100,000 to build and appears in old photographs and postcards to be a precursor of Disney's Matterhorn.

Fraser had built his pier to last—or so he thought—by using reinforced concrete piles meant to weather winter storms. They would support a 300-foot-wide pier featuring a dance pavilion, vaudeville theater, restaurant, carousel, and other attractions. Perhaps the weirdest of the bunch was an infant incubator, where premature babies were put on display while they were nursed (hopefully) to health. The whole place lit up at night to provide a dazzling display of electrical energy over the water, and related attractions sprang up next door: Looff built his own carousel on the beach, where another roller coaster called the Dragon Gorge Scenic Railroad also appeared.

Built for a staggering $250,000, the 1.25-mile Dragon Gorge reportedly carried more than 10 million passengers without accident in its first year.

As with any elaborate enterprise, however, there were problems: The Grand Canyon roller coaster shut down after just a month for renovations that included a new, scenic tunnel and 2,000 more feet of track that made the ride nearly a mile long. But that hiccup paled in comparison with what was to come: a fire on September 3, 1912, just 15 months after the "Million Dollar Pier" opened, that destroyed the Grand Canyon Railroad and everything else atop the pilings.

The fire started in the servants' quarters below the casino restaurant, ignited by a cigarette.

Afternoon breezes fanned the flames, and hundreds of people in the dance hall and other venues scrambled for the exits. Some, finding their route of escape blocked, jumped off the pier and into the water. Almost everyone made it out alive, but H. S. Locke didn't. Kellogg Van Winkle, who stayed behind in an effort to save one of the pier's attractions, told Locke to follow him down a rope into the ocean below the pier, where the water was only knee-deep. But Locke refused, declaring, "I was never in the water in my life, and I will not go in it now until I have to."

Eventually, however, that moment came. Locke was the last man to jump from the pier, and he drowned almost immediately, one of two people who lost their lives in the fire.

The flames also spread to the beach attractions, destroying the uninsured Dragon Gorge ride as well as the Looff carousel. Initial damage estimates ranged from

Abbot Kinney Pier in 1907. Kinney, a tobacco tycoon, had opened his Venice of America development—which featured several miles of canals on the Southern California coast—on Independence Day two years earlier. *Public domain.*

$1.8 million to $3 million, but Fraser vowed to rebuild his pier, making it bigger and better than ever. "I am broke," he admitted, "but Los Angeles capitalists have placed $1 million at my disposal for rebuilding a better Ocean Park."

Despite a court fight with the city of Santa Monica over the rights to ocean frontage at the entrance to the pier, Fraser managed to pull it off, albeit on a slightly smaller scale than before. By 1914, however, he'd added a new roller coaster (the Ben Hur Racer), a 7,000-seat bandstand, and a carousel. The roller coaster didn't last long, though. It and several other attractions were consumed in a Christmas night fire.

Ernest Pickering bought the pier in 1919, added new rides, and did a brisk business when they opened the following summer. Meanwhile, a group of investors led by Charles Lick built an adjacent pier to the south.

At this point, there were no fewer than four piers within shouting distance of one another in the Santa Monica-Ocean Park-Venice area, and Lick's pier was a worthy rival for the others. It boasted a distinctive domed dance pavilion, an 85-foot-high roller coaster called the Giant Dipper that featured a 55-degree drop, and various other rides. The Giant Dipper opened on Memorial Day 1923, but the pier lasted only a few months after that—the victim of (you guessed it) yet another fire.

This time, the loss was pegged at more than $3 million.

Lick did manage to rebuild his pier and even reconstructed the Giant Dipper, a small section of which had survived the fire. Frank Prior and Fred Church created the Giant Dipper and sold the design to other amusement parks, as well. Two of their coasters—both called the Giant Dipper—are still in existence, one at Mission Beach's Belmont Park in San Diego and the other on the Santa Cruz Beach Boardwalk. The builder of the Santa Cruz coaster, which opened in 1924, was none other than Arthur Looff, son of carousel builder Charles Looff. The San Diego coaster is a little more than a mile off the old U.S. 101 alignment along the coast south of La Jolla.

Other attractions on the new Lick Pier included a couple of wax museums, one of which had a Chinatown theme and featured graphic scenes from an opium den, torture exercises, and a wedding of slave girls and tong hatchet men—paid enforcers for Chinese gangs. Not exactly family-friendly fare. One of the most popular features was the new Bon Ton Ballroom, with its 22,000-square-foot dance floor.

Park attendance declined after World War II, despite continued renovations and, mercifully, a lack of major fires. The exception was the ballroom, which having been rechristened the Aragon Ballroom, brought in bandleader Lawrence Welk for televised broadcasts on KTLA. The show became so popular that ABC picked it up for its national network, where it ran from 1955 to 1971, followed by more than a decade in first-run syndication.

DUELING WITH DISNEY

This brings us to 1957, when it was announced that the pier would be closed, completely overhauled, and reopened the following year as a major amusement park: Pacific Ocean Park. (You knew I'd get back around to that sooner or later, right?)

The park was the brainchild of Charles "Doc" Strub, a former dentist who had made a fortune as the driving force behind Santa Anita Park, which had opened in 1934. Strub had found further success at Lake Arrowhead Village in the San Bernardino Mountains, which he purchased after World War II and turned into a topflight resort that attracted celebrities as well as tourists looking for a fun weekend getaway within driving distance of L.A.

Strub's next project was supposed to be Disneyland. He offered $10 million to become a partner in Walt Disney's grand vision for a new kind of theme park, but the deal went south because Strub wanted to build the park beside the ocean. Disney and his brother Roy were firmly opposed to the idea, and with neither side willing to give in, they parted company. Strub took his $10 million and went home.

But that money was still burning a hole in his pocket, and Strub wasn't willing to give up on the idea of a seaside amusement park.

If he couldn't join Disney, he'd try to beat him.

That's how Pacific Ocean Park was born. Strub put the full weight of his Los Angeles Turf Club (the entity behind Santa Anita Park) behind the project, then brought CBS television on board, as well.

Strub's group signed a contract to lease the pier for 25 years and set about remaking it as an "oceanic wonderland," L.A. County's answer to Disney's Orange County Magic Kingdom. They even hired a 30-year-old wunderkind named Fred Harpman, who had helped create Disneyland's Main Street U.S.A. attraction, to design the park. It would be a rival to Disneyland and, with the added attraction of an ocean view, P.O.P. made the most

The midway at Pacific Ocean Park during its brief heyday. The pier amusement park, conceived as a rival to Disneyland, only remained open about a decade in the late 1950s and '60s. *Public domain.*

of its location and billed itself as a nautical theme park. If you crossed Disneyland with Sea World and threw in a healthy dose of the Googie-style architecture that looked "futuristic" in the 1950s, you'd have a fair idea of what the 28-acre park looked like.

A water fountain and statue of Neptune, along with a gateway arch shaped like a stylized "starfish" (with *six* legs) topped with seahorses welcomed visitors. Truth be told, it had more in common with the elevated restaurant at nearby Los Angeles International Airport, designed a year later, than it did with any real starfish. You'd enter the park via the arch, then make your way immediately to an attraction called Neptune's Kingdom. There, you'd descend in an elevator to a faux "ocean bottom" featuring windows to real aquatic creatures and, as the coup de

grâce, an elaborately designed scene made to resemble an underwater kingdom.

A larger-than-life sculpture of King Neptune, holding a golden trident, presided over a room full of ocean creatures, including a suspended shark and sawfish. Dick Wallen, an All-American receiver at UCLA the previous year who had been called a "model collegian" by the *Los Angeles Times*, became a real model for the Neptune sculpture, which even had some moving parts.

If all this sounds elaborate, it was. The Turf Club and CBS threw gobs of money into the project and signed on corporate sponsors like Coca-Cola and Westinghouse. Then they took out a loan with Bank of America to bankroll the rest of the $10 million project, which kept going over budget anyway.

But despite the huge capital outlay and a concerted effort to make the attraction seem more like a theme park and less like the carnival that had preceded it, some of it was still window dressing. Many of the attractions from the old Ocean Park pier carnival—such as a funhouse, the 1926 High Boy Roller Coaster (renamed the Sea Serpent), and the merry-go-round—were retooled and incorporated into the new design. Perhaps the most transparent example of a post-carnival makeover was the giant façade built over the front of the Enchanted Forest, which was housed in the former Ocean Park Municipal Auditorium.

Some attractions, however, were built from scratch, among them the Sea Circus and Mystery Island Banana Train Ride, two of the park's showpieces.

Though it all had to be packed onto a limited pier space, the park offered plenty to see and do. Up to 2,000 people could watch performing sea lions and dolphins at the Sea Circus, or you could immerse yourself in the ocean itself courtesy of two "diving bells"—another carnival-era holdover.

Other rides, however, had little or nothing to do with the ocean. As with many other amusement parks, there was a sky gondola ride (to the end of the pier and back).

The old Dome Theater housed a flying carpet monorail with an Arabian Nights theme. There was a Flight to Mars spaceship ride meant to outdo Disney's Rocket to the Moon concept, and a Safari Ride in which children used electronic rifles to hunt big game in a pseudo-African jungle.

The best ride, many agreed, was the Mystery Island Banana Train Ride, a trip through a tropical plantation that featured an artificial volcano, waterfall, and simulated earthquakes. At one point, the tracks passed over a gap in the pier.

Top that, Disney.

The park had some other advantages over its slightly older competitor, too. One press report noted that it was "more compact than Disneyland, has improved on some of the Disney rides, is closer to Los Angeles (and) has a dramatic ocean setting." On the other hand, it stated, "Disneyland offers more variety and imagination, is more accessible to freeways (and) has better parking."

Admission to the two venues was comparable, and P.O.P. booked some big-name acts to play at the Aragon, including Welk, Frank Sinatra, and later the Byrds, Janis Joplin, and even the Syd Barrett-led Pink Floyd. Over the years, it would serve as a backdrop for such shows as *The Twilight Zone*, *The Man From U.N.C.L.E.*, and *Route 66*, and scenes from a couple of movies were filmed there, as well.

The timeline they'd set to open the park turned out to be too ambitious, and the owners lost a month of the crucial summer season when the park opened late, but to much fanfare, on July 28, 1958.

P.O.P. drew 20,000 people on opening day, a Saturday, and nearly doubled that to more than 37,000 the following day. Things looked promising: During its first six days, more people visited P.O.P. than Disneyland. But the novelty soon wore off. Visitors found it harder to reach the pier, and the neighborhood surrounding it wasn't the best. The salt-heavy sea air posed a challenge when it came to maintaining the attractions.

Nearly 2 million people visited the park in its first year, but despite the addition of some new rides, attendance fell in 1959. With the park bleeding red ink, CBS and the Turf Club bailed on the concept, selling the park to 37-year-old Paso Robles landowner and developer John M. Morehart for $10 million.

Morehart changed the admission to a flat fee of $1.50, marketing the concept as "Pay One Price," and stopped

Mystery Island was widely considered the most impressive attraction at Pacific Ocean Park. *Public domain.*

trying to compare it to Disneyland. Instead, it would be a family-friendly destination for a fun weekend at the beach. He brought in local deejay Wink Martindale (later more widely known as a game show host) to emcee an American Bandstand-style program on the pier that was broadcast in the Los Angeles area. It was a big hit, drawing teens to the pier along with big names such as Sam Cooke, Chubby Checker, Jan and Dean, the Beach Boys, Johnny Cash, and the Everly Brothers, to name a few. The Beach Boys even paid homage to the park in a lyric to "Amusement Parks USA," declaring that "Disneyland and P.O.P. is worth a trip to L.A."

The teen angle was so successful that Morehart approved a Teen Age Fair there in 1962 that also drew the younger set in droves.

But in catering to the teen crowd, the park lost its original focus as a family theme park. Attendance kept falling despite the changes, and Morehart eventually sold the park himself—to San Francisco developer Irving Kay—in 1963. But by the time the new year rolled around, Kay had relinquished control to a group headed by Jack Roberts.

Roberts' takeover was the final step in the park's gradual return to its carnival roots. Roberts was a traditional carny who emphasized midway booths and "step right up" games at the expense of the elaborate Disney-style attractions the original owners had installed. Only a few new rides were added during his tenure, and they were old carnival mainstays that had little or nothing to do with the park's nautical theme. Meanwhile, many of the original exhibits started to break down as a result of lax maintenance.

Despite all this, however, the picture began to look a little brighter after Morehart's departure. Attendance rose nearly 37 percent from 1963 to 1964, when 1.66 million customers passed through the gates to enjoy a few new rides that had opened at the park.

But the following year marked the beginning of the end for P.O.P., as the city of Santa Monica launched a massive urban renewal project that closed streets and created obstacle after obstacle with construction zones throughout the Ocean Park neighborhood. Many of the old residents who had frequented the eating establishments just outside the park were relocated, and business inside the park suffered, too.

In 1966, attendance plummeted to barely a third of what it had been the previous year, and it fell further to less than 400,000 in '67. In a last-gasp effort to draw people to the pier, the Aragon Ballroom was rechristened the Cheetah Club, part of a chain with other locations in New York, New Jersey, and Chicago. It opened at Easter time, and was designed as "a psychedelic's vision-come-true," catering "strictly to America's restless and dizzying youthquake," according to an article in the *Los Angeles Times WEST Magazine.*

The interior, shaped like a triangle, featured 3,000 rainbow-colored lightbulbs cued to various sound frequencies and flashing to the music of two live bands. The house band was an act called Nazz, which soon had to rename itself to avoid confusion with Todd Rundgren's band of the same name. The name they chose was Alice Cooper. The club also booked big-name rock acts like the Doors, Pink Floyd, Eric Burdon and the Animals, Steppenwolf, and Quicksilver Messenger Service, charging $2 admission during the week and $3 on weekends. The club opened at Easter and proved popular, but it didn't translate into better business for the park itself.

Roberts wasn't able to pay his bills to the city of Santa Monica on time—in fact, he hadn't paid his rent on land leased from the city since 1965 and had racked up a debt of more than $17,000. But the problem was, at least in part, the city's own doing: Its renovation project was making it impossible for the park to turn a profit. First, the city accused Roberts of not being properly insured, but he arrived in court at the eleventh hour and produced the required insurance papers, so the city backed off.

But then, he said, "They closed the streets."

"People would actually telephone me, there at the park, and say that they could see the rides moving but couldn't

The sky ride at Pacific Ocean Park took visitors to the end of the pier and back again. *Public domain.*

Pacific Park on the Santa Monica Pier is a modern amusement area featuring free admission. *Panoramio photo, public domain.*

find any way to get there. How could they possibly expect us to survive that way?"

It couldn't. The park closed "until further notice" in October 1967 and never reopened. In the year after it closed, the park was still used in episodes of TV's *Get Smart* ("The Wax Max"), *The Fugitive* (its climactic episode), and *The Mod Squad*, but it wasn't long until many of the rides were dismantled and its assets used to pay off creditors. The massive $16 million auction in the summer of 1968 sold off 36 rides along with 16 games and amusements, restaurant and bar equipment, office furniture, electrical and plumbing fixtures … you name it. Most of what remained burned down in a series of arson fires from 1970 to 1973. The second of these, in 1970, destroyed the Cheetah Club and the entire Lick Pier.

These days, all that's left are a few underwater remnants of the pier, along with accompanying signs warning swimmers in the area to watch out for them.

But the Pacific Ocean Park name lived on, in a manner of speaking, and minus the "Ocean."

A new Pacific Park opened in 1996 where we started this account, on the Santa Monica Pier. It's the last of its kind: the only amusement park on the West Coast to be located on a pier. It's not nearly as ambitious as P.O.P. was: There are a dozen rides, including the world's only solar-powered Ferris wheel and a steel roller coaster dubbed the West Coaster. You have to pay to use the rides, but admission to the park itself is free, the only L.A.-area amusement park that can make that claim.

When the park opened, an article in the *Los Angeles Times* described it as "reminiscent of Pacific Ocean Park" and a throwback to the carnival days of yore.

The more things have changed, the more they've stayed the same—except that, so far at least, there haven't been any more fires.

HIGHWAY 101 IN COLOR

THE ROAD

U.S. 101, facing north from Fourth Street in Arroyo Grande, 2016.

The old alignment of U.S. 101 through the redwoods in northern California, Avenue of the Giants is a 31-mile stretch of scenic road now signed as State Route 254 in Humboldt County.

Concrete on the old U.S. 101 alignment between San Luis Obispo and Santa Margarita; the modern Cuesta Grade highway is to the right of this photo (not pictured).

This section of old U.S. 101 northwest of San Luis Obispo is now on private property in the Santa Lucia Range; this photo was taken looking down from the modern highway.

You can still walk out onto the 1918 concrete arch bridge over Arroyo Hondo Creek near Gaviota. The modern highway, farther inland, replaced it in the 1980s.

A billboard advertises Pea Soup Andersen's on the old highway, now called Jonata Park Road, just north of Buellton.

A strip of old concrete, foreground, runs past the historic Octagon Barn off the old highway (Higuera Street) at the southern end of San Luis Obispo.

This strip of old concrete once carried the highway around the large outcropping at Point Mugu on what's now State Route 1, formerly the northern end of the U.S. 101 Alternate in southern California.

Old concrete survives beneath the asphalt of the San Juan Grade, an old and winding alignment of U.S. 101 northeast of Salinas.

A stroll out onto the old Eel River Viaduct north of Leggett will produce this view of the river for which the abandoned section of highway is named.

An old section of
highway in
San Miguel, near
the mission.

THE SIGNS

Bill's is an old drive-in burger joint on old 101, Broadway, in Santa Maria. It was still serving up fast food when this photo was taken in 2016.

The Buckboard Motel's large sign hearkens back to an era when Broadway was U.S. 101 through town.

A fixture along Ventura Boulevard (old 101) in the San Fernando Valley community of Encino, this was where the author learned to bowl … or sort of learned.

The Farmhouse Motel in Paso Robles is at the southern end of Spring Street, historic/business 101.

The Fremont Theatre opened in 1942 on Monterey Street in San Luis Obispo. Movies are still shown there, and the theater hosts live events, as well.

Foster's Freeze operated in San Luis Obispo for 65 years on Marsh Street, a section of old U.S. 101, before it shut its doors in 2014. This photo was taken just after it closed.

A crescent moon rises at twilight above the neon sign at the Homestead Motel, just off the highway in San Luis Obispo.

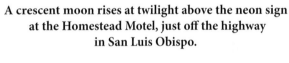

This neon sign in Garberville still lights up at night; the pancakes were made to flash on and off in sequence, giving the impression that the chef is flipping them above his pan.

The sign for the Motel Inn at the north end of Monterey Street, old U.S. 101, in San Luis Obispo. The first inn to be called a "motel," it was being rebuilt and refurbished as of this writing.

The sign on the Star Theatre on North Coast Highway (U.S. 101) at Civic Center Drive provides one of the visual highlights along this section of the road. The theater was built in 1956.

The irony of this sign shouldn't be missed: It's an outpost all its own these days, pointing the way to a motel that's no longer there, near the Eel River Viaduct in northern California.

A cowboy rides an oil rig at the western entrance to San Ardo on a bypassed section of U.S. 101 east of the modern highway in the Salinas Valley.

THE SIGHTS

The 101 Café along the Coast Highway in Oceanside features a mural
on its south side that evokes memories of the 1950s' drive-in, cruiser culture.

The Benbow Inn beside the Eel River in Garberville offers deluxe accommodations, tasty meals … and a reputation for being haunted.

This totem pole is one of many attractions and carvings at Confusion Hill in the Leggett area, off a section of the old Redwood Highway that has since been abandoned and now serves as the roadside stop's parking lot.

The Chandelier Tree in Leggett is one of many redwood attractions in the area.

The Del Mar Racetrack, closely associated with legendary actor-crooner Bing Crosby, is seen from Camino Del Mar, a section of U.S. 101 later bypassed by Interstate 5.

A historic house on the Long-Bonetti Ranch at Higuera Street (old U.S. 101) and Tank Farm Road in San Luis Obispo. The ranch house, which dates to 1908, was to be converted into a restaurant under redevelopment plans in the works by 2014.

The One Log House off U.S. 101 in Garberville is a tourist attraction that once traveled the country; it was hollowed out from a single log in 1946 and features connected rooms inside.

Rod's Auto Body in Arroyo Grande sits along old U.S. 101, where it's known as Traffic Way.
It dates from the 1930s and previously housed Standard and Chevron service stations.

The Tustin Garage is now a seafood restaurant, but it began as a garage a century ago.

A bell tower greets visitors exiting the highway at the southern end of San Miguel, site of one of California's historic missions.

Now a sixplex in the Regal chain, this theater was built
in the 1940s by Redwood Theatres with a single screen.

PART II:
A TOUR OF OLD 101

THE CARLSBAD HIGHWAY

M y wife worked for a few years as a claims adjuster for an insurance company in San Diego, where she'd get calls from all over Southern California. When she started working there, she was mystified by callers who said they'd been in an accident on the "101 freeway" because, for her, U.S. 101 wasn't a freeway at all—it was Main Street for San Diego County's northern coastal communities. Sometimes two lanes, sometimes four, it broke off from Interstate 5 and sliced its way down through the heart of Oceanside, Carlsbad, Encinitas, and Del Mar. Like State Route 1 farther north, it's called the Coast Highway in some places, with local designations such as Carlsbad Boulevard, Camino Del Mar, and Torrey Pines Road taking over in others.

A sign across U.S. 101 welcomes motorists to Encinitas. It's relatively new but follows a tradition of signs that spanned California highways dating back more than a century.

Interstate 5 bypassed this section of highway in the 1960s, just as it bypassed old U.S. 99 in the San Joaquin Valley far to the north. But unlike 99, which became a state route, 101 retained its federal designation.

It began as an even older highway that snaked its way down into San Diego over the Torrey Pines and Biological grades, winding down through La Jolla before moving back close to the current alignment north of Mission Bay. This portion of the road was bypassed in 1933 by what California's highway department called the "Million Dollar Highway"—because it was completed for just slightly more than $1 million. (Today, the same project would cost a lot more, with inflation raising the cost to $18.5 million in 2016 dollars.)

The improvement was dramatic. District engineer E. E. Wallace described the old road as "a tortuous, steep and narrow roadway" featuring about 50 curves between Del Mar and La Jolla and a grade as steep as 18 percent in some places. Wallace wrote: "This last link provides a most attractive entrance to the city, as well as a rapid and uninterrupted access for traffic."

Up from San Diego

Traveling north from the border, you can still follow the surface streets that served as U.S. 101 before it was replaced in stages, first by the Carlsbad-Oceanside Freeway in the early 1950s and later by Interstate 5.

A cyclist makes his way south on U.S. 101 in northern San Diego County, where U.S. 101 retains much of its historic charm.

Starting at the San Ysidro border crossing, take Beyer Boulevard northwest; it'll curve more directly north and turn into Broadway through Chula Vista and then National City Boulevard in National City.

From there, the alignment shifted over the years. An official Highway Department map from 1944 shows the route jogging westward at 8th Street in National City, then funneling traffic onto the coastal Harbor Drive, bypassing downtown San Diego. Harbor became the Pacific Highway north of downtown San Diego and Rose Canyon Road north of Mission Bay.

An earlier alignment, though, sent the road straight into the heart of San Diego. Instead of veering west on 8th Street, traffic in 1933 continued north on National Boulevard for another half mile or so before veering northwest on Main Street, turning north for a short block on 31st, then east on a different National Avenue, north for two short blocks on 26th, and northwest on Logan until it curved due north as 16th Street. From there, it was maybe a quarter mile to Broadway, where the route turned westward just south of Balboa Park. (A later alignment followed Market, just south of Broadway, turned west instead.)

After about a mile on Broadway, 101 turned north again on India—two blocks east of the later Pacific Highway route—and curved around, following the outline of San Diego Bay before continuing north.

Instead of following Rose Canyon Road north from there, an earlier alignment, seen on a 1922 map, shows the route veering off west again north of Mission Bay on Garnet Boulevard all the way to the coast, where travelers were sent north again along Mission Boulevard/La Jolla Boulevard. This route followed the contours of the La Jolla peninsula and went through the heart of La Jolla before pushing more directly north again along Torrey Pines Road.

This road led to the modern "old" 101 along the coast, otherwise known as the Carlsbad Highway—a stretch of about 20 miles through the seaside towns of Del Mar, Solana Beach, Cardiff, Encinitas, Carlsbad, and Oceanside.

Preserved in Time

This section of highway still exists today. If you want to see what U.S. 101 once looked like, there's no better place to start than the Carlsbad Highway. Cyclists drawn to the sunshine and sea breeze pedal past on a tree-lined highway that parallels the old Atchison, Topeka and Santa Fe rail line. These tracks still carry "Coaster" trains along the old coastal strip between San Diego and Oceanside.

Although the cities have nearly grown together now, they're still separated by lagoons and strips of undeveloped sandy beaches, and each retains its own flavor.

Del Mar, with its iconic racetrack, is where the wealthy still come to play. Shoppers and diners—both locals and tourists—still make Stratford Square a popular destination. The English Tudor-style structure at the southwest corner of 101 and 15th Street was built in 1927. Now home to a variety of shops and restaurants, it was built by Herman Kockritz as a companion building to the Hotel Del Mar across the street. It originally housed a pharmacy, soda fountain, market, barber shop, dress shop, and doctor's office, providing essential services to the community and tourists at the hotel.

A new owner bought both Stratford Square and the hotel in 1943, but he didn't care for the Tudor style, painting over the wooden planking and brick. Stratford Square outlasted the hotel, which was torn down in 1969, and the Old English flavor of the building was all but forgotten until the paint was removed, revealing its original character. The building fell into disrepair and might have been torn down itself, with its second-floor apartments having become a hippie hangout by 1971. But Jim Watkins purchased it, converted the apartments into retail spaces and renovated the building, which was designated a historical landmark in 1978.

The Watkins family still owned the building which, as of 2017, housed two restaurants and five retail shops on the ground floor, with offices and a museum on the second story.

Up the coast in Encinitas, you'll pass a large piece of property fronted by a massive, square structure with four arches topped by a decorative golden dome. It looks like something you'd see at the Taj Mahal, and it marks the front entrance to the Encinitas Temple of the Self-Realization Fellowship, founded in 1920 by Paramahansa Yogananda. The site, dotted with tall, swaying palm trees, was still open as of 2016, featuring lush meditation gardens and a full schedule of inspirational lectures and programs.

Stratford Square offers shopping and dining to locals and travelers on 101 in the upscale San Diego County community.

Yogananda liked to visit the place to pray and meditate in two caves that were built into the face of the ocean bluff. He wrote his *Autobiography of a Yogi* on the site, an isolated promontory overlooking the ocean that became home to a lavish 16-room mansion in the mid-1930s. He didn't build the hermitage on the site himself: It was a surprise gift from a Kansas City insurance executive that greeted the yogi when he returned from India for a visit.

"I saw a building jutting out like a great white ocean liner toward the blue brine," Yogananada recalled. "The stately central hall, with immense ceiling-high windows, looks out on an altar of grass, ocean and sky: a symphony in emerald, opal and sapphire."

The hermitage was part of a $400,000 improvement project—more than $6.6 million in 2016 dollars.

Unfortunately for the yogi and his followers, his Golden Lotus Temple turned out to be on shaky ground—literally. Just five years after the expansion was completed, adherents in the temple gardens heard the sound of the building's frame and stucco creaking. The original plan was to move the building inland, but the cliff face underneath it was eroding so rapidly that the yogi's followers had to be content with saving the furnishings, oriental rugs, and fixtures from the interior. The building itself collapsed into the ocean—all except for the temple tower, which was salvaged and relocated to the front of the grounds along Highway 101. It's that tower, with its four archways and golden dome, that greets visitors passing by there today.

Over the years, the site's lavish architecture brought attention to the area at the south end of Encinitas, with the yogi's presence inspiring the name of Swami's State Beach, a popular surfing spot nearby. The Beach Boys even mentioned Swami's (right before Pacific Palisades) in their musical tribute to point breaks and pipelines, "Surfin' USA." Across the highway, Swami's Café and Bar serves up a full menu that includes everything from a Swami's granola Belgian waffle to a Swami club sandwich and a Swami's Surprise smoothie.

Encinitas residents had a love-hate relationship with the 17-acre temple, which was at times rumored (falsely) to be a nudist colony and front for wild parties. Making matters worse, the temple negotiated the closure of two public streets through the compound, funneling local traffic out onto the highway and spawning protests about congestion. But the fellowship made up for it by donating time and money toward the effort to build the Interstate 5 bypass.

The fellowship expanded internationally, with more than 500 sites around the world, including seven temples in California (the others are in Hollywood, Glendale, Fullerton, Pacific Palisades, San Diego, and Berkeley). The Hollywood temple was founded in 1942, the same year the Encinitas temple fell into the ocean.

Yogananda died in 1952.

The Golden Lotus Temple of the Self-Realization Fellowship inspired the name of Swami's State Beach in Encinitas.

UP THE ROAD

Other, less ostentatious but equally historical landmarks lie northward along the Old 101. La Paloma Theatre, one of a few historic theaters that still line the highway, is a Spanish-style cinema built in 1928 that sits a stone's throw away from the Encinitas arch spanning the highway. It's not the original sign but a replica installed in 2000 that helped restore the feel of an era when steel and stucco arches welcomed visitors to many towns along this and other California highways.

Carlsbad followed suit with its own replica sign over 101 at Carlsbad Village Drive in 2014, modeled after a sign that stood nearby in the 1930s. In re-creating the sign, the community only had a black-and-white photo as its guide and had to guess at the central color—eventually choosing navy blue. The neon-lit sign, measuring 82 feet across, cost $225,000, with a local company footing the bill.

Also in Encinitas is the Daley Double, a bar and cocktail lounge that opened as the Village Rendezvous in 1934, right after the repeal of Prohibition, and has been serving drinks ever since. The original owner was

Maurice DeLay, who reportedly ran an illegal poker parlor upstairs before selling the place in 1942. He shouldn't be confused with Frank Daley, a former hockey player who bought and renamed it in 1957.

Daley, also known as "Dapper Dan," played five games at left wing for the NHL's Detroit Cougars—since renamed the Red Wings—in 1930. He didn't score a goal and spent the rest of his career in the minors with teams in Cleveland, Seattle, and elsewhere before retiring in 1945 and winding up in Encinitas.

The bar was the scene of a bizarre incident in 2002, when an off-duty U.S. Secret Service agent assigned to Vice President Dick Cheney's detail bit off part of another man's ear during a fight outside. A jury eventually ruled that the agent, Kelly Ward, had been ambushed by the other man and had acted in self-defense.

A couple of local fast-food institutions, Angelo's and Roberto's, have multiple locations along the highway.

Angelo's Burgers is a family-owned business that dates back to 1977 and has four locations in northern San Diego County—all of them along the Coast Highway. The Encinitas location is a funky building with a pair of dining rooms separated by a covered drive-through lane that runs between them. It looks almost as much like an old gas station/garage as it does like an eatery.

There are three more locations to the north in Oceanside, one of which features a statue named Angelo Man greeting customers outside. He wasn't always Angelo Man, though. That big frosty mug of root beer in his right hand is a dead giveaway that, in a previous life, he was Papa Burger, one of the "Burger Family" of mascots for A&W. As mentioned earlier, you can find other members of the Burger Family on Highway 41 at the 41 Café in Laton and just off Highway 99 in Selma, but Angelo Man may be the only one left in southern California.

The restaurant where Angelo Man stands was the first Angelo's. It's actually a former A&W, but it's not Angelo Man's original home: Owner Tony Regakis bought the statue from the other A&W location in town, at Coast Highway and Mission Avenue. The price? A paltry $100. Angelo Man was originally on the roof, like his "twin"

Angelo's Burgers in Oceanside features a mascot it calls Angelo Man; in an earlier incarnation, he was known as Papa Burger and carried a mug of A&W root beer.

Papa Burger at Winkins' in Selma, but was later lowered to street level.

If Mexican food is more your speed, there's Roberto's. It's the original "-berto's" Mexican restaurant in San Diego County, which is saying something. One count, made in 2000, found 15 fast-food businesses with 123 outlets countywide making use of the suffix in their names, from Alberto's and Aliberto's (yes, two different places) to Jilberto's and Hilberto's. Not confusing at all, right?

Roberto Robledo grew up in a home built of mud and hay in San Luis, Mexico. A railroad and migrant farmworker, he spent $30 on a machine to make tortillas and $40 more on a station wagon to deliver them. A friend persuaded him to open his own restaurant, and in 1964, he and his wife Dolores started what the company website calls "San Diego's first taco shop" in San Ysidro.

The business expanded, and Robledo died in 1999; today, family members run various eateries. Locations along Old 101 in San Diego's North County include Encinitas and Solana Beach, but the chain reaches far beyond the coastal strip: As of 2017, the website listed 15 San Diego County locations and even more in Nevada, which boasted more than four dozen locations in the Las Vegas-Henderson area.

Oceanside has preserved its share of historic sites, including the Dolphin Hotel, which as of early 2017 closed for renovations. Opened in 1927 as the Hotel Keisker, the two-story, 25-room hotel is part of a block of buildings on the west side of the Coast Highway.

Down the street is the 101 Café, which former owner John Daley calls "the oldest café on Highway 101."

It opened in 1928 as a 20-seat diner and tripled in size nine years later after Greyhound installed a bus stop in front of the building. The café eventually changed hands, and when the new bypass opened to the east in 1953, the owner changed course. Starting in the 1950s and continuing through the 1970s, John Graham operated it as a Graham's Drive-In—one of three in the area—adding the overhang and a sign near the front of the building that advertised "car service." When the drive-in craze began to wane, he converted it into a coffee shop, which was later rebranded as Randy's by another new owner.

The décor at the 101 Café in Oceanside pays tribute to a simpler time along the highway.

When Daley bought the place with partner David Ranson in the 1980s, new customers started calling him "Randy," so he restored the original name, transforming it into a nostalgic trip back in time with a 1950s flavor and a colorful mural on the south side of the building depicting its drive-in and "cruisin' " days. Daley was meticulous about restoring the café, making it look just the way it did in 1954. The same booths in use at that time were rebuilt and reupholstered to ensure its authenticity.

Daley and Ranson sold the 101 Café after three decades to Cesar Galvez of Del Mar, who has, as of this writing, preserved the café's distinctive character.

The military town also has a pair of vintage movie houses within little more than a block of each other on Old 101. On the east side is the Star Theater, which opened in 1956 with a distinctive neon sign that still lights up the night.

Across the street is the older Sunshine Brooks Theater, which opened 20 years earlier as the Margo, the first major construction project downtown since the onset of the Depression. It was later renamed the Towne and takes its current name from former owner Hattie Hazel "Sunshine" Brooks.

The theater went downhill after 1953 when a highway bypass was built—the precursor to Interstate 5—and was, at one point, converted into a karate studio. These days, it's a theater again, hosting live theater productions by the Oceanside Theatre Company.

SLAUGHTER ALLEY

That 1953 bypass—known as the Oceanside-Carlsbad Freeway—was the first segment of freeway built in San Diego County. The 10-mile stretch of road largely followed was completed in two phases The first consisted of widening Carlsbad Boulevard (still Old 101) for about three miles from La Costa Avenue north to Palomar Airport Drive. The second, longer section veered inland to follow the modern Interstate 5 alignment all the way to Oceanside.

Even with the bypass, though, traffic remained a major concern farther north, on an 18-mile stretch of the Old 101 between San Clemente and Oceanside, where 50,000 vehicles a day sped across a strip of highway known as "Slaughter Alley" in 1964.

The highway more than earned that name.

Five people died in a head-on collision there in August 1964, and an even more tragic accident occurred there just two weeks later, when eight people were killed and 40 injured in a head-on crash that involved a church bus and seven other vehicles. The adopted 12-year-old daughter of Roy Rogers and Dale Evans was one of those who lost their lives, along with another child who was traveling on the bus. Six people in a station wagon also died.

Those were just two of many crashes that occurred on the infamous stretch of asphalt. By the end of 1964, a record 39 people had been killed on that section of

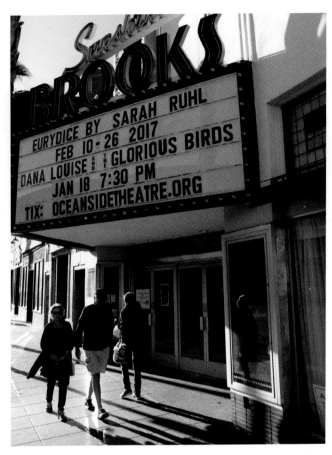

Sunshine Brooks was the first major construction project in downtown Oceanside since the start of the Great Depression, opening in the mid-1930s.

101, and some of the worst was yet to come. On a foggy morning in February 1966, seven people died in an inferno ten miles north of Oceanside that began when two cars collided in the southbound lanes. A Greyhound bus pulled over, and someone got out to carry flares to the accident, stalling northbound traffic as motorists waited for the person to cross. That's when a tanker truck filled with gasoline swerved to avoid a transport vehicle carrying seven new cars and slammed into the steel cable center divider.

A compact car carrying a man and his pregnant wife stopped between the tanker and auto transport just in time … but a supermarket food van wasn't. It slammed into the couple's car and threw it forward into the tanker, which exploded into a fireball, spilling burning gas over the gridlocked highway. The couple and their unborn

Welcome to Carlsbad, just south of Oceanside on U.S. 101.

child died, along with the driver of the supermarket van, as traffic backed up all the way to San Clemente.

Still, the tragedy wasn't over. Ten minutes later, about two miles north of the main accident, a second fuel tanker pulled to a halt, and a third tanker—unable to stop—pushed a stalled car into the tanker ahead of it. Both gasoline-filled transports burst into flames, along with six passenger cars in the area, a conflagration that left one of the tanker drivers and two other people dead. The seven people who died in the twin accidents were so badly burned that dental records were needed to identify them.

Cars were still smoldering four hours after the accident, while potatoes and onions spilled from the supermarket van "literally were 'cooking' on the pavement," according to the *Long Beach Independent*. More than a dozen cars were wrecked, and 100 others were damaged. The accident claimed another victim three weeks later.

In the aftermath of the crash, California's State Highway Division announced it would seek bids within a month to widen Slaughter Alley from four to eight lanes. And just four months after February's highway inferno, a 25-mile portion of freeway known as Interstate 5 opened south of Carlsbad. The $33 million project bypassed the communities of Del Mar, Solana Beach, Cardiff, Encinitas, and Leucadia to the south—an area also prone to accidents that was considered an extension of Slaughter Alley.

With the improvements, injuries and accidents between San Clemente and Oceanside both fell by 50 percent in 1968.

THE FLOWER FIELDS OF CARLSBAD

Today, that stretch of highway, flanked by the Camp Pendleton Marine base, crosses the only stretch of undeveloped land between the Los Angeles and San Diego metroplexes, but it wasn't always that way. The towns of northern San Diego County, which have merged into an unbroken string of homes and businesses along Old 101, were once separated by plenty of open land. One vestige of that earlier era remains visible on the east side of Interstate 5: the Carlsbad Flower Fields, which these days are neighbors to a modern outlet mall.

Luther Gage, the son of a Presbyterian minister from Colorado, ran a nursery in Montebello and moved to Carlsbad in the 1920s. The South Coast Land Company had begun to develop the area, buying up land and bringing in water from the San Luis Rey River. Gage set up shop at Tamarack and Jefferson (then called Fourth Street), about three quarters of a mile east of Old 101 and barely more than a stone's throw away from where I-5 would be built.

If there's any doubt the area was still countryside back then, you could just ask the frequent visitors to Gage's fields: flocks of owls that swooped in over the flowers, inspiring him to name his place Tecolote Gardens and sell his bulbs under that label ("tecolote" being Spanish for owls). He crossed strains of ranunculus from France, Australia, and Austria to produce a larger bloom, also growing baby gladiolas, corn lilies, and harlequin flowers, among others. He sold them to a Los Angeles-based wholesaler, which in turn distributed them across the United States and Europe.

His flower fields, however, were causing more of a nuisance than he could tolerate. Gage once remarked to someone who had stopped to look at his fields, "Publicity only means a lot of visitors, and as we do only a whole-sale business, we have nothing to sell to visitors."

Ultimately, it wasn't Gage but one of his workers who made the flower fields famous. In 1928, Frank Frazee ventured out on his own, growing bulbs along with two of his sons on 1,000 acres on the Agua Hedionda Lagoon—a body of water in Carlsbad that runs about three miles inland from the sea under both Old 101 and I-5.

At one point, Frazee Flowers grew more ranunculus flowers than the next four biggest growers combined. Frazee and his sons moved the operation up the road to Camp Pendleton in 1938, but returned to the Carlsbad area two decades later, planting his bulbs on a plot of land owned by Paul Ecke Jr.

Today, more than 100,000 people flock to the fields during the first week of March every year, when the flowers are in bloom across 50 acres of Ecke's land. The dazzling display is a multicolored reminder of a time when the 101/I-5 corridor wasn't just office buildings, resorts, and tourist shops.

NORTH OF OCEANSIDE

Part of historic 101 survives in Camp Pendleton as a bike route that between Las Pulgas Road and Cristianitos Road. An old mileage sign remained there until a fire destroyed it in 2007, many of its letters having peeled off by that time. It showed a distance of 12 miles to San Clamente, 48 miles to Anaheim, and 76 miles to Los Angeles.

El Camino Real heads north from Cristianitos Road for a couple of miles before crossing under the modern freeway into San Clemente. The huge sign for Tommy's Family Restaurant just beyond the freeway underpass welcomes you to the city. Tommy's has been there ever since I can remember—I stopped there with my parents back in the 1970s—and today it's a '50s-themed diner with plenty of seating. Richard Nixon, a San Clemente resident, reportedly dined there frequently.

The old highway winds through the center of town and down toward the ocean, where it continues north to Dana Point as the Coast Highway and diverges into State Route 1, the old 101 Alternate and Camino Capistrano, the main route north into San Juan Capistrano.

Farther north, there's about a four-mile stretch of old highway called Cabot Road west of and parallel to the modern freeway into Mission Viejo, where the old road was overlaid by the current freeway. It emerges again to veer northeast for about a mile on Sand Canyon Road, then doubles back along Trabuco Road, which now ends at Culver Drive but once upon a time hooked up with El Camino Real into Tustin.

The roads had different names back in the day: 101 passed El Toro as San Juan Road, then became Laguna Road from Irvine into Tustin.

Tommy's Restaurant, with its huge sign just off the freeway, is impossible to miss at El Camino Real in San Clemente.

2

THE SANTA ANA FREEWAY

It's hard to believe it these days, but Orange County, godfather of the subdivision, was once at the center of Southern California's fertile crescent, a swath of land that extended up U.S. 101 and eastward across to San Bernardino along U.S. 99/60/70. If you can't find that on the map, it's because that highway has been replaced by Interstate 10.

U.S. 101 in Orange County, for its part, has been renamed Interstate 5, although it's still the same road. As an aside, this is the only place in California where 101 no longer exists. It starts up as a freeway in Hollywood, and the old highway can be found—still signed as 101—along surface streets in coastal San Diego County.

Whatever you call it, it's best known in the county south of Los Angeles as the Santa Ana Freeway, named for the county seat (no, the city of Orange isn't the capital of Orange County) and renowned for its anytime-of-day rush-hour traffic. That's in part because, as you head north toward the L.A. County line, it's squeezed like an orange into three lanes each way, in contrast to the wider but still congested San Diego Freeway that runs parallel a few miles to the west.

The Hotel Laguna, seen here in the 1930s on the Coast Highway (101 Alternate), is still open to guests.
Orange County Archives.

Today, Orange County has more than 3 million inhabitants, but back in 1948, it had even more oranges: 5 million in all, growing on 67,000 acres. There were towns in the area, to be sure, but they were just that—towns. Not cities or the elements in a seemingly endless asphalt-and-concrete playground, as they are today. Old photos of Highway 101 and the network of now-busy boulevards that crisscross the landscape show them in their infancy as dusty roads lined by mile after mile of orchards.

Camino Capistrano, a section of old U.S. 101 through San Juan Capistrano, in 1959. *Orange County Archives.*

In the middle of the 20th century, this region was the citrus capital of the world, so it was fitting that the county and one of its main cities should both be named for the orange. But ironically, when the name was chosen, oranges weren't the dominant commodity they would become. In fact, the city of Orange originally had a different name, Richland, but when it opened a post office, early city leaders found that a city in northern California had chosen that name first. An alternative had to be found, so "Orange" it was.

So why isn't Orange the capital of Orange County?

For one thing, the county name was actually suggested while the town was still called Richland (which consisted of just four houses)—and six months before the first orange seeds were even planted there. As county historian Jim Sleeper once declared, "In 1871, oranges were merely a promise, *not* our most promising crop." According to Sleeper, the only orange trees in the county were in pots at that stage, and most of the farmland was dedicated to corn, grapes, sheep, and hogs. Despite this, oranges sounded more exotic, and had a nice ring to real estate developers seeking to lure new residents.

"The organizers of Orange County chose that name for the sordid purpose of real estate," said J. M. Guinn, who witnessed the naming attempts firsthand. "They argued that Eastern people would be attracted by the name and would rush to the county to buy orange ranches, forgetful, or perhaps ignorant, of the fact that there were more than a hundred other places in the United States named Orange."

The proposal didn't pass the legislature, and a couple of other attempts over the next few years also went nowhere. Still, residents of the area wanted to separate from Los Angeles and form their own county, and they needed a name. Santa Ana was suggested—and promptly rejected, with one critic calling it a devilish idea: "There may be a certain propriety in making a *satanic* division of the county of Los Angeles, but when we try again, suppose we leave the saints in peace." (Coincidentally, the hot, dry Santa Ana winds that blow in the area are also called "devil winds.")

Finally, in 1889, the legislature approved formation of the new county, along with the name Orange, selecting Santa Ana as the county seat. By that time, a blight had wiped out the region's grape industry, and oranges had begun to take root in its soil—and its soul. The name made sense at last, even if today, with the orange groves having given way to tract homes, it no longer does.

Two Alternatives

In 1940, before the age of freeways, you could choose two routes from San Diego to Los Angeles: U.S. 101 and the 101 Alternate. The former roughly follows the path taken by the current Santa Ana Freeway (Interstate 5), while the latter traces a course similar to that of the San Diego Freeway (I-405).

Those two paths diverge now in Irvine, but before World War II, northbound travelers had to decide earlier which course to take: The fork in the road came just seven miles north of San Clemente at Doheny Park.

The coastal or "Alternate" route would take you up through Dana Point and the "Beach" cities: Laguna, Newport, Huntington, Seal, Long, and westward to Redondo. From there, the road curved north again past El Segundo and Venice and on to Santa Monica, passing through the resort town of Malibu before rejoining the main arm of the 101 at Oxnard.

In all, this route covered a distance of about 125 miles and allowed travelers to skirt central Los Angeles—an attractive option in a time when the coast was less populated and the central city was already becoming congested. Just ask the cities along the "main" inland route of the 101, which were complaining about the traffic within a few years after the federal route was established.

And no wonder.

The "highway"—if you could call it that—was really just a series of surface streets cobbled together and held in place by little more than street signs and road maps. Before the Santa Ana Freeway went in, U.S. 101 took you on a roundabout, in-and-out, zigzagging tour of the Southland.

TUSTIN GARAGE

Drivers who had just covered what was then a long stretch of rural road coming up from San Diego needed a place to gas up. The road passed through small towns like San Juan Capistrano and Irvine on its way north, but those were little more than dots on the map. Just before World War II, in 1939, San Clemente had just 667 people and San Juan Capistrano was a metropolis, relatively speaking, at 1,200.

Tustin itself had just under 1,000 residents at the time, but it must have seemed like an oasis to travelers coming into town from the south with their fuel tanks trending toward empty. At one time, a parade of 10 service stations greeted travelers as they entered Tustin from the south. Outlets selling Signal, Shell, Texaco, Gilmore, Associated, and other brands competed for motorists' business. Most are gone now, but interestingly, the first automotive business established in the area still stands—although it's no longer a garage but (as of this writing) a seafood restaurant. Will Huntley and Nick Gulick opened the Tustin Garage a block off the old highway on New Year's Day, 1911, then moved to its current location at El Camino Real and Sixth Street in 1915, a decade after the main road was paved but still twelve years before the city was incorporated.

The pair kept the place open until midnight, offering "a first-class auto repair shop and a full line of automobile accessories." The owners advertised pump work as a specialty and proudly sold Diamond Tires, a brand they said "had proven to be the best value on the market." Its motto: "Service is our slogan."

"Our automobile repairing is done speedily and well," a 1922 ad in the Santa Ana Register proclaimed. "We do not loaf on your job because we know at once just what is wrong and what must be done to remedy it. We do not tinker. We do not deliberate. We repair."

The garage drew attention in 1954 when a pair of employees tore down an old shed at the back of the property and, while digging with picks and shovels, unearthed an oddly shaped rock. As it turned out, though, the rock was actually a bone: a six-by-eight-inch specimen that a geology professor identified as an ancient fossil, possibly part of an extinct animal's backbone. The garage owner donated the fossil to a geology instructor at Santa Ana College for further study, but there was no further report in the press as to where it had come from.

The garage was in the news again a quarter century later when it served as a base for the Double Eagle III, successor to the Double Eagle II, which had become the first hot-air balloon to cross the Atlantic a year earlier. The DEIII was in town preparing for an international balloon race, which its pilots, Ben Abruzzo and Maxie Anderson, ended up winning. The garage was used to store and check the balloon's equipment as it arrived.

The garage changed hands in the 1990s and became Transmission & Clutch Express. It was converted into a seafood and barbecue restaurant around 2008.

The Tustin Garage dates to 1915; this photo shows it when it was still a garage (lately, the building has operated as a seafood restaurant). *Orange County Archives.*

The surface streets were the puzzle pieces of the route's earliest alignments, strung together like a daisy chain held across the landscape. From Tustin, you'd go west on First Street into Santa Ana, then turn north on Main Street toward Anaheim.

At the spot where modern I-5 hits Katella Avenue (these days, the gateway to Disneyland), you'd head north on Los Angeles Street, then jog a block west to Spadra Road. If you can't find these names on the map, it's because the former was renamed Anaheim Boulevard, and the latter has been rechristened Harbor Boulevard.

Spadra/Harbor would carry you north for several miles to Whittier Boulevard—known then as Whittier Road—and by this time, you'd be a good 12 miles east of the current freeway. So if you wanted to reach L.A., you'd have to head back west in a gentle arc toward downtown. Not only did it make no sense for motorists to drive so far out of their way, it also transformed cities along the way, such as Whittier and Montebello, into traffic traps of the first order. Motorists didn't

like it. The cities didn't like it. Nobody liked it.

So, it wasn't long before plans were being made to abandon this route and create a bypass that would give drivers a straighter shot into Los Angeles. The 101 Bypass, as it was called, followed a diagonal route that was much more closely aligned to that of its ultimate successor, Interstate 5. In fact, much of the route—old Manchester Boulevard between Anaheim and Norwalk—lies underneath the modern interstate's pavement today.

From Norwalk, the 101 Bypass veered left from the path taken by the current interstate at Firestone Boulevard. For many years after I-5 was completed, the Firestone off-ramp offered a glimpse at how the highway had evolved, exiting the freeway from the left-hand lane. Only recently, in the spring of 2013, was the rare left-lane exit closed for good, destroying the most direct point of access to the earlier alignment. (To see another left-hand exit on 101, head southbound through Santa Barbara, and you'll find one at the east end of town, near the Santa Barbara Zoo.)

A sign over U.S. 101 serves as a "Direct Route" to "Santa Ana and Coast Cities," and a Gilmore Gas Station offers Lion Head Motor Oil in this historical photo. *Orange County Archives.*

The Orange Drive-In Theatre operated at U.S. 101 and Plascentia Avenue in 1946, one of many drive-ins that lured passing motorists from the highways during the height of the outdoor film era.
Orange County Archives.

With the addition of the bypass, there were not one, not two, but *three* routes labeled 101 through Los Angeles County. And none of them was exactly the same as modern Interstate 5.

You can follow the old bypass route today by turning off Firestone north onto Lakewood Boulevard, then turn north on Telegraph Road shortly after you pass under I-5. Telegraph, which runs directly parallel to the freeway, ceded the 101 designation for a couple of blocks to Downey Road, a north-south connector to the older alignment at Whittier Boulevard. The 101 Bypass ended there.

KNOTT'S BERRY FARM

Orange County and orange juice should have naturally gone together. But ironically, Frank Pohl's chain of Giant Orange stands, which dispensed orange juice and were shaped like (what else?) giant oranges, didn't extend south into the county named for oranges. One of Pohl's roadside stands did operate during the 1950s on Spring Street, the old alignment of U.S. 101 in Paso Robles, but that and Bakersfield on Highway 99 were about as far south as the chain went.

Pohl's stands, covered extensively in my book on U.S. 99, were far from the only roadside options for travelers in the first half of the 20th century. Fruit stands were, then as now, familiar sights along California's highways, serving then as oases on the dusty roads connecting farm towns such as Tustin, Buena Park, Anaheim, and Orange. One such stand belonged to a couple named Walter and Cordelia Knott, who operated it beside the road on State Route 39 (Beach Boulevard) barely a mile south of its junction with 101.

The Knotts started their enterprise in 1920, selling berries, pies, and preserves from a wooden roadside stand that consisted of a single room opening onto a sales counter that was shaded by a canopy.

His father had grown oranges in the Pomona Valley, but he died in 1896 when Walter was just 6 years old, and his mother had to sell the orange grove in order to make ends meet. Walter Knott would make his mark growing fruit, as well, but he dropped out of Pomona High School after two years, and it would be more than a decade before he founded the berry farm that bears his name.

He married Cordelia, his high school sweetheart, in 1911, and the next few years brought a series of ventures, some more successful than others. He worked as a construction foreman in Pomona, on the silver mines in Calico, and on a crew that helped build a road through the Mojave Desert that would become Route 66. He finally got back into farming near Shandon, in San Luis Obispo County, working on a strip of land as a tenant farmer. The deal was simple: He could grow fruits and vegetables for the ranch hands, and sell whatever they didn't eat. Cordelia brought in money of her own by making candy for shops in the area, and within a couple of years, they had enough to consider an offer from Walter's cousin, Jim Preston, to start a berry farm in the Buena Park area.

Walter took him up on the offer, and in late 1920, the pair leased a 20-acre plot of land along Grand Avenue, about a mile west of the future U.S. 101.

By 1924, they had expanded their operation to 35 acres, a little more than half of that devoted to blackberries, with the rest divvied up among raspberries, strawberries, dewberries and loganberries (a blackberry-raspberry hybrid). That same year, the *Los Angeles Times* documented their success, even in the midst of what it called an "agricultural depression."

Sales that year from the Preston and Knott farm reached 200,000 baskets, the most in their four years of doing business.

"Conditions in local farming sections are not normal by any means," the article read, "yet we sometimes come upon those who, through hard work and careful planning, have been making a steady return from their efforts. Such is the case with Preston and Knott …, who, in spite of recent embargoes restraining shipping to their most profitable markets, are able to report a very successful season on all berries."

Preston and Knott paid their workers by the day, instead of by volume, to ensure they didn't rush their work and focused on picking the best quality fruit. They increased productivity with the help of a wheelbarrow-like mechanism designed by Knott to carry trays of berries. Consisting of a bicycle wheel on an iron frame, it was made specifically to traverse the rows between the crops.

The pair shipped their fruit to markets in Los Angeles and Orange Counties but also did a booming business at their roadside stand, where daily sales averaged $100 and sometimes went as high as $200.

Despite their success, Preston decided to bow out of the partnership when their lease ran out in 1927, starting his own berry farm in Norwalk. Knott decided to stay put, but he wanted to own the land. The oil boom was on in southern California, and growers were selling their land left and right to speculators hoping to strike it rich. Land prices were skyrocketing as a result. But Knott saw an opportunity to increase his share of the market if he made the right investment.

Walter and Cordelia Knott stand in front of their "original" Knott's Berry Farm stand. *Orange County Archives.*

Part of that investment would be a new tearoom with seating for 20 customers, where Cordelia Knott could sell sandwiches, berry pie, and ice cream. But to make it work, Knott would need to buy the land with no money down. In exchange, he offered the landowner a premium price of $1,500 an acre. "It isn't worth fifteen-hundred an acre, and you know it," Knott later recalled saying. "But I'll pay you fifteen-hundred an acre anyway."

When the Depression hit two years later, though, the land's value plummeted to 20 percent of what it had been when he bought it—and Knott was still making payments. Still, despite a drop in sales and the failure of a second stand in Norco to take off, Knott persevered and kept promoting Knott's Berry Place, as it was known then, in the media. He started carrying boysenberries— a variety created by Anaheim grower Rudy Boysen—in 1933 and added fried chicken to the tearoom menu. Customer traffic increased to such an extent that the Knotts increased its seating capacity to 225 with two new rooms in 1937 and decided to keep it open year-round, instead of just during the berry season.

It still wasn't enough to keep up with the demand, with Knott's serving 265,000 chicken dinners in 1938. Two more dining rooms brought the seating capacity to 400, but even so, lines of customers waiting for a table were stretching down Grand Avenue. It occurred to Walter that it might be a good idea to give the customers something to do while they were waiting, so he added a rock garden and waterfall, along with collections of fluo-rescent minerals and antique music boxes. They weren't exactly the Boomerang or the Xcelarator (roller coasters of more recent vintage at the farm), but they were the beginning of a new era in which non-edible attractions would become as much of a draw as berry pies and fried chicken.

The first big step in that direction was a man-made volcano, made of rock trucked in from the Mojave Desert, that belched steam from a boiler accompanied by the ominous roar from a noise machine. The idea was to shield patrons from the unsightly view of a 12-foot-high pipe stand, visible from the restaurant's latest expansion, that was used to irrigate the berry fields.

The biggest attraction yet, a full-fledged ghost town, was added in 1941. That same year, however, the United States entered World War II, and in 1945, the berry farm—specifically, the volcano—became the object of what the sheriff described as a "vicious and unfounded" rumor. The Orange County sheriff, that is, not the sheriff of Knott's replica ghost town. According to this rumor, the enemy was somehow using the volcano as a secret short-wave radio base. The rumor grew (as rumors are wont to do) to include gossip about an FBI raid, multiple arrests, and a supposed sale or lease of the berry farm to enemy agents.

The head of the FBI office in San Diego didn't know anything about it, but did investigate and found no substance to the allegations—nor any way of tracing them to their source.

A story in the *Los Angeles Times* was accompanied by a photo of Walter Knott scratching his head.

"At first I didn't want to dignify such fantastic stories with a denial," Knott said, "but the thing has reached such proportions that I called on Sheriff (Jesse) Elliott and the FBI to try to track down the instigator of this campaign. I'd pay $1,000 if I knew who started it."

Knott's business survived the innuendo and continued to grow, adding various attractions over the years. Among them, a lagoon with a steamboat dubbed the Cordelia K., a picnic area, horse show, and covered wagon camp. El Camino Real served as the inspiration for a miniature King's Highway that featured 21 miniature models of the original Spanish missions.

In 1951, Knott's fascination with ghost towns and his own personal history led him back to Calico, where his uncle had owned a silver mine and where he himself had worked briefly as a young man. After closing escrow on the 75-acre town site, he restored it and eventually donated it 15 years later to San Bernardino County, where it became a county park. A year later, back in Buena Park, he used the ghost town as the inspiration for his Calico Railroad, featuring a narrow-gauge train that dated to the early 1900s.

In many ways, Knott's success with fried chicken and his ghost town mirrors that of Pollardville in Stockton, where Neil and Frances Pollard set up a similar attrac-tion on a slightly smaller scale (see my book *Highway 99* for more). One key difference was that the Pollards never added large-scale theme rides to their site, which closed—and was dismantled—in 2007. The Knotts did.

The Disneyland sign on Harbor Boulevard, just off U.S. 101, in 1974. *Orange County Archives.*

The Calico Log Ride (now known as Timber Mountain) was added in 1969, with John Wayne and his son taking the first official ride. And the first roller coaster with a 360-degree element—a repeating spiral loop—was added in 1975.

By 2016, it had 10 roller coasters.

Walter Knott lived on the farm until his death in 1981, and his family operated the park until 1995, when it was sold to Cedar Fair, an amusement park company that—as of 2016—also operated California's Great America (opened in 1976 as Marriott's Great American) off U.S. 101 in Santa Clara. But there's still a down-home element to Knott's: These days, the park serves up syrups and berry preserves produced at Linn's, a family-owned business known for its own pies in Cambria, an unincorporated town of 6,000-plus residents along the Pacific Coast Highway in San Luis Obispo County.

A MAGIC KINGDOM

Knott's Berry Farm served as a key inspiration for another attraction that would set up shop just seven miles down the highway in Anaheim. Knott's had started out as a fruit stand that became an Old West town and then an amusement park. Its more famous neighbor began with a similar Old West concept, but it eventually morphed from a Mickey Mouse project into the quintessential amusement park.

What most people probably don't know is that Disneyland wasn't supposed to be in Anaheim. It was originally intended to be in Burbank, across the street from Walt Disney's studios on Riverside Drive.

How it got from there to its ultimate location in Anaheim is a fascinating tale.

Anyone who's traveled Santa Ana Freeway is familiar with the sight of a mountain rising up beside the freeway in the middle of a valley where there aren't any mountains. Although it's eye-catching, it's not nearly as big as it should be, and it's always capped with snow, even in the midst of a sunny Southern California summer. Despite its small size (it rises just 147 feet high), it's so famous that, when many people think of the Matterhorn, they think of this man-made replica alongside the freeway rather than the real mountain by that name, which rises more than 14,000 feet above sea level in the Swiss-Italian Alps.

It's fitting that Disney's Matterhorn is a miniature replica of the real thing, because that's how his vision for Disneyland started out. In 1947, he set up a miniature electric train next to his office, a setup he expanded until it was large enough, according to biographer Neil Gabler, to fill up half of a two-car garage. This gave way to a larger railroad project on a five-acre plot of land in Westwood that he purchased specifically for this purpose.

Disney started to buy up other miniatures, with the goal of creating an entire village patterned after the town where he'd grown up, Marceline, Missouri. Disney, it seemed, wanted to go home again. He'd once written to the *Marceline News* that "To tell the truth, more things of importance happened to me in Marceline than have happened since"—words penned in 1938, a year after the breakthrough success of his first full-length animated feature, *Snow White and the Seven Dwarfs*. It was this feeling of nostalgia for his boyhood home that spurred

Disney to ask a layout artist to design two dozen scenes from an Old West town, which he planned to construct out of miniatures and display in a traveling exhibit he dubbed Disneylandia.

He originally intended to carve some of the miniatures himself but later enlisted the help of a sculptor. His first project was "Granny Kincaid's Cabin," based on Disney's movie *So Dear to My Heart*, and featuring a narration by the actress who played Granny in the film, Beulah Bondi. The scene eventually went on display at the 1952 Festival of California Living at Los Angeles's Pan-Pacific Auditorium, and work was done on two other scenes—one in which a barbershop quartet would sing "Sweet Adeline" and a second with a dancer performing in a frontier music hall. (The dancer used as the model for this scene was none other than Buddy Ebsen, who rose to greater fame as Jed Clampett in TV's *The Beverly Hillbillies*.)

**Walt Disney Studios in the San Fernando Valley, the original proposed site
of a proto-Disneyland conceived by Walt Disney.**

The idea for a traveling exhibit never got off the ground. Instead, Disney turned his attention to creating something bigger. Other movie studios had taken to offering public tours of their production lots; Universal Studios Tours would eventually develop into a theme park of its own. Disney was intrigued by the idea of doing something similar, but worried that the public wouldn't be too interested in watching a team of animators hunched over picture storyboards all day.

Still, fans had been sending letters to the studio for some time, asking to meet his animated characters in the flesh. As early as 1939, Disney had envisioned a Bavarian village with a carousel and train ride that would include a tunnel through the mine from *Snow White*, which would feature characters from the movie. The war had forced Disney to shelve that project, but he revisited the idea a decade later when the idea occurred to him that he could build a railroad attraction and village at his Burbank studios. Among the sites he visited while researching the project was none other than Knott's Berry Farm, which already had an Old West town of its own similar to what Disney had envisioned for his traveling replica exhibit.

A 1951 visit to Tivoli Gardens in Copenhagen—which remains the world's oldest operating amusement park,

Walt Disney, center, goes over plans for his amusement park in 1954. *Orange County Archives.*

having opened in 1843—fired his imagination further, and he returned home with a request for illustrator Harper Goff to produce sketches of what a similar park might look like. Goff would go on to work on projects such as *Willy Wonka and the Chocolate Factory* and Tokyo Disneyland, his final project before his death in 1993.

Goff's sketches of a "Proposed Disneyland in Burbank"—also called Mickey Mouse Park—largely followed the Old West theme Disney had been enamored with for some time. There would be a railroad encircling much of the grounds, a livestock area behind "Granny's Farm," a stagecoach, "Indian Village," donkey pack train, petting zoo, and picnic area. A large portion of the park would be devoted to a lagoon, with an island at its center, where a Mississippi

An aerial view of Disneyland in 1962, with the Matterhorn prominent at top center. *Public domain.*

The Tom Sawyer ride at Disneyland in 1960.
George Louis, public domain.

steamboat would ply the waters. There would also be an opera house and bird sanctuary, along with select tributes to more fantasy-themed Disney creations, such as a castle and a "Dwarfs' House," presumably from *Snow White*.

As with most amusement parks, there would be a carnival area, and there would be rides, too. One would feature the giant whale from *Pinocchio*, another would put visitors on board a submarine. Other attractions foreshadowed elements that eventually found their way to Anaheim: a haunted house and a mock spaceship, the ancestor of Tomorrowland. But in contrast to many parks, with their loud carnival atmosphere and roaring roller coasters, Disney wanted Mickey Mouse Park to be a more laid-back, family-friendly place.

The Burbank Parks and Recreation Board liked the idea and approved the plans in 1952, but the Burbank City Council shot them down, with one council member declaring, "We don't want the carny atmosphere in Burbank. We don't want people falling in the river or merry-go-rounds squawking all day long."

Fortunately, Disney had a backup plan: Four months before the council's decision, he had spoken of buying another site, "something up to 200 acres" that would "give us control of the surrounding area, which we feel is important." To fund this more ambitious project, he agreed to produce a television series for ABC, which would invest in the theme park and take a 35 percent stake in it. The television show, which debuted in 1954, was titled (appropriately enough) *Walt Disney's Disneyland* and would later be retitled *The Wonderful World of Disney*. In a bit of irony that demonstrated how successful Disney was to become, the company he started eventually turned around and bought the ABC network.

Disneyland would maintain some of the Old West flavor of Mickey Mouse Park, but Frontier Country (later Frontierland) would be just one of seven themed areas planned for the new project. The others would be True-Life Adventureland, World of Tomorrow, Lilliputian Land, Fantasy Land, Recreation Park, and Holiday Land. The steam train, unsurprisingly, also made the leap from Burbank to Anaheim.

World of Tomorrow would eventually become Tomorrowland, and True-Life Adventureland merely Adventureland. Some of the concepts were dropped, though. Among them, Lilliputianland and Holdidayland, envisioned as a land that would change along with the holiday seasons. Recreation Park, an area with a relaxed feel envisioned for Mickey Mouse Park, which had been intended as an area that could be reserved by schools or other groups, was also lost in the transition, but several other attractions intended for the Burbank park survived in one form or another.

Among them are the castle, the town square, and Main Street, USA, which owes its inspiration at least in part to Marceline. The steam train was, not surprisingly, preserved as well, and the Storybook Land Canal Boats pass through the mouth of a giant whale, just as they did in Goff's sketch of the Pinocchio ride for Mickey Mouse Park. Ironically, the carnival idea that led to Burbank's rejection of Disney's original proposal wound up being dropped at Disneyland.

Plans for the Burbank park had included a Riverside Café, and Disneyland offered food, as well, such as Aunt Jemima's Pancake House on New Orleans Street.

Another early vendor, which set up shop not too far away, was Frito-Lay. In 1955, shortly after the park opened, Disney contracted with the company to open a Mexican restaurant in Frontierland called Casa de Fritos. It wasn't what you'd call "authentic" Mexican food. Heck, even its mascot at the time, the Frito Kid, was a blond-haired, blue-eyed cartoon cowboy. And while the menu at Casa de Fritos included standard Tex-Mex fare such as enchiladas, tacos, and tamales, it also featured (naturally) Fritos. It's no surprise, then that Casa de Fritos would eventually produce a dish that owed something to Mexico but was, at the same time, uniquely American.

The Frito Kid served up Fritos corn chips at Disneyland during the 1950s and early '60s. *Public domain.*

That innovation wasn't a result of anything the Frito company did, because the Frito folks didn't actually make the taco shells or tortillas it used at the Disneyland restaurant. A company called Alex Foods did. It's not as famous as Frito-Lay, but it's become pretty successful in its own right: You might know the company by its more recent name, Don Miguel Foods, and if you live in southern California, you've probably seen the frozen Mexican dishes it supplies to your local supermarket.

By the time Disneyland got built, Alex Foods had already gobbled up a sizable share of the distribution market in Orange County, where its factory was located. It landed a contract to supply Casa de Fritos, and one day, one of its salesmen noticed that the workers there were dumping old, slightly stale tortillas in a trash bin.

He took one of the cooks at Casa de Fritos aside and told him the restaurant was wasting perfectly good tortillas. Instead of throwing them away, he suggested, why not fry them up and sell them as chips?

The idea caught on, and the chips became a hit. But it wasn't until about a year later that a company executive for Frito-Lay stopped by and took notice. He suggested that the chips be mass-produced and marketed nationally as a new snack food.

Alex Foods was only too happy to oblige, and in 1966, the snack hit the market. Within a few years, Frito-Lay took over production of the chips itself, while Alex went on to success in the frozen food aisle.

The name of the popular snack? "Little golden things," which, translated, is Doritos.

THE HOLLYWOOD FREEWAY

"There's gold in them thar hills!"

It was a rallying cry for California prospectors in the 19th century, but most of them were talking about the veins of ore that ran through the mountains themselves, not a lost treasure worthy of a sea pirate.

Less than a year before highway workers were to break ground on the Cahuenga Pass Freeway in 1939, San Francisco mining authority Henry Jones assembled a team to dig for a treasure he believed to have been buried along the route—long used by travelers heading north and south across the Santa Monica Mountains.

Some of Jones's associates, armed with a metal detector, were convinced they'd found the lost treasure of Diego Moreno, buried beneath the parking lot of the Hollywood Bowl.

How the treasure (allegedly) came to be buried there had become a folktale of some renown, and by the time Jones and his colleagues came along, the curse that had kept it there had become a legend in its own right.

The story begins at the time of the American Civil War, when the French captured Mexico City and staged

This off-ramp from the Hollywood Freeway funneled traffic onto Santa Monica Boulevard in 1953, when that street still was part of iconic Route 66. © *California Department of Transportation, all rights reserved. Used with permission.*

a referendum to set up an imperial government. At the invitation of Napoleon III, Archduke Maximilian of Austria agreed to assume the title of Emperor Maximilian I of Mexico and rule there with his wife, Carlota.

The year was 1863.

Horses and wagons navigate the Cahuenga Pass before the era of the automobile, in 1892. *Public domain.*

Not surprisingly, France's aggression didn't go over well with Mexico's sitting president, Benito Juarez, who staged a resistance movement that—once the United States had resolved its own bloody conflict—earned the support of Juarez's neighbor to the north. In the meantime, he set about organizing his own forces in a high-stakes insurgency against Maximilian, who for his part sought to consolidate his power by bringing some of his European supporters to Mexico.

Juarez, in need of weapons to arm his insurgents, sent four of his agents north with some $200,000 in gold and jewels for the purpose of buying weapons in San Francisco. This is where the treasure's "curse" began to take its toll. When one of the four agents died under mysterious circumstances, suspicion immediately fell on French agents who, when the group arrived in San Francisco, appeared to be everywhere.

Unable to purchase the weapons as planned, Juarez's three remaining men withdrew to San Mateo, where they decided to divide their treasure into six parts and bury it.

They managed to evade the eyes of the French agents who had been tracking them, but they failed to account for a Mexican shepherd named Diego Moreno, who happened to see where they hid the valuables and—once they had departed—promptly dug them up and made off with the goods, heading back toward Mexico.

The "curse" next claimed two of the agents and, ultimately, Moreno himself. Upon discovering their treasure was missing, two of the agents got into a violent argument and ended up killing each other (the third would also die violently, intervening in a bar fight). As for Moreno, the first indication he had that things might not end well for him was a dream he had upon stopping for the night at a Cahuenga Pass tavern called La Nopalera—the Cactus Patch. According to the dream, Moreno was destined to forfeit his life should he enter Los Angeles with his loot.

The panicked shepherd, taking no chances, buried the treasure under an ash tree and continued on his way.

But the dream turned out to be wrong: He died anyway.

He fell ill during his trip to Los Angeles. But before he left this world, the ailing Moreno managed to tell a friend named Jesús Martinez where he had buried the treasure. The directions he wrote down were explicit: "One night, everything being quiet in the tavern, I slipped out with the treasure to a previously selected spot on the side of the pass, about halfway from the inn to the summit on the hillside, opposite the main road, and buried it. I buried it in six different holes, taking measurements from the fresno (ash) tree east, west, south and north. It is the only fresno tree in that locality."

U.S. 101 through the Cahuenga Pass, entering Hollywood, with trolley tracks separating the north- and southbound lanes, in 1940. © *California Department of Transportation, all rights reserved. Used with permission.*

After Moreno died, Martinez followed his friend's instructions and trekked to the site with his stepson, José Correa. But before he could start digging at the base of the tree Moreno had described to him, he suffered a fatal seizure. His stepson fled, and the treasure remained right where it was.

Many years later, Correa would think twice about leaving the loot where it was and seek to recover it—only to be thwarted by the curse when his brother-in-law shot him dead during a family quarrel.

More than twenty years after Martinez's death, another shepherd—this one of Basque descent—is said to have found a bag of jewels and coins under a tree in the same area. If the other five bags of treasure remained in the same area, he didn't know to look for them, but that didn't stop the curse from striking him, as well. On a ship headed home to Spain, he is said to have tumbled over the railing and been carried to the bottom of the ocean by the weight of the treasure, which he had taken the precaution of sewing into his clothes.

The collective fatal failures of those several attempts to cash in on the lost treasure seem to have deterred others

from trying their luck—until, that is, Jones came along. He and his cohorts received permission from L.A. County to dig for the treasure underneath the Hollywood Bowl parking lot, with the understanding that they'd split the profits with the county if they found anything.

That turned out to be a big "if."

The Jones team dug and dug and dug some more, spending a full two months in pursuit of Diego Moreno's elusive trove. All they had to show for it at the end of that time was a collection of old tin cans and other worthless metallic items.

Jones, perhaps distraught over his failure, killed himself in January 1940 and thus became the latest victim of the "curse." For all anyone knows, the treasure is still buried where Moreno described it, though perhaps now beneath the pavement that makes up the northern expanse of the Hollywood Freeway through the Cahuenga Pass.

BOWLED OVER

The Hollywood Bowl is a treasure in its own right, an instantly recognizable amphitheater on a plot of land once known as Daisy Dell.

The Hollywood Bowl as it appeared in 1922.
Public domain.

For the longest time, I thought the "bowl" referred to the shell of amphitheater stage, with its concentric arches forming what seemed to be half a sugar bowl sticking up sideways out of the earth. But no, the bowl is actually the natural depression of the land itself. That amphitheater shell wasn't there when residents started using the place for outdoor gatherings, and the first version wasn't shaped like sideways sugar bowl, either.

Christine Stevenson, heiress to the Pittsburgh Paints fortune, wanted a place to hold religious plays and other performances outdoors, so she formed the Theater Alliance and enlisted a man named William Reed to find a suitable location. He and his son searched the area until they came upon Daisy Dell. Reed put it to the test by speaking to his son across the small canyon and found the acoustics to be exceptional.

"I scaled a barbed wire fence, went up to the brow of a hill," the younger Reed said. "Dad stood near a live oak in the center of the bowl-shaped area and we carried on

a conversation. We rushed back to the Alliance with a glowing report."

Based on the Reeds' recommendation, Stevenson and developer C. E. Toberman promptly plunked down $49,000 to purchase the site. They cleared away the rocks and created a level surface in the bowl; then, in 1920, they staged the first known performance on a small, makeshift wooden stage, featuring Gertrude Ross, Anna Ruzena Sprotte, and a single piano. Soon, Easter sunrise services were being held there, with attendees spreading out blankets or sitting on temporary wooden benches.

The Los Angeles Philharmonic played its first concert there in 1921, using a larger wooden stage atop a dirt mound, and a covered stage was added shortly after that, flanked by half a dozen huge, decorative, Greek columns on either side. The seating consisted of wooden benches. But it wasn't until 1926 that a group known as Allied Architects was enlisted to regrade the Bowl and provide permanent seating and a "shell" to shield the stage from the elements.

Myron Hunt designed the first shell, an elliptical arch that grew thicker near the bottom on both sides, allowing room for a pair of murals that depicted sailing ships at sea.

It didn't work.

The acoustics were bad, and the people didn't like the design, either, so it was torn down after a single season, and the job of designing a new shell was awarded to Lloyd Wright, the son of Frank Lloyd Wright. Using leftover lumber from a production of *Robin Hood*, he created a shell that looked nothing like the sloping arch that graces the bowl today. Instead, it took the shape of a step pyramid, meant to serve as a contrast to the rolling hills around the canyon.

A 1927 article in the *Los Angeles Times* stated that Wright "particularly desired to attain such a contrast."

The writer seemed to approve of the design, though he admitted to some reservations: "Perhaps the new stage does not at first sight seem so inviting to the eye—so unobtrusive as those previously in vogue, but it appears to have commendable acoustic qualities."

In fact, according to at least one account, the acoustics were the best ever attained at the Bowl. The aesthetic appeal of the pyramid, however, was something else

The Hollywood Bowl today.

Yes once filled the pool with dry ice and used it to give rise to a huge inflatable dinosaur. The pool was eventually filled in to make room for more seats, but Wakeman was neither the first nor the last pop musician to play the Bowl.

Frank Sinatra was the first, during the 1940s, and the parade continues to this day. The Beatles performed there in 1964 and '65, and other acts to grace the stage have included everyone from Lady Gaga to Nine Inch Nails, from Elton John to Jimi Hendrix.

None of them, however, holds the record for the most attendance at a Bowl show. That honor goes to French-American soprano Lily Pons, who drew a crowd of 26,410 back in 1936. (If you include early events, you could have counted 50,000 people at an Easter sunrise service at the dell back in 1922.)

Nonmusical acts have appeared there, as well, including President Franklin D. Roosevelt, dancers Fred Astair and Mikhail Baryshnikov, and the comic teams Abbott and Costello and Monty Python.

THE RISE AND FALL OF PACIFIC ELECTRIC

The Cahuenga Freeway, as it was known at first, was the linchpin in a grand plan to create an extensive network of roads that would become known as the freeway system. Or perpetual gridlock. Or both: Take your pick.

It's easy to forget that Los Angeles was once known for a different transportation system that was also, at one time, the biggest in California: the Red Car.

The brainchild of Henry Huntington, the Red Car—a.k.a. Pacific Electric Streetcar System, an octopus with tentacles that stretched out over 1,100 miles of track by the 1920s. They even *called* it "the Octopus." It extended south into Orange County, both inland and along the coast, reaching as far as Santa Ana and Newport Beach. It reached northward to San Fernando and eastward to San Bernardino and Riverside.

entirely. It lasted just one year, before being demolished and replaced the following season by a shell much closer in design to the modern version: a series of nine concentric arches descending back toward the rear of the stage. The arches in this design, however, were more gradual and elliptical rather than semicircular. One advantage: They were movable and could be adjusted to "tune" the acoustics. But this shell, too, lasted only one year before it had to be removed because of weather damage.

The first lasting shell, installed the following season, was similar to Wright's but with tighter, semicircular arches. This 55-ton "classic shell," which most people associate with the bowl, lasted until it was replaced by a similar (but not identical) shell in 2004. Its acoustics, however, were never as good as those of the shells Wright had designed, and various attempts were made over the years to improve them, ranging from gigantic hollow "sonotubes" to hollow fiberglass spheres, both of which obscured part of the shell itself and spoiled the aesthetics.

In 1940, a statue called the *Muse of Music* was added to the entrance, which was accessible from Cahuenga Boulevard—Old 101—where it morphs into Highland Avenue. And up until 1972, a pool filled with 100,000 gallons of water separated the seats from the stage; during intermissions, it was featured in a water show. Keyboardist Rick Wakeman of the progressive rock band

Cars share the road with trolley tracks near the Los Angeles city limits in this undated photo.

Think New York City's rail system is big? Pacific Electric's network had 25 percent more track.

Huntington's uncle had controlled Southern Pacific Railway, but when he died in 1900, the board of that company ousted the younger Huntington and seized control. So, he did the next best thing: He founded his own railway company in the West's most expansive, fastest-growing population center, also building lines in Fresno and Santa Clara. A second "Yellow Car" line or Los Angeles Railway, a narrow-gauge system that focused on downtown L.A. and the surrounding neighborhoods, actually carried more passengers.

Huntington didn't just want to make money on trolley fares; he wanted to expose riders to his real estate developments. So, he built the rail lines strategically, in order to connect his subdivisions. The Red Car line brought in more than $90,000 in 1905, which turned out to be its best year, but his real estate endeavors were far more successful, with profits of $151,000 that same year and more than $400,000 two years later.

But the trolleys weren't necessarily taking people where they wanted to go: How many people really wanted to hopscotch around L.A. from one subdivision to another? They wanted to get to work, to the retail district, to the beach, etc. And they didn't want to have to wait for a trolley to take them there. More to the point, they didn't want to have to wait once they were onboard the trolley. The Southern California freeway system didn't invent the concept of gridlock. Indeed, it was supposed to be the antidote to "hurry up and wait."

The trolleys helped create the concept of the traffic jam before there were enough cars on the road to even matter. Huntington had designed them as a means to an end: a way to get prospective buyers to the myriad subdivisions that helped L.A. pioneer the concept of urban sprawl. So, he hadn't invested much in making them comfortable or efficient. Instead of building subways and viaducts to separate them from surface street traffic, he plunked his rail lines down smack in the middle of city streets. It was cheaper that way.

It also made those streets a lot more congested—especially Main Street, where Huntington built his main terminal. With Red (and Yellow) Cars descending on Main from all directions, the result was a line of trolleys all headed the same place but barely moving. It could take riders an hour to get from Los Angeles to Santa Monica, a distance of just 14 miles. The Hollywood Boulevard trolley was even slower, lurching along at a stodgy clip of just 11 miles per hour.

It wasn't as if riders were traveling in the lap of luxury, either. Huntington's economical (read: cheap) approach to building the system meant the cars themselves left a lot to be desired when it came to comfort. There wasn't much incentive to maintain them, either. Huntington sold his subdivisions and, in 1910, sold the Red Car line, as well—to the very firm that had spurned him a decade earlier, Southern Pacific. (He and his heirs did, however, retain control of the Yellow Car line until 1945.)

In the years that followed, the Red Cars became the streetcars that weren't desired. They fell into such a state of disrepair that riders mocked the system as a "slum on wheels." Besides, they had a better option in the form of ever-more-comfortable and increasingly reliable automobiles, which offered them more flexibility to travel on their own terms.

Los Angeles's obsession with the automobile hurt Pacific Electric in more ways than one. Not only did Angelenos forsake the trolleys by getting behind the wheel, their cars clogged the streets they shared with the Red and Yellow lines even more. Drivers, of course, blamed the trolleys. It's hardly surprising that Southern Pacific's proposal to improve the system using tax money went down in flames. Residents had little reason to put their faith in the railroad. If it had failed to maintain the system with its own money, how could it be trusted with public funds?

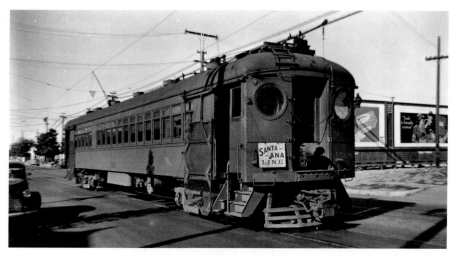

The Pacific Electric Santa Ana Line in 1943.
Orange County Archives.

The company was also known for its anti-union stance and hardball tactics in breaking strikes. Not only did that make it unpopular with labor forces—many of whom rode the dilapidated trolleys to and from work—it also didn't sit well with everyday residents, who viewed it as a sign of the railroad's insistence on cutting corners so it could operate on the cheap. Labor wanted the city to take over the lines, but Southern Pacific balked at the idea, in part because it stood to lose significant revenue from the freight cars that shared the lines with the trolleys.

The railroad did undertake at least one project to improve the streetcars' efficiency: a tunnel through downtown L.A. roughly parallel to what would become the 101 route.

The Hollywood Subway, which opened December 1, 1925, and was built at a cost of $1.25 million, was supposed to cut 15 minutes off commute time.

When the Cahuenga Pass Freeway was dedicated in 1940, its north- and southbound lanes were separated by two sets of Red Car trolley tracks. At least there, the streetcars weren't competing with automobiles, but by that point, only time—and a world war—stood between the Red Car's glory days and oblivion. Ridership spiked during World War II with the advent of gas rationing to conserve rubber for the war effort (instead of using it on tires). But once the war ended, residents flocked to their cars with greater enthusiasm than ever … and in greater numbers.

A newspaper ad for the Hollywoodland development, dated January 6, 1924, touts it as combining "the luxury of metropolitan living with the glorious freedom of the hills."

Freeways were being built at a rapid pace, and a plethora of plans—some of them realized, others not—for even more of them were on the drawing boards.

The writing was on the wall, and Pacific Electric soon started scaling back its service, dropping the Santa Ana and Baldwin Park lines in 1950, and abandoning the Pasadena and Monrovia-Glendora lines a year later. Some of the lines were converted into bus routes, and the last rail line—the Los Angeles-to-Long Beach interurban route—was shut down for good on April 9, 1961.

The Hollywood Subway was closed in 1955, just 30 years after it opened, and the trolley tracks on the Cahuenga Pass were paved over, to make room for more freeway lanes and more automobiles.

HOLLYWOOD ICON

Perhaps the most famous landmark associated with the Hollywood Freeway area is a massive nine-letter sign overlooking the freeway in the Hollywood Hills.

The "Hollywood" sign, which originally featured a less-lucky complement of 13 letters that spelled out "Hollywoodland," was the brainchild of *Los Angeles Times* publisher Harry Chandler. He paid $21,000 to build the sign—which featured 4,000 lightbulbs to illu-

minate it at night—as a clarion call across the city below announcing his Hollywoodland real estate development. Each of the letters was 43 feet tall by 30 feet wide, and they blinked out a three-part message at night: first "Holly," then "wood," then "land."

At the time, it was touted as the largest sign in the world.

Workers had to drag the letters and other construction up Mt. Lee, where the sign was to be located, on foot and by hand. But a couple of weeks after the sign's debut, an actor named Harry Neville decided to see whether the site could be reached by car. Taking the wheel of an Oakland Six touring car, Neville ascended the roadless mountainside at an incline ranging from 20 to 57 percent and reached the sign almost an hour later.

That, it turned out, was the easy part.

Some onlookers suggested he'd be better off using a cable to get back down, but Neville "had implicit confidence in the four-wheel brakes of the Oakland, and amid the misgivings of onlookers, he let the car slide forward," a representative of the San Bernardino Oakland dealership reported. It was, of course, a publicity stunt—the ad manager for Hollywoodland had cameramen clicking away, as well—and it was necessary to inject the account of Neville's feat with the highest possible level of drama:

"Once the car took a sudden lurch to one side of the hogsback and it looked for the instant as if it was doomed to be dashed to the deep canyons below," the account continued. "But Neville, with his uncanny knowledge of Oakland's ability, stepped on the throttle and with a dart as swift as a deer it leaped forward and away from danger."

Never heard of Harry Neville? You might recall the Tasmanian-born actor from such movie classics as the *Man Hater*, *The Blindness of Love*, and *The Pretenders*. Then again, you probably won't. The last of these hit the silver screen in 1917. As for the Oakland car brand, it faded into obscurity after 1931, when it was absorbed into General Motors' Pontiac line.

The Hollywood sign (minus the -land) as it appears today.

The sign was more tragically linked to another actor, aspiring starlet Lillian "Peg" Entwistle, who had come to Hollywood—like so many others—looking for her big break. Born in Wales, she'd had some roles on Broadway before heading west, and her role in one of them reportedly inspired a young Bette Davis to remark, "I want to be exactly like Peg Entwistle."

Entwistle, however, had seen her share of heartache: In 1927, she had married a fellow actor named Robert Keith—who neglected to tell her he was the father of a six-year-old boy. They divorced two years later, with Entwistle charging cruelty and that they had been married under false pretenses. The young boy in question, incidentally, went on to an acting career of his own. Brian Keith starred on the big screen in Disney's *The Parent Trap* and on TV in the situation comedy *Family Affair*, which aired from 1966 to 1971.

Entwistle's bad luck continued on her arrival in Hollywood, where a part in a play featuring Billie Burke (who played Glinda the Good Witch in *The Wizard of Oz*) failed to earn her much attention from the studios. She did manage to sign on for a bit part in one picture with RKO: *Thirteen Women*, starring Myrna Loy. But the studio failed to pick up her contract after that.

Apparently distraught over her waning fortunes, Entwistle left her uncle's home on Friday, September 16, 1932, the official release date of *Thirteen Women*, telling him she was about to keep a "rendezvous" with a friend. Instead, she made her way into the hills and climbed up a ladder used by repairmen to replace the lights on the mammoth sign. Reaching the top of the letter "H," she flung herself forward and fell 50 feet to her death.

Her broken body rolled 100 feet away from where she hit and landed near the letter "A," where she was found by a woman hiking in the hills, who phoned police with an anonymous tip.

"I was hiking on Hollywood mountain and near the Hollywoodland sign I found a woman's shoe, jacket and purse," the woman told police. "In the purse I found a suicide note. I looked down the mountain and saw a body. I don't want any publicity in this, so I wrapped up the purse, shoe and jacket and laid the bundle on the steps of the Hollywood police station."

Before police could question her further, she hung up.

The note found in the purse was signed "P.E." and read, "I am afraid I am a coward and I am sorry for many things. If I had only done this long ago I could have saved a lot of pain."

Entwistle was just 24 at the time of her death.

In the ensuing years, the Hollywoodland sign fell into a state of disrepair. The Depression had pulled the rug out from under the real estate market, and the developers no longer had the money to maintain it. By 1949, the "H" had fallen over (leaving the sign to spell out "Ollywoodland") and the sign was becoming an eyesore, so the Hollywood Chamber of Commerce offered to step in and repair it—on condition that the last four letters be removed so that the sign could serve as a symbol for the entire community.

The "H" was returned to place, and the sign assumed its present shape, but what had been created as a temporary advertising gimmick (it had never been intended to last longer than 18 months) was now more than a half century old. So, it wasn't long before it began to deteriorate again. An arsonist set fire to the bottom of the second "L," while the top of the first "O" crumbled and the entire third "O" fell down.

In wasn't until the late 1970s that a group of celebrities took it upon themselves to save what one newspaper article described as the rickety, rotting sign. *Playboy Magazine* founder Hugh Hefner held a $100-a-person fund-raising party at his mansion, attended by the likes of Jack Haley Jr., Rita Hayworth, Bob Newhart, and Andy Williams. Football star-turned-actor Jim Brown also attended, while Hefner, rock star Alice Cooper, and Warner Brothers Records each donated $27,000 to the cause. With the help of additional pledges, they raised an estimated $200,000 toward the $250,000 cost of restoration, which was described as "an exact, though materially tougher replica of the original."

Even after all these years, the Hollywood name most closely associated with the sign is Entwistle's.

Griffith Park Rangers have, at various times, reported coming upon the ghost of the Hollywood sign: an attractive, young, blond woman with a sad expression, dressed in 1930s clothing. Once, a couple walking their dog on the park's Beachwood Canyon trail noticed their dog whimpering and cowering. Just then, they said, a woman in antique clothing appeared on the trail, looking confused, before vanishing just as suddenly.

A resident of Beachwood Canyon once came upon a woman who "seemed to almost glide" along. Before she could catch up to her, however, the woman had disappeared, leaving behind only an intense scent of gardenias.

It was reportedly the aroma of Entwistle's favorite perfume.

BEFORE THE FREEWAY

Those interested in retracing the course of the pre-freeway 101 alignment through Los Angeles can still do so—if you want to contend with the traffic on downtown's surface streets. (Freeway traffic these days can be just as bad, though, so why not, right?)

As with many other routes that cobbled together existing surface streets, the Old 101 changed over time.

A California state road map dated 1944 shows the route entering the city from the southeast on Whittier Boulevard, then turning north at Boyle Avenue just

The Spring Street exit from U.S. 101 in downtown Los Angeles, as it appeared in 1953. *© California Department of Transportation, all rights reserved. Used with permission.*

before the L.A. River and veering northwest briefly at Pleasant Avenue. It then turns east again along Macy Street (rechristened Cesar E. Chavez Avenue in 1994) and across the river. It becomes Sunset Boulevard about a mile and a half later—close to the four-level "stack" interchange completed in 1949 to link the new Hollywood Freeway version of U.S. 101 with California's first freeway, the Arroyo Seco Parkway.

The 1939 WPA Guide, however, charts a slightly different course. It omits any mention of Boyle Avenue and describes U.S. 101 as entering the city via Whittier Boulevard, then taking "several turns," before it "follows Spring Street in the center of Los Angeles." The book doesn't say what those turns were, but earlier maps provide a clue.

Some sections of the route were in place before being incorporated into the federal highway system in 1926. A map from five years earlier shows the main route already entering L.A. on Whittier Boulevard—but instead of turning *north* on Boyle Avenue, it jogged *south* for a single block before resuming its eastward course along Seventh Street until it got to Broadway (just past Spring Street).

A 1929 map shows that that route remained the same through downtown once it was signed as U.S. 101.

Once on Broadway (or Spring, if you're going by the WPA Guide), the motorist would travel for a mile or so to Macy/Chavez, then turned northwest from there.

Descriptions of the route are fairly consistent from that point forward. Macy became Sunset, and Sunset funneled traffic back eastward to Highland Avenue, where the route turned north again across the Santa Monica Mountains as Cahuenga Boulevard, running parallel to the modern freeway. (The two roads had to share a narrow corridor; the pass is only so wide, after all.)

Cahuenga, in turn, morphed into Ventura Boulevard in the San Fernando Valley.

VENTURA HIGHWAY

A view of Ventura Boulevard, old U.S. 101, lined with palm trees in Studio City.

There's something about this section of the highway that lends itself to vibrant memories and vivid imagery. It's even found its way into our musical folklore.

In Tom Petty's "Free Fallin'" from 1989, the old highway alignment—today's Ventura Boulevard—was a hangout for vampires. Not real vampires, but the shadowy figures who congregate off the sidewalks along the busy road.

The Everly Brothers recorded a song called "Ventura Boulevard" in 1968, and four years later, the band America released a song called "Ventura Highway" based on guitarist-vocalist Dewey Bunnell's reminiscence of a trip down the road interrupted by a flat tire. He and his brother waited there as their father changed the tire, feeling the sun on their faces and gazing at cloud formations that reminded him of alligator lizards. The childhood scene became the inspiration for the song.

My personal memories of this section of road are just as vivid. I spent six years of my childhood in Woodland Hills, a slice of suburbia where we lived sandwiched in between then-Dodgers outfielder Bill Buckner on one

The Ventura Freeway, then called the Calabasas Freeway along this stretch, replaced Ventura Boulevard as U.S. 101. Here, it's seen in 1958. Note that fractions of a mile are given in tenths, rather than halves and quarters.
© California Department of Transportation, all rights reserved. Used with permission.

side and Shelly Cohen, who served as the assistant music director for *The Tonight Show*, on the other. It was on Ventura Boulevard that, at the age of nine, I was introduced to my favorite Mexican restaurant, El Torito, which has since become a massive chain. Unfortunately, that location's no longer there. But Corbin Bowl, just up the road in Tarzana, is still open. It was there that I bowled my first game at about the same age, racking up the fantastic score of 81. Built in 1959, it survived the Northridge quake of 1994 and has been used as a set for TV shows such as *Moonlighting* and *Quincy*.

Ventura Boulevard was the artery that kept the lifeblood pumping across the San Fernando Valley—and inspiration for Frank and Moon Zappa's song "Valley Girl," where it's linked with "bitchin' clothes." It's the world's longest roadway of contiguous businesses, running some 20 miles from Calabasas at its west end to Studio City, where it morphs into Cahuenga Boulevard.

It served as the alignment for U.S. 101 through the San Fernando Valley until 1956, when construction began on the new Ventura Freeway just to the north.

It's a funny thing about the Ventura Freeway: It's still technically U.S. 101 north and south, even though it actually runs east and west. (This was enough even to confuse the signposters, who set up signs bearing the words "east" and "west" in some San Fernando Valley locales, but "north" and "south" in others.)

Another oddity: At the so-called Hollywood Split, the interchange where the 101 morphs from the Hollywood Freeway into the Ventura Freeway—or vice versa—the Hollywood Freeway continues northward as State Route 170, while the Ventura Freeway keeps right on going eastward as State Route 134.

The Studio City Theatre on Ventura Boulevard was transformed into a bookstore.

Pictures in Motion

Lights, camera, action. The first light—traffic light, that is—in the San Fernando Valley flashed red at the corner of Ventura and Lankershim Boulevards in a place called Studio City.

The motion picture industry was coming into its own in the second decade of the 20th century, but Hollywood didn't spill over the hill into the San Fernando Valley until 1927—a year after Ventura Boulevard became U.S. 101. It was in the summer of that year that Mark Sennett announced plans to construct a studio on 500 acres, which would include a five-story office building on the highway at Radford Street.

The $20 million development was to front Ventura Boulevard for a full mile, and it would include an administration building, two dressing buildings, and "two immense stages," with plans for two more stages to be built later, *The Van Nuys News* reported. The newspaper hailed it as "one of the greatest single development projects ever launched in the history of the San Joaquin Valley." Other stucco buildings planned for the site would house a machine shop, cutting and projection rooms, film vault, and wardrobe and property rooms.

Sennett's studio wasn't the only one eyeing the site. Three other film production companies, including MGM, were poised to open studios in the new district.

The highway itself would be widened to accommodate the increased traffic, and the Pacific Electric trolley company planned to extend its service with a new line.

Before it was Studio City, the area where the highway bends southward from the valley toward Los Angeles was known as Laurelwood, an area bisected on the north-south grid by the similarly named Laurel Canyon Boulevard. In the second decade of the 20th century, Laurel Canyon was already becoming a haven for film players such as Tom Mix and Clara "It Girl" Bow, along with famed escape artist Harry Houdini, who took refuge in this scenic hideaway nestled in the Hollywood hills. (Errol Flynn had a large mansion of his own north of Houdini's, which burned down in 1958. Tales arose that the rest of the estate was haunted.)

But earthmovers and pavers didn't connect plush Laurel Canyon Boulevard all the way across the mountains—connecting Hollywood to the San Fernando Valley—until the 1940s. It was Studio City that first brought the film industry across the Santa Monica Mountains in a big way.

Jungle Love

West of Studio City on the 101 lies Tarzana, a name that sound like it was lifted out of Edgar Rice Burroughs's famous stories—because it was.

Burroughs used some of the fortune he'd made writing his Tarzan stories to buy a 540-acre estate in 1919. Before he purchased the land in a rural area informally known as Runnymede, it had belonged *Los Angeles Times* publisher Harrison Gray Otis, who had christened it Mil

Tarzana Safari Walk pays tribute to the city's namesake, Edgar Rice Burroughs's fictional ape-man, Tarzan.

Flores. Burroughs bought the estate for $125,000 after Otis died and renamed it Tarzana. It wasn't exactly a jungle, but the author did buy animals to raise and breed on the ranch: cows, chickens, draft horses, and Angora goats, among others.

The centerpiece of the rancho was a 4,500-square-foot Spanish-style mansion, which was also the social center of the rural area that surrounded it. Every week, Burroughs would invite his neighbors to the theater underneath the servants' quarters to watch a free movie. As many as 200 people would show up to pack the place on any given Friday.

By 1922, though, he had grown weary of being lord of all he surveyed and decided to subdivide the land, offering tracts for sale in a nascent community that took its name from the estate—and the fictional hero. His description of it made this new vision for Tarzana sound something like a proto-hippie commune.

He advertised it as "an artistic colony on high class residential acres," open to all "who expressed artistic desires through the medium of pictures, flowers or vegetables, furniture, drugs, plumbing,

poetry or the screen—but artists, each in his own field, and each a lover of the beautiful. The mere desire to join this art colony will not in itself be sufficient unless you have the artistic urge."

Unfortunately for Burroughs, such an art colony was probably too far ahead of its flower-power time. He wasn't able to sell many of the lots, so he simplified his pitch with a newspaper ad that read simply, "Tarzan of the Apes to Sell Lots in Tarzana." A few more lots sold, but not enough for Burroughs, who decided to move out of his mansion and converted it into the clubhouse at a country club he started.

In 1926, he moved into a smaller cottage along Ventura Boulevard—Old 101—and two years later, members of the nascent community decided to honor its founder by adopting the name he'd used for the rancho: Tarzana. Burroughs eventually left the Valley completely; he and his first wife divorced in 1934, and he remarried a year later, resettling with his new bride in Santa Monica. A few years later, he sold the land to developers who could achieve what he'd failed to accomplish: find buyers for subdivided

This walnut tree was planted as a memorial to author Edgar Rice Burroughs in front of his office on Ventura Boulevard (old U.S. 101).

plots from the old rancho. He got just $30,000 for it, less than a quarter of what he'd originally paid, the bottom having dropped out of the real estate market during the Depression.

The community, meanwhile, took a long time to fully embrace its identity: In 1936, a total of 300 residents signed a petition to change the name to Otono, with one of the people who argued for the change lamenting that the post office was likely to be annexed to Reseda, Van Nuys, or Canoga Park unless a better name were found.

"Edgar Rice Burroughs, who lives in Santa Monica, is the heaviest patron of the Tarzana Post Office," Droege said. "His books published in the east are forwarded here so they can be mailed out with a Tarzana postmark. And I can't even find a Tarzana library."

Another name considered at the time was Walnut Hills. The chamber of commerce, though, opposed the idea, and it ended up dying—for the time being, anyway. In 1949, a year before Burroughs's death, residents launched another drive to adopt a new, less kitschy-sounding name. Options on the table included West Encino, South Hills, and Southridge. Burroughs, who once remarked that "City of Tarzana" sounded like the name of a steamboat, gave his blessing to the idea of a name change, but again, the idea failed to take hold.

Tarzana stayed Tarzana.

Burroughs came home himself—posthumously—when his ashes were scattered in Tarzana under a walnut tree on Ventura Boulevard, outside his old office.

Still, it wasn't until 1987 that the community really got into the spirit of things, holding its first Tarzan Movie Festival with showings of two 1970 films, *Tarzan's Deadly Silence* and *Tarzan's Jungle Rebellion*. The event featured T-shirts, posters, a costume contest, and free comic books printed in languages from Swedish to Portuguese. Eleven years later, Tarzana renamed its business district "Safari Walk." No matter how hard it tried, it couldn't escape the shadow of the lord of the jungle. So, in the end, Tarzana finally submitted to his rule.

GIRARD'S TURKEY

One of the busiest on- and off-ramp exchanges on the modern freeway is at Topanga Canyon Boulevard, a major crossroads since before the route was a freeway or even a federal highway.

Before Topanga Canyon was even paved, it was a natural pass through the Santa Monica Mountains connecting the western San Fernando Valley with the coast. A huckster from Kentucky named Victor Girard Kleinberger knew an opportunity when he saw it and promptly bought up 3,000 acres of land in the vicinity with the intent of marketing it as an exotic new settlement with a Turkish theme.

Kleinberger dropped his last name in an act he touted as repudiating his German heritage during World War I. He built a series of structures near the then-rural intersection to resemble a Turkish city—complete with fountains, light standards, domes, and minarets. Everyone else was building in the Spanish Mission style, and he wanted something that would stand out. Besides, he had an affinity for southwest Asia, having previously worked as a door-to-door salesman hawking knockoff Persian rugs. His favored tactic: rolling the rugs out across a homeowner's doorstep to keep the door from being slammed in his face.

He announced his new development with great fanfare in 1923.

Some of the buildings were nothing more than facades, meant to create the illusion of a thriving business district, something Girard hoped to create: a kind of "half-build it and they will come" approach. A huge sign adorned with a pointing index finger advertised Topanga Canyon as a "scenic mountain drive" across a state highway with an easy grade. In typical P. T. Barnum fashion, Girard stretched the truth just a tad by boasting that ocean breezes would cool future residents—even though the ocean itself was some 13 miles away. But perhaps the biggest attractions were the trees. The valley back then was an open plain of pastureland, so Girard decided to spruce things up by planting more than 120,000 trees across his land: eucalyptus (later a staple along western highways), acacia, pine, sycamore, and pepper trees.

Girard subdivided the land to maximize his potential profits by creating some 6,800 lots that were just 25 feet across at a time when land was still plentiful and the typical parcel was measured in acres, not feet. Then he launched a campaign that included newspaper ads,

This vintage ad points the way to Girard, a development in the western San Fernando Valley, later renamed Woodland Hills.

along with pamphlets placed in hotels and train depots to catch the interested traveler's eye. Among his promotional innovations was the so-called "sucker bus," a tactic used widely in time-share promotions decades later: He offered a seat on the bus, a free lunch, and a tour of the area—highlighted, of course, by a visit to his nascent development. A ticket for one of these tours could be redeemed for a free 80-mile trip to the town of Girard: "Ride in comfortable busses and have lunch with us. No obligation."

Named, naturally, Girard.

Girard even started his own newspaper to promote the development, then made it more attractive by spending some $300,000 on new streets and adding features such as stables and a golf course. Meanwhile, he pushed for a new highway across the Santa Monica Mountains, which eventually came to fruition as Mulholland Drive.

How did Girard pay for all this?

By taking out loans that he'd never have to repay. Instead, he put a lien on every lot he sold that left the buyers on the hook for the money. Undeveloped lots could be purchased for $500, but Girard's sales staff would accept almost anything offered as a down payment to get the buyer on the hook, sometimes selling the same piece of property to multiple buyers.

Girard built homes in the development, too. Or, rather, cabins made with log siding and placed on wooden foundations built directly on bare earth. About 100 of them were built, starting at just 500 square feet and without any running water or electricity. A few still remain in an area known as Spaghetti Canyon in honor of its winding streets.

The community, like so many other high-flying speculations, came crashing down to earth with the stock market in 1929, and many of the residents—faced with those nasty liens they couldn't pay on top of their regular

A 1917 billboard touts Calabasas as "an entrance to Santa Monica." *Public domain.*

bills—simply abandoned the place. Girard found himself saddled with a slew of lawsuits and more than 1,300 acres of land he had been unable to sell, so he folded his Boulevard Land Company.

By 1932, the community that bore Girard's name had dwindled to 75 families, but that wasn't the end of the story.

Unlike the development he'd built, the trees he'd planted to attract prospective buyers flourished—and eventually began to attract a new generation of residents to the area. In 1941, mindful of the stigma associated with Girard, they decided to erase his name from the map and replace it with a more elegant and descriptive moniker.

Woodland Hills.

Ventura Boulevard

and beyond

Old 101 was a maze of surface streets in Los Angeles and Orange County before the dawn of the freeway era, but that wasn't the case in the San Fernando Valley.

Indeed, following the Old 101 is a relatively simple matter once you cross the Santa Monica Mountains: Just stay on Ventura Boulevard for 20 miles until you reach the west end of the San Fernando Valley at Mulholland Drive. Then cross under the freeway and keep going on Calabasas Road. You'll head through Old Town

Calabasas and past the Sagebrush Cantina. Built in the early part of the 20th century, it was once the Oak Garage and general store that sold RC Cola and Associated Gas. An El Camino Real bell stood in the parking lot underneath the 12-foot-tall oak tree that gave the garage its name, celebrated locally as the "hanging tree."

There's no solid evidence anyone was actually hanged there (although the town jail stood where the parking lot is until the early 20th century), but a noose was hung from the tree around 1970 for the fun of it. Unfortunately, the tree—which had been dead for some time—toppled over during a storm a quarter century later. The town, however, not to be so easily deprived of its heritage, saved the pieces of the old oak and reassembled it.

That doesn't mean the place didn't see its share of Wild West mischief. A 1921 headline in the *Oxnard Press-Courier* proclaimed, "Calabasas Garage Is Looted by Bandit Gang." The bandits made "a complete robbery of the building," blowing open the safe and taking a hefty sum of cash in addition to making off with tires, motor oil, and other merchandise.

The garage had been in business at least 4 years by that time at the westernmost outpost in the San Fernando Valley.

From Calabasas, the Old 101 continued west into the hills, crossing back under the highway on Las Virgenes Road before heading west again as Agoura Road and into Thousand Oaks as Thousand Oaks Boulevard. There it disappeared beneath the modern freeway before resurfacing again in Ventura as Main Street and Thompson Boulevard.

One of the most challenging obstacles along the way was a steep descent (or climb, going the other direction) between Thousand Oaks and Camarillo called the Conejo Grade. The modern freeway negotiates a steep 7 percent grade that's a fairly straight downhill run into Camarillo—at least compared to its predecessors.

A paved two-lane state road, built in 1914, replaced an earlier gravel passage down the mountain, but even that was a winding, switchback-laden course with no fewer than 49 twists and turns. Plenty of motorists were seriously injured or even killed in the early part of the century when their cars skidded off the precipitous incline and tumbled down the hill. Among them was a

The **Calabasas Garage on old U.S. 101 is seen in 1932.** *Calabasas Historical Society.*

rancher named Ernest Thompson, a passenger in a car driven by one Frank Wadleigh. While traversing "one of the most dangerous pieces of mountain road in the state, the car suddenly skidded and went 200 feet down the mountainside, turning several somersaults and instantly crushing the life out of" Thompson. Wadleigh, amaz-ingly, made it through with no more than a few bruises, according to an account in the *Bakersfield Californian.*

That first state road, later designated a portion of U.S. 101, was replaced in 1937 by a three-lane highway (one lane in each direction, plus a central passing or "suicide" lane) and finally, in 1958, by the modern freeway.

THE CABRILLO HIGHWAY

A section of Highway 1 facing north as it passes through Pismo Beach, just before rejoining U.S. 101.

The Cabrillo Highway is U.S. 101. Sometimes. And in some places. It's also State Route 1—even though that scenic highway is better known as the Pacific Coast Highway for much of its length.

Confused yet?

It's easy to lose your bearings when one road is sometimes two and, at various times in our state's still-young history, has been called by different names.

Until 1964, the segment of road that ran along the coast in the Los Angeles area was called U.S. 101-A. The "A" identified it as an alternate to the main alignment of U.S. 101, which was later converted into Interstate 5 south of the Hollywood Freeway. The "alternate" coast route in that area became State Route 1 when the federal government turned over responsibility for its maintenance to California.

Along some segments along the Central Coast, however, the state and federal highways share the same strip of asphalt.

They have to.

Pavement from an old alignment of the U.S. 101 Alternate goes nowhere, stopping where the ocean has eroded the coastline at Point Mugu.

In areas where the coastal mountains hug the seashore, there's simply no room for two roads, and the Cabrillo Highway takes on a split personality as both 1 and 101. If you drive up the coast between Ventura and Santa Barbara, you'll see what I mean. Before the construction of the coast highway, the only viable north-south route here was inland, along the Casitas Pass Road (now State Route 150), still the only alternative for travelers along this stretch of coastline.

My wife and I discovered that firsthand in December 2015, when a fire closed the coast highway for several hours as we were heading south for a holiday meal with her family. With all traffic diverted onto the mountain road that wound around the backside of Lake Casitas, we spent more than two hours covering a distance we would have traversed in one quarter that time had the coast highway been open.

This scenic back route, which had been used for stagecoach travel since 1878 and opened to automobiles in 1897, was once as deadly as it was picturesque for travelers heading north from Los Angeles through the foothills to Santa Barbara. In the late summer of 1911, for instance, a particularly jarring tragedy claimed the lives of a physician and his wife, Arthur and Grace Pillsbury.

The Pillsburys and their three children had set out from their home in Hollywood at 8:30 on a Sunday morning on a trip to Stanley Park, a popular mountain resort on Rincon Creek in the Santa Ynez Forest.

Just a mile away from their destination was Shepherd's Inn on the Ventura-Santa Barbara County line, a rustic way station popular with travelers up and down the coast.

The Pillsburys never got that far.

Instead, as their six-cylinder Auburn 30 traversed the Wadleigh grade 10 miles from Ventura, they came upon a slide that cut into the roadway so severely that it barely left room for a single car to pass. Undaunted, Dr. Pillsbury steered as close to the embankment as he dared--too close, as it turned out. His inside fender plowed into the earth and, in attempting to correct his course, the good doctor failed to negotiate a sharp turn. Instead, his car went plunging over the edge, rolling repeatedly as it fell almost 50 feet to the bottom of the canyon beside the road.

The children (a girl and two boys, ages 13 and 6) screamed as they were thrown from the back seat of the car as it hurtled down the incline. Landing in the brush, they suffered bruises and, in the case of the 13-year-old, a badly sprained left ankle. They were, sadly, left as orphans. Rescuers discovered Dr. Pillsbury's body 15 feet from the Auburn, which finally came to rest after striking a tree. They found his spouse, also lifeless, a short distance away.

Friends attributed the accident in part to the physician's "mania for speed." He had informed his wife a few months earlier that he was "going in for racing as a pastime," a development that had worried her to such an extent that she told neighbors of a premonition before they departed that she might not return alive.

Motor Age magazine's Paul Gyllstrom wrote that the pass had, indeed, taken its toll in human lives, "but chiefly among the careless," and described it as one of the scenic wonders of the West.

"Motorists who visit southern California and fail to go through it at the proper time of year will have missed one of the sights," he said. "One might just as well go to Seattle without seeing Mount Rainier, or Tacoma without seeing Mount Tacoma, and the Yosemite (Valley) without gazing on Half Dome, as come to this part of the country without traversing the Casitas."

Despite this, the *Oxnard Courier*, in reporting the tragedy that claimed the lives of Mr. and Mrs. Pillsbury, noted that the condition of the road was at least partly to blame. In an editorial comment embedded in the news report, the *Courier* remarked that "the grades and curves on the Casitas are extremely dangerous, especially so to drivers whether or not they are experienced when they do not know the roads and all the ins and outs." The accident, the newspaper declared, "brings forcibly to mind the urgent necessity of the immediate construction of the Rincon sea-level road between Ventura and Santa Barbara, thus doing away with the travel over the dangerous Casitas Pass."

CAUSEWAY AND EFFECT

The Rincon Road was meant to provide a more direct (9 miles shorter) alternative to the winding mountain pathway, running directly along the coast from Ventura to Santa Barbara. The challenge was carving out a path for the roadway between the sheer mountains and the surf that slammed into their base at high tide.

The solution? A series of three wooden causeways—20 feet wide and 2,000, 400 ,and 4,000 feet in length, respectively—to raise the road above the pounding surf.

"The method of construction is simple," Paul Gyllstrom wrote in the October 17, 1912, issue of *Motor Age*. "Eucalyptus piles are driven, cross beams are laid, then the floor of the causeway and the wooden railings on each side."

The causeways, like piers running parallel to the coastline, gave the waves somewhere to go without inundating the road that now ran over the top of them. Passengers could peer out the window and stare down through the spaces between the planks, where they could see the white foam crashing up against the shoreline beneath them.

The causeways—built at a cost of $47,000—opened in November 1912 to great pomp and celebration, with a crowd estimated at 20,000 to 30,000 in attendance.

But the new road wasn't perfect. The steep hills beside the road were prone to mudslides, such as one in 1922 that buried a couple of cars to the tops of their doors between two of the causeways and deposited boulders on the highway. From the other side, the pounding surf took its toll on the causeway pilings, which required extensive maintenance, and nails sticking up through the wood punctured their fair share of tires.

Despite the hazards and a large number of accidents reported on the sea road, motorists hummed along at a speedy clip that came to be known as the "Rincon gait." Was the new route really safer than the Casitas Pass? That was open to question.

Regardless, it wasn't long before the highway builders found a better way to navigate the coastline than a rickety wooden road: The causeways were in use for just slightly more than a decade, replaced in 1924 with a paved road set down on earth fill.

The Rincon Sea-Level Road, a wooden plank causeway, was an early attempt to create a coastal highway in Ventura County. © *California Department of Transportation, all rights reserved. Used with permission.*

U.S. 101 at Olive Mill Road in Montecito, 1938. © *California Department of Transportation, all rights reserved. Used with permission.*

THE (LEGAL) BATTLE OF GOLETA

As the Cabrillo Highway enters Santa Barbara, it remains both 1 and 101, and it's common to encounter slower traffic along the highway through town.

It was once even slower than it is today, with the town being the site of the only traffic lights on 101 between L.A. and San Francisco. Beginning in 1948, four stoplights signaled motorists to stop and spend a little time in Santa Barbara—even if they didn't feel like it. The last of the four, at Anacapa Street, winked off for the last time at midmorning on Wednesday, November 20, 1991.

"These lights are almost an anachronism of the '40s and '50s," Caltrans engineer Mike Mortensen told the *Los Angeles Times* on the eve of the light's demise. "They kind of remind me of Route 66, with the motels shaped like wigwams—part of a more simple life."

"I think of it like the Golden Spike," that linked east and west via the transcontinental railroad, he added. "In a way, it's a closing of the frontier."

The Cabrillo continues as an east-west highway along the coast for more than 30 miles from Santa Barbara through Goleta and past El Capitan State Beach to Gaviota. An earlier alignment, west of the modern freeway, is a wide boulevard known as Hollister Avenue that runs about 14 miles on either side of Goleta. That's where you'll find the historic Barnsdall-Rio Grande service station that dates from 1929.

If "Hollister" sounds familiar as the name of a city to the north—in San Benito County, a couple of miles east of U.S. 101—there's a reason for that. Both that town and the street are named for the same man: William Welles Hollister, who founded a sheep ranch near the present site of Hollister (the town) and made a fortune by selling wool during the Civil War. After the war ended, he traveled south and began buying large tracts of land in the Santa Barbara area.

One of those tracts was Tecolotito Canyon, which belonged to Nicholas Den, whose daughter, Katherine

If you exit at Mariposa Reyna in Gaviota and drive a short way inland, you'll be treated to this view of old concrete on the west side of the road.

Den Bell, would famously predict the Ellwood oil strike several decades later. Den, who died in 1863, had decreed in his will that his land could not be sold until his youngest child—then just one year old—reached adulthood. But Hollister had two important assets: money and determination. He offered the Den heirs between seven and a hundred times what the land was worth, and the family, hit hard financially by a devastating drought, accepted.

Hollister built a lavish estate at the end of a private road through the canyon, which extended from the county road that would later be named Hollister Avenue (old U.S. 101). He widened the county road to 100 feet, lined the entrance to the estate with palm trees, and renamed the canyon Glen Annie, in honor of his wife, Annie James Hollister. Unfortunately, Hollister's wife and sister didn't get along, and even though they shared an expansive mansion, Annie insisted that her husband choose between her and his sister.

He refused, instead building an entirely separate, second mansion for his wife. The mansions and their gardens—planted with flora that ranged from olive trees and grapevines to banana trees and lilies—became a showplace, and everyone was happy.

Except for Katherine Den Bell.

Nicholas Den's eldest daughter didn't like the way the family lawyer had handled her father's will, so she hired another attorney—a man from San Francisco named Thomas Bishop—to investigate the matter. As it turned out, Hollister had bought the land from the estate without bothering to seek the probate court's approval. It was just the sort of loophole Bishop needed. He agreed to take the case on the promise that he would receive half of the disputed land if he won, and nothing if he lost. To Bell's way of thinking, 50 percent of a possibility was better than 100 percent of nothing, so she accepted. Thus began an epic courtroom battle that one historian dubbed the "legal drama of the nineteenth century" and dragged on for fourteen years.

Hollister won the first round, but lost on appeal, and his own appeal was ultimately rejected. By the time the California Supreme Court had decided the case, Hollister had been dead for four years, and his widow was left to retrieve her belongings from the home that was no longer hers. Just 15 minutes after she departed, the mansion went up in flames, but though suspicion immediately fell on her, no one could ever prove that Annie Hollister was guilty of arson. She died in 1909, steadfastly claiming that she had no idea what caused the fire.

Bishop, as promised, received half the land in payment for winning the case. That land—a parcel bordered by U.S. 101, Glen Annie Road, Cathedral Oaks Road, and Patterson Avenue—remained in his family until 1959 and is still known as Bishop Ranch.

A bridge from an old alignment of U.S. 101 crosses Arroyo Hondo along the Santa Barbara County coastline near Gaviota. The current alignment can be seen in the background.

West of the ranch, El Camino Real continues a more-or-less direct path toward Gaviota, but it wasn't always that way. A 1903 map shows Hollister Avenue (which would become the first alignment of 101) veering abruptly inland at a 45-degree angle on what is now Las Armas Road—a short stretch of pavement that's cut off by the modern 101. On the other side of the highway, the old road starts up again as Winchester Canyon Road, then veers westward onto private land and undergoes another name change, to Armas Canyon Road.

The reason for the directional change was a steep hill that stood directly in early travelers' path.

In 1912, Santa Barbara County got so fed up with the detour that it commissioned road builders to smooth the way westward by leveling the hill. Even so, El Camino Real's route then still wasn't as straight as the modern freeway's. It meandered a bit here and there to the north of the modern alignment, becoming quite curvaceous indeed as it approached Gaviota. If you exit the freeway at Mariposa Reina and drive up the hill northward a short way, you'll be able to see a well-preserved segment of the original concrete curving down over a gently sloping hillside west of the road. (Another, much less well-defined segment of the old highway is visible on the east side of the road).

A much newer segment of the road on the other side of the current highway is also visible in the same general area. It's the old Arroyo Hondo Bridge, built in 1918 and now accessible via a lookout point if you're traveling east on 101. Its concrete arches retain both their beauty and their functionality, but they're no longer open to vehicle traffic, having been closed in the mid-1980s. You can still walk the length of the bridge and see its pavement disappear at the west end in a mosaic of cracked asphalt, weeds, and wildflowers. To the south, the last thing you see before the Pacific Ocean is a steel railroad trestle bridge that runs parallel to the concrete arches and makes the scene even more impressive.

Gaviota Pass, early 20th century.
California Historical Society, public domain.

The modern freeway doesn't travel over a bridge at all, its foundation having been laid on solid ground. It's a bit east of Gaviota on the modern freeway.

Speaking of Gaviota, its population is listed as less than 100 people, but you'll be hard pressed to see any sign of a community from the highway. The Hollister Estate Company built a general store there in 1915, and it was so far away from anything else in either direction that it quickly became a hub of activity. It featured a service station—at one time selling Chevron gasoline—an auto court, a dance hall, and post office while offering telephone access along with groceries and clothing for sale.

Free-spirited surfers drawn to the waves and truckers lured by the prospect of some hot coffee wandered in and out of the café until it was sold in the late 1960s and demolished in 1970 by a big-city concern that wanted to develop 17 miles of coastline into a residential and recreational community. Among the planned attractions: a clear plastic tunnel through which people could walk down to the beach, and a lighthouse.

The developer started by reinventing the wheel—or in this case, the rest stop—by building a Cape Cod-style restaurant and service station. Further plans called for a

"Drake Point Park" with shops, a coin-op laundry, a teen center, swimming pools and courts for shuffleboard, badminton, tennis, and paddle tennis.

None of it ever happened.

The company went bankrupt, and the restaurant went through a series of owners, among them a commune that specialized in organic farming. One of the few events considered newsworthy by the press was the Gaviota Village Bicentennial Backgammon Tournament, in which Diane Stephens defeated Andy Smith for the championship. The restaurant eventually closed after someone stunk up the place by stuffing sea snails into the ventilation. The abandoned building burned to the ground in 2002, and six years later, the land once destined to be a grand development became, instead, Gaviota State Park.

THE GAVIOTA TUNNEL

Gaviota, where it veers abruptly northward and through the Gaviota Tunnel, was carved out in 1953 for the highway's northbound lanes. (There's no tunnel for the southbound lanes, to the west, which use the narrow Gaviota Pass—a key site in the Mexican-American War of 1846. Mexican forces waited in ambush here for John C. Frémont's troops, but the U.S. forces never came. Learning of the ambush, they traveled southward by the San Marcos Pass instead and captured Santa Barbara.)

The pass was a challenging obstacle for early travelers, who had to find a way across Gaviota Creek, which had carved out the narrow canyon that linked the coastal plain with the Santa Ynez Valley to the north. The canyon was so narrow in the mid-19th century that workers had to chisel away the rock to create an opening large enough for stagecoaches to pass through. William Brewer, who worked on the first geological survey of California in 1861, remarked that the Gaviota Pass was the only break in the sandstone of the Santa Ynez Mountains for "a hundred miles or more."

"At the Gaviota," he wrote, "a fissure divides the ridge, but a few feet wide at the narrowest part and several hundred feet high."

Just two years before Brewer worked on that survey, workers used dynamite to carve out the first county road at a cost of $32,000 and built a wooden bridge over the

creek. Standing guard over that bridge was—and still is—a rock overhang that early visitors to the place imagined looked like an "Indian head." The name stuck, and the rock became such a familiar sight that plans for its removal for safety reasons were scrapped in response to a protest, and other adjustments were made to ensure travelers safe passage.

Over the years, more improvements to the road were made, as well. In 1915, workers replaced the wooden bridge with a steel suspension bridge that served to guide motorists across the creek for the next 16 years. After that, highway workers installed a narrow concrete bridge that preserved the zigzag course over the canyon and forced any driver crossing to stay alert and maintain a safe (read "slow") speed.

Still, it was an improvement over its predecessor. Workers actually realigned the creek itself to create a more direct pathway. Three years later, in 1934, they straightened the road on the ocean plain, reducing the number of curves there from 41 to just 10.

Gaviota Pass in 1935, before the modern tunnel widened the highway to four lanes through the close quarters between the mountains. © *California Department of Transportation, all rights reserved. Used with permission.*

The Gaviota Tunnel, which opened in the 1950s, as seen today.

It wasn't until 1952 that the Department of Highways set about widening the road through the pass by carving out a tunnel from the rock on the eastern side of the canyon. Workers had to do all their digging from the south end of the mountain because blind curves on the north side made it impossible for earthmovers to cross the existing highway safely. When they completed their work in May 1953, they had carved out a passage that measured 435 feet long, 35 feet wide, and 18 feet high, encased in 18-inch-thick concrete. The lights inside operated on the first power lines to be installed in Gaviota Valley.

The tunnel's been featured in everything from Dustin Hoffman's breakthrough film, *The Graduate*, to the *Saturday Night Live* spinoff comedy *Wayne's World 2*— which both featured actors driving the wrong way in the northbound tunnel, heading south. The landmark also makes appearances in the film *Sideways* and the video-game *Grand Theft Auto V* (where it's called Braddock Tunnel).

The 11-mile stretch of road north of the Gaviota Pass to Buellton was among the last paved sections. Opened to traffic in 1922, it eliminated a detour via Solvang that one report described as "very provoking indeed to the motorist who was used to paved highway, and quite a shock to his car."

GHOST TOWN

Shortly after you leave the Gaviota Tunnel heading north, U.S. 101 and State Route 1 diverge again at a crossroads known as Las Cruces, which evolved over time from a Spanish rancho into a stagecoach stop, then a highway crossroads.

There's not much there now, and if you blink, you'll pass by without seeing it. Even if you get out of the car and stare, you're liable to miss it. There's very little left except for a single building and an old truss bridge just to the west of 101 south of its junction with Highway 1. The Park Road Bridge, as it's called, was originally made of wood and dates back to 1909.

Las Cruces dates from an 18th-century graveyard in the area, where the Chumash buried more than 100 of their dead. Franciscan friars later replaced the tribal grave markers with crosses: hence the name Las Cruces. Miguel Cordero, a career soldier, built an adobe home there in 1833 and received a land grant of more than 8,000 acres four years later. On his death in 1851, the land passed to his children, who built six more adobe structures—including the one now referred to as the Las Cruces Adobe.

In the early 1860s, a grasshopper infestation and two years of drought all but wiped out many ranchers in the area. During this time, the Corderos sold a number of undivided interests in the rancho to keep their heads above water. Such sales gave each buyer a common—but not exclusive—claim to all the rancho's assets.

Among those buyers was a sheepherder named Wilson Corliss, who saw an opportunity to boost his profits when he heard about a plan to reroute the stage line closer to Las Cruces. The new route was approved, and Corliss lost no time in building a new house not far from the crossroads that would double as a way station.

Las Cruces, north of Gaviota, was a highway stop with services and food available in the 1930s. Now, it's largely deserted, and the businesses that once thrived there are long gone.
Curt Cragg and the Buellton Historical Society.

But what looked like a shrewd business move turned out to be a fatal mistake.

A few days after Corliss and his wife moved into their new house, they were beaten and locked inside—and the place was torched. The body of a shepherd who lived with them was found a couple of weeks later, wedged between some rocks.

Suspicion eventually fell on Bill, Elize, and Steve Williams, three brothers who lived in the building now known as the Las Cruces Adobe and had been competing with the Corlisses to set up a stagecoach stop. They'd even gone so far as to remodel the adobe's interior so it could serve as a hotel, as well as building a barn and corral for stage horses. They certainly had a strong motive for murder, but what was the evidence?

One woman testified that the Williams brothers had offered her money to lace the Corlisses' milk with strychnine, but without any corroboration, the case was deemed too weak to secure a conviction. Some suggested that the brothers be sent to the gallows to elicit a confession, but their accusers decided that would be going too far and, seeing no other alternative, released them.

If you believe in karma, what happened next would surely qualify: Shortly after their acquittal, two of the three brothers were murdered in an apparent robbery while they were camping in San Luis Obispo. Authorities later arrested a man wearing one of their gold watches and hanged him for their murders.

The adobe, meanwhile, and some of the ranchland eventually fell into the hands of William Welles Hollister—the same man who built the palatial Glen Annie estate in Goleta—and two local landowners named Thomas and Albert Diblee. They had built a wharf in Gaviota to facilitate shipping exports overseas, and acquiring a stage stop up the road made perfect sense. The Williams brothers might have failed to develop the adobe as a stage stop, but the Corliss murders and the destruction of their home left it as the most suitable location.

Hollister built a new barn to replace the one the Williams brothers had constructed there, and the stage road passed between it and the adobe—which was serving as a hotel, general store, and post office under the management of R. J. Broughton by 1877. It also, at various times, housed a saloon, a gambling hall, and even a brothel … an interesting combination considering that Broughton became sheriff of Santa Barbara County in 1882, a position he held for 13 years until his death. After that, the adobe no longer housed a hotel, but confined its business operations to a café and bar.

When the railroad and highway replaced the stage line, it became a highway stop during the 1920s and '30s. Service stops like Las Cruces sprang up along major highways during this era between major towns like Santa Barbara and Santa Maria. There wasn't much in either direction, and at a time when cars moved more slowly and frequently broke down, Las Cruces was well situated for travelers who needed to stretch their legs, refill their gas tanks, or grab a bite to eat.

Such highway stops still exist today on roads such as Interstate 5, which rambles across mile upon mile of empty land on the west side of the San Joaquin Valley. Clusters of gas stations, diners, and convenience stores huddle around the highway at exits for Patterson, Los

**This trestle bridge, visible from U.S. 101, is one of the few indications
that a town once existed at Las Cruces.**

Hills, and Kettleman City, beckoning travelers with soaring lighted signs visible from miles away on a clear summer night.

Things were simpler in the heyday of Las Cruces. A Model T might rumble across the Park Road Bridge and into town at 15 or 20 mph and pull up to get some Chevron gasoline at the El Camino Garage, the first stop on the short strip of roadside buildings. Eugene and Marguerita Tico Hess ran the Hess Garage, offering "general repairs" and "accessories for all cars" until about 1938, when they packed up and left the area. Farther on were the Las Cruces Store and Las Cruces Station, which dispensed Shell brand gasoline.

In the meantime, cattle drives continued through Gaviota Pass on until the end of World War II, with highway patrol officers warning motorists of oncoming bovine traffic.

The town withered after a new highway alignment passed it by, and newer, more dependable cars that could go farther on a tank of gas rendered it an unnecessary detour on a trip up the coast. If you could make it to Buellton on 101—or Lompoc on the Pacific Coast route—why bother to stop at Las Cruces?

Fewer and fewer people did, and eventually, the businesses all closed. All that's left there now is one old, falling-down structure, and you can't even get to the town from U.S. 101 today. There's a locked gate between the highway and the Park Road Bridge, and you have to go up Highway 1 toward Lompoc and double back on San Julian Road if you want to see the place up close.

Legend has it that the ghosts of three prostitutes from the old stagecoach-era brothel still haunt what's left of the rickety old building, one having committed suicide and the other two having been strangled by a crazed customer. The spirit of a man wearing a long black coat and a wide-brimmed hat also supposedly haunts the place, the veteran of a long-ago gunfight in which he came out on the losing end.

SPLIT ROAD

North of Buellton, at Los Alamos, the highway splits again, and for a short distance, there are three north-south alternatives for heading up the coast.

The original route for U.S. 101 between Los Alamos and Santa Maria ran between the Cabrillo/Pacific Coast Highway and the current 101 Alignment until 1933, following the route now occupied by State Route 135. This Old 101 Alignment merges again briefly with Highway 1 south of Orcutt, then enters Santa Maria as Broadway, the main north-south thoroughfare through town. Despite an abundance of modern development, this section of road retains much of its historic character. Old motels and a few vintage neon signs are visible along the length of the old highway through Santa Maria, and a short section of the original, narrow concrete is visible at its north end, where the road veers back to rejoin the modern 101 Alignment. (Just look for the white picket fence on the left near Priesker Lane as you head north).

In years past, at the south end of town, travelers were greeted by a brightly lit tower in the shape of a tall, slim oil derrick, one of about 30 such towers lining the highways in California, Oregon, and Washington. Twenty of those were in California, with the majority along U.S. Highway 99 but about one third of them at various points on U.S. 101.

The 125-foot towers, with Richfield spelled out vertically on one of its three steel-beamed sides, were built in the late 1920s and placed strategically along the highway to signal motorists that it was time to stop and fill 'er up. They were also designed to act as points of light to guide aviators along what became known as the "Great White Way." On 101, you could find them just north of the Mexican border at Palm City, as well as in Capistrano Beach, Santa Maria, Paso Robles, Chualar, and Santa Rosa. There was also a beacon—but no station—in Santa Barbara, and the toll gate to the San Francisco Bay Bridge bore two 135-foot towers with the Richfield name, although no towers were placed there.

The era of the Richfield Beacons was fleeting. The company ran into financial problems with the onset of the Great Depression, and within a few years, aviators no longer needed the beacons to serve as their guides. In the span of a decade, the lights went out on most of them, and several were torn down. These days, all the 101 towers are long gone, although a couple of examples remain along Highway 99 in northern California,

Old gas pumps in Los Alamos.

Peeking inside the old Richfield Beacon station through a circular window.

at Willows and Mount Shasta. (See my book *Highway 99* for photos and a detailed look at the Beacon stations).

The beacon tower three miles south of Paso Robles remained in place until it was finally removed in 1995, but the long-closed gas station is still there on Theatre Drive, a segment of the old alignment bypassed by the current freeway. The locked Spanish Mission-style building now serves as a bus stop in front of a modern big-box shopping center that's home to such retailers as Target, Bev Mo, and Orchard Supply Hardware.

The Santa Maria tower lasted a while, too, flickering on for the first time during a rainy opening-day celebration on April 18, 1929 and making its curtain call in 1971. Both the gas stations were built a bit south of town, because the intent was to catch travelers before they reached the city limits—and other service stations, of which there were plenty in Santa Maria at the time. By one count, a two-mile stretch of Broadway was packed with some two dozen businesses that sold gas, even though Santa Maria's population at the time was just 7,000.

Plus, the beacon stations were designed to be outside the city limits because Richfield had big plans for them:

They weren't supposed to be just service stations, but hubs for small communities that the company envisioned growing up around them. Richfield itself planned to open cafés and "taverns" (actually motels) alongside each of the towers and gas stations, but that phase never reached fruition at most of the sites because of the Depression's toll on the company. Barstow on Route 66 was the only place where a "tavern" was actually completed, and although Santa Maria was next in line for one—along with Capistrano and Visalia—none was ever built there.

Instead, private operators unaffiliated with the company—but eager to cash in on the "beacon" name and landmark—stepped into the void. An entrepreneur named Virgilio Del Porto advertised a competing gas station on the same stretch of road as offering "BEACON SERVICE," even though he sold (at various times) Standard, Texaco, Economy, and St. Helen's brands, but never Richfield.

The Beacon Motor Apartments (later renamed the Beacon Motel) went in across the road to offer lodging in lieu of Richfield's shelved "tavern." And in 1932, a Beacon Coffee Shop went up just north of the tower, the final element in the planned community Richfield itself had failed to produce.

In 1936, the state improved the highway between Orcutt and Santa Maria, widening it—although it remained just two lanes—and replacing the original pavement. About this time, development started creeping southward from town toward the beacon tower, a move accelerated by an oil strike in March of that same year. Before long, soaring wooden oil derricks nearly as tall as the Richfield tower began sprouting up on land across the highway from the beacon and nearby, competing for the traveler's attention. One photograph shows half a dozen of them clustered across the road, behind the M&M Motel, which opened next to the Beacon Motel in 1939.

Oil rigs remained in the area into the 1970s, by which time Atlantic Oil had purchased Richfield and changed the name to ARCO.

That took place in 1966, and within a few years, the Richfield name had become obsolete. Already, during the 1950s, the original mission-style Richfield station had been replaced by a modern, generic "box" service station with mechanics' bays and an overhang to shield motorists from the elements as they pumped their gas. Now, it was time for the iconic tower to go, as well: On March 2, 1971, a crane almost as tall as the tower itself lowered the steel-beamed behemoth to the ground intact.

It was later sold off as parts to an Oxnard milling company, which used its steel to build a gravel conveyor.

The Santa Maria Inn on Broadway, an old alignment of U.S. 101, housed Cecil B. DeMille when he directed his first version of *The Ten Commandments* in 1923. Scenes were filmed at the nearby Guadalupe dunes.

SPHINXES ON THE BEACH

In 1923, the legendary director Cecil B. DeMille checked in at the Santa Maria Inn on Broadway. He wasn't the only Hollywood legend to stop at the luxury hotel: Douglas Fairbanks, Rudolph Valentino, and Charlie Chaplin all spent the night there, as did Bob Hope, Bing Crosby, Mary Pickford, William Randolph Hearst, and Joan Crawford. Stars adorn the doors to rooms where they stayed. Rumor even has it that Valentino's ghost haunts one of the rooms.

Some of the hotel's famous guests came to get away from it all, but DeMille was there on business. He was filming the next big Hollywood extravaganza, and although he was a long way from Hollywood, he'd originally planned to travel much farther afield for this portion of the movie: to Egypt.

That's where *The Ten Commandments* was set, but even someone with as much clout as DeMille had to live with certain budget constraints, and Paramount wasn't about to fly him and his crew all the way to the land of the pyramids for the sake of authenticity. We should note before continuing that the movie in question isn't the Charlton Heston/Yul Brynner blockbuster—also

directed by DeMille—which didn't hit theaters until 33 years later. (Unlike the '56 remake, which was set entirely in the biblical era, the second half of the original was set in the modern day).

This was still the era of silent films, but that didn't mean DeMille's production was small potatoes. Anything but.

Although DeMille had been thwarted in his request to film a portion of his movie in Egypt, that didn't mean he was going to settle for half-measures when it came to realizing his vision. Craftsmen created a set modeled after the gates of Karnak—a famous temple complex that was, incidentally, a good 500 miles south of the Nile Delta, where the main action in the biblical narrative is supposed to have taken place. Historical concerns aside, the set was nothing if not spectacular. Rising 10 stories high and spanning 700 feet from end to end, it was fronted by giant statues and adorned with huge engravings of Egyptian charioteers. (Actual charioteers were used for the movie, too, with men from Battery E of the U.S. Cavalry filling those roles.)

The set featured 500 tons of plaster statuary, including four seated images of the pharaoh and no fewer than 21 sphinxes. The former were 35 feet tall, and the latter were

On the set of *The Ten Commandments*, some of which lies buried beneath the shifting sands at Guadalupe even today.
Collection of Cecilia de Mille Presley.

The *San Luis Obispo Telegram* reported that "one of the most impressive scenes, actors yesterday freely agreed, was the yoking of several hundred people to a huge vehicle on which was placed a sphinx."

When filming wrapped up, the question arose of what to do with the mammoth sets. Hauling everything back where it came from would be too expensive, and then where could it be stored? On the other hand, DeMille didn't want to simply leave it there, where some other filmmaker might run out and shoot scenes on *his* set—or, worse yet, make off with some of the statues. So, in a large-scale example of "if I can't have it, nobody can," DeMille told his crews to simply bury the whole thing. To put it another way, he was simply protecting his patent.

In effect, DeMille had left a buried treasure in Guadalupe for someone to find—an ancient Egyptian city that wasn't ancient and wasn't in Egypt.

He wrote in his autobiography: "If a thousand years from now archaeologists happen to dig beneath the sands of Guadalupe, I hope that they will not rush to print with the amazing news that Egyptian civilization extended all the way to the Pacific Coast."

As it happened, though, it didn't take a thousand years.

Over the next few decades, a group of eclectic bohemians, drifters, artists, and free spirits gravitated toward the dunes, where they lived in driftwood shacks, eating fish and Pismo clams. Some of the folks who ended up there were transients left homeless by the Depression who had nowhere else to go. Others were utopians who believed in the lost continent of Lemuria and eccentrics such as Gavin Arthur, grandson of President Chester A. Arthur, whose resume included forays into writing, acting, and astrology.

John Steinbeck, Ansel Adams, and Upton Sinclair all visited the community at one time or another, but the Dunites, as they were known, came and eventually went.

so large their heads had to be removed before they could be shipped north from workshops in L.A. to the beach at Guadalupe, where the scenes were to be filmed. The sand dunes there, part of a 30-mile stretch that makes its way up the coast through Oceano to Pismo Beach, would serve as a stand-in for the Egyptian desert, with the Pacific Ocean playing the Red Sea.

It was about a half-hour drive from the Santa Maria Inn, where DeMille was staying on the road that would become U.S. 101, west to the dunes, closer to today's Highway 1. There, some 2,500 actors, extras, and crew members gathered in a temporary city of 600 tents called "Camp De Mille" that covered 24 square miles. Their task: to film scenes designed to evoke the grandeur of the biblical narrative. In one such scene, some 2,000 people and 4,000 animals lined up in a procession against a backdrop of dunes and seashore—with the line holding formation all the way from 10 a.m. to 5 p.m.

Storefronts on Los Berros Road (old U.S. 101) in Nipomo date back to the late 19th century.

Meanwhile, in 1956, DeMille remade *The Ten Commandments* with Heston in the role of Moses, Brynner as the pharaoh, and Henry Wilcoxon as captain of the pharaoh's guard. Wilcoxon, who also served as associate producer for the film, had been an A-list star in the 1930s, playing Marc Antony opposite Claudette Colbert in *Cleopatra* and Richard the Lion-Hearted in *The Crusades.* Both were DeMille films, and although the second was a box-office flop that knocked Wilcoxon off that A-list, DeMille tapped him for a series of projects in the 1950s that included the new *Ten Commandments.*

Henry Wilcoxon wasn't involved in the original version of the movie—which was filmed eight years before he made his acting debut—but a cousin of his, Larry Wilcoxon, was … a long time after the fact.

The younger man, an archaeologist at UC Santa Barbara, had been hired by an oil company that wanted to drill out on the dunes. But in the course of conducting his studies there in 1977, he stumbled upon something else:

"We essentially discovered what was left of the movie set," he told a reporter in 1984, describing it as "one of the last of the great movie sets left from that era" and estimating that as many as 16 of the sphinxes from the original film might be buried there.

But it would cost an estimated $50,000 to dig up the "lost city," and despite media coverage from the likes of *NBC Nightly News* and *People Magazine*, the treasure hunters raised less than a quarter of what they needed over the next decade—enough to do a high-tech search beneath the sands and some preliminary survey work. An environmental roadblock emerged, as well: Because the dunes were home to the western snowy plover, listed as threatened under the Endangered Species Act, special permits were needed to do any kind of work there.

A limited excavation in 1990 turned up such things as cough syrup bottles and tobacco tins, but it wasn't until 2012 that more extensive work turned up large-scale finds from the buried set itself. Archaeologists uncovered the head of a sphinx they said was about the size of a pool table, and the wind that spreads the shifting sands across the seashore helped uncover the body of another sphinx. One of the sphinxes discovered at the site was still in just about the same place it had been during filming.

These days, some of the artifacts from the set are on display at the Dunes Center in Guadalupe, and work continues to excavate more of the set that DeMille thought might remain buried for a millennium.

It isn't quite King Tut's tomb, but it's about as close to ancient Egypt as most motorists on U.S. 101 are ever going to get.

GOING TO SLO

When you leave Santa Maria, the landscape changes: The flat, agrarian valley gives way gradually to rolling hills and an ocean view.

If you exit Santa Maria at Thompson Avenue heading north, you'll be on the Old 101 for several miles through Nipomo. This section of road, which served as the highway alignment between 1930 and 1958, runs parallel to the current highway, a little to the east. The Nipomo Barber Shop, constructed in 1886, is still standing, right next to the general store, which was built eight years earlier.

North of town, the old alignment crosses back under the present highway at Los Berros Road. A still-older, pre-1930 version of the road veers north just after the underpass onto Quailwood Lane, which today is just a short spur that crosses an old bridge onto private land. There's another short strip of the old road a little farther north at Hemi Road, which is the next exit, and still another at Tower Grove Drive.

Entering Arroyo Grande, the old highway diverges from the new once again at Traffic Way, which takes you past a series of businesses that date from the 1930s to the '50s. Among the oldest is a 1930s-era gas station that's been converted into Rod's Auto Body. The original alignment continued up Bridge Street across a 1909 bridge to Branch, at which point travelers made a 90-degree left turn back west and (across the current freeway) north again on El Camino Real. In 1932, though, a short, gently curving bypass was built across a new bridge at Arroyo Creek, eliminating the Bridge-to-Branch-and-back-again portion of the route.

On El Camino Real, you'll pass Francisco's Country Kitchen, which you might recognize from the architecture as an old Sambo's Pancake House.

Once you hit Pismo Beach, the oldest alignment of state Route 2—before it was designated U.S. 101—took an angular detour to the northeast on a narrow little drive called Frady Lane, then crossed Pismo Creek on an old bridge that dates back to 1912. The steel bridge is still there, but it's closed now, so you can't drive across it to the other side, where the route continued on Bello Street until it merged with Price Street at the north end of town.

If you travel up Bello today, you'll pass a series of small, blue gable-roofed apartments as you head in toward town from the old steel bridge. The structures are obviously an old auto court that probably dated from before 1925, when the route was shifted away from Bello and west down Ocean View Avenue to Price Street, where you'd turn north again. Price Street through town remained the route's alignment from then until 1956, when the current freeway bypass opened.

State Route 1 runs parallel to 101 through Pismo, a block west of Price Street, then merges with the federal highway at the north end of town, and the two highways share the same road from there to San Luis Obispo. Before the freeway went in, that road was Shell Beach Road through Shell Beach.

To stay on the old highway, turn west at Avila Beach Drive, then immediately north on Ontario Road, which will take you up to the south end of San Luis Obispo, crossing under the modern freeway and becoming Higuera Street. A very old alignment of the route—dating to the 1910s or early '20s—runs on concrete between Higuera and the freeway. To find it, turn left at the distinctive white Pereira Octagon Barn and then

Francisco's Country Kitchen is an old Sambo's Restaurant that survives along Business 101 in Arroyo Grande.

south on the old road, which will take you across an old bridge before the pavement ends a few hundred feet farther on.

The Octagon Barn itself is a notable feature of the old highway. The 5,000-square-foot structure was built in 1906 as part of a dairy farm and was used to house beef cattle beginning around 1950. Although the design was popular in the Midwest, the barn is the only one of its kind on the Central Coast. It was in danger of collapsing in the late 20th century: Its structure was sagging and its shingles were coming apart in 1997 when a 15-year restoration project began that succeeded in rescuing it. The barn was placed on the National Register of Historic Places in 2014.

Another barn on Higuera dating to the same era, on the Long-Bonetti Ranch just past Tank Farm Road, was on the verge of being torn down as of this writing. Developers were in the process of converting the site into

This 1915 bridge is closed to traffic these days, but it once ferried drivers along an old and not-very-direct highway route through Pismo Beach.

a retail hub. And while the ranch house on the property, built in 1908, was to be preserved—and reborn as a restaurant—plans called for the demolition of the rickety old wooden barn.

The old highway continues on Higuera, past some vintage highway businesses. A keen eye will spot a couple of old motels on the east side of the road, and be sure to check out the old 1930s-era Texaco station at the intersection of Pacific Street; as of 2016, it was operating as a wine and beer shop called (appropriately) the Station. Just before you get there, take a detour left on Bianchi Lane, which crosses San Luis Obispo Creek on a 1905 bridge. It may not have been part of the original state route, but the age of the bridge makes it worth a look.

From there, the old highway alignment curved northeast through the heart of town on Marsh Street before jogging left briefly on Santa Rosa Street. If you continue on Santa Rosa, you'll be on State Route 1, but to stay on the Old 101, turn right again in just a couple of blocks onto Monterey Street, which was the old highway through the remainder of town. At the northeast end of the strip is a series of motels, culminating in the historic 1925 Motel Inn, the last structure on Monterey before it rejoins the modern freeway.

The Station on Higuera Street, an old 101 alignment in San Luis Obispo, sold gas once upon a time; later, it sold wine, instead.

6

THE SALINAS VALLEY ROAD

When you hit the Cuesta Grade, it's like hitting a wall that separated one world from another. To the south are verdant, rolling hills rising gently above inland valleys that open out onto the blue Pacific. To the north, on the other side of that wall, is the Salinas Valley, a flat and often dry agricultural plain; the Salinas river at its center runs between the Santa Lucia Range on the west and the Diablo Range to the east.

That wall was, to travelers of old, a formidable obstacle. Today's U.S. 101 ascends a steep, seven percent grade, hugging the hillsides to the east, well above the floor of a narrow canyon. The old alignment entered that canyon at its south end along the old Stage Coach Road. You can still walk that section of road for a short distance, staring up at the imposing retaining wall built to keep the modern highway in place.

You can also continue on the State Coach Road over a distance of three or four miles until it spits you back onto

A horseshoe curve on the old concrete alignment of U.S. 101 traverses the narrow Cuesta Pass north of San Luis Obispo on what is now private land. This photo was taken from the modern alignment, which lies at a higher elevation to the east.

the highway near the summit. Also known as the Padre Trail, it's the oldest route through the narrow pass, heir to an 18th century dirt road that carried travelers between the San Luis Obispo de Tolosa mission to the south and San Miguel Arcángel mission to the north.

The old road between San Luis Obispo and Santa Margarita is seen in this pre-1920 photo. © *California Department of Transportation, all rights reserved. Used with permission.*

Old 101, meanwhile, veers off to the right, but you can only go so far before you come to a gate that bars your path onto what is now private land. Beyond that gate, the narrow concrete road ascends the canyon's eastern flank via a horseshoe curve—still visible from the current freeway, especially to southbound traffic. The ribbon of concrete winds its way around three-quarters of a solitary hill before intersecting the modern road and crossing it, climbing farther up the hillside before disappearing into the underbrush. Before an upgrade in 1937, this section of highway had 71 curves; afterward, that number was reduced to a dozen.

"La Cuesta, the steep and tortuous grade that since the days of the Franciscan friars has been the bogey of travelers on El Camino Real, no longer will impede the flow of motor vehicle traffic over The King's Highway," engineer Lester H. Gibson exulted.

It was the latest, if not the last, in a series of improvements dating back to 1876, when the first upgrades to the old trail were made using $20,000 in bonds. A road of gravel and oil more suited to automobiles replaced it in 1915, and a concrete road was installed seven years later. Still, the circuitous route created a bottleneck over the grade for travelers midway between Los Angeles and San Francisco, and the state dedicated more than $1 million to construction of the four-lane highway that took its place.

Before that, Gibson wrote, "it was a frequent sight to observe a line of 20 or more automobiles creeping along behind a large truck throughout their crossing of Cuesta."

A short section of roadway called Cuesta Springs Road coming down out of the pass northbound is another section of the old highway, which followed the current route to the intersection with State Route 58. There, it turned east along the state highway, making its way through the center of Santa Margarita in a route that would later be bypassed by the current 101 alignment.

Old West-style architecture in central Santa Margarita, north of the Cuesta Pass.

This old route can still be driven today.

Santa Margarita, which has the look of an old Western town, is one of those almost-boomtowns that never quite made city status. It was a hopping highway stop in the roaring twenties, when it boasted six gas stations, pool halls, restaurants, bars, and even a couple of baseball teams—one made up of ranch workers from the surrounding area and the other of Southern Pacific Railroad workers.

But the Depression took its toll, and fewer than 300 people lived there in 1939. Two years later, the government confiscated ranch land to build a reservoir—Santa Margarita Lake—to provide water for Camp San Luis Obispo, original home to the California National Guard. Any hopes for a substantial rebound were dashed when the new 101 freeway bypassed the town in 1956, and six decades later, the population was still less than 1,300.

The Carlton Hotel is the most distinctive feature of the skyline in Atascadero, where the old 101 Alignment, El Camino Real, parallels the modern freeway.

The old road leaves State Route 58 at the east end of town and curves northward again along El Camino Real, a two-lane road that parallels the rail line as it stretches out across a lazy flatland of grasses dotted by oak trees here and there. Eight miles up the road, the old highway reaches Atascadero, paralleling the freeway through town until it rejoins the current alignment at the city's north end.

Atascadero was founded in 1913 by a magazine publisher named Edward Gardner Lewis, who bought 23,000 acres and envisioned a utopian colony there (you'll still see the word "colony" used at various spots in town). The first "homes" in the new colony were actually tents, pitched by homesteaders who came from across the country and waited while permanent housing was constructed. The Atascadero Printery, a brick building that still stands but was boarded up after an earthquake in 2003, published the first edition of the *Atascadero News* in 1916. It's located just two blocks east of El Camino Real, on Olmeda Avenue.

On the old highway itself, you'll pass the Carlton Hotel near the center of town. It opened just a month after the stock market crash of 1929 ushered in the Great Depression and played host to the likes of Bette Davis, Jack Benny, Fred MacMurray, Ralph Bellamy, and Dick Powell. Despite the hard times, the Annex—as it was originally called—attracted J. C. Penney, Safeway, and Sprouse-Reitz to open retail outlets on its main floor.

Its name and ownership changed shortly after that to the Hotel Halfway and Coffee Shop, then again in 1931 when new owners adopted the current name in an attempt to play off the East Coast cachet it afforded them. Another owner added the distinctive clock tower in 1952, and the hotel went downhill over the next several decades, being converted into a senior housing complex and subsequently lying vacant for several years. Recent renovations, however, have restored it, and it opened for business as a hotel once again.

More affordable overnight stays could be had near the south end of town at the Beautysleep Motel, which dates to at least the 1940s and remained in business at this writing as a Mexican restaurant and apartments. Closer to the center of town was the Atascadero Motor Lodge, which originally consisted of cabins but was later remodeled to become a two-story motel and renamed the

Rancho Tee. The distinctive golf ball atop the sign was hard to miss as you passed through town. It's a long tee shot to the nearest fairway, though: The Chalk Mountain Golf Course is more than a mile south of the motel.

As it turns out, there *used to be* a golf course right behind the Rancho Tee. Bing Crosby led a parade of famous stars out onto the course in the summer of 1944 to boost the war bond campaign. One Atascadero resident remembered there was a green right behind the motel, and an errant tee shot could send the ball flying out onto El Camino Real (or, presumably, through a window at the motel!). The golf course was scaled back to nine holes in the 1960s and eventually closed. A large, modern movie theater complex was built where part of it had once been.

The Rancho Tee survived a bit longer, but as of 2017, a large red banner online labeled the place permanently closed.

The name "Atascadero," incidentally, comes from the Spanish word for a bog—not a particularly romantic designation. More like a place to get stuck. TV producer Garry Marshall got stuck there once when his car broke down, but the incident served as the inspiration for something that really *was* romantic: a character named Pinky Tuscadero, whom Marshall introduced as the girl-friend of Arthur "Fonzie" Fonzarelli on the 1970s hit sitcom *Happy Days*.

Six miles north of Atascadero, the old highway reappears briefly through Templeton as Main Street. Look for sections of old concrete near the south end of Main and near the Legion Hall, just north of Templeton High School. A couple of old gas stations can be found off the old highway, as well: an abandoned 1940s-era Chevron station at 8th Street on the east side, and a smaller stop—converted into a fast-food joint called the Burger Station—on the opposite side of the road a block farther north.

Another sight worth seeing: a funky larger-than-life milk bottle, once used to promote the Rossi Dairy, that was partly overgrown by a large tree, off Rossi Road at the south end of town (this is on the west side of the freeway, opposite Main Street, so you'll have to take the Vineyard Road exit and double back south in order to see it).

At the north end of Templeton, Main Street crosses the freeway and continues north as Theatre Drive—named for the old Oaks Drive-In that stood just south of the junction with State Route 46, not far from the old Richfield Beacon station. The theater opened in 1950, a year after the River Lodge Motel was built on the north side of 46. That motel, the latest in modern lodging when it was built, was still in business more than six decades later. The theater, however, was long gone, a dream that died with the era of the drive-in. Original owner Al Stanford, who opened the theater after selling stock to 15 local businessmen and farmers, kept the dream alive for 27 years before selling the theater; it was eventually abandoned and torn down in 1995 to make way for a Target store.

Continuing north to Paso Robles, you'll find one of the most well-preserved sections of Old 101 in the form of Spring Street, which takes you off and modern bypass and straight through town. A few of the old motels remain along the route, notably the Farmhouse Motel at the south end of town, which dates to the late 1930s and still sports a distinctive neon sign. The Melody Ranch Motel farther north was built in the mid-1950s, and other roadside inns still visible include a TraveLodge that dates to the late '40s,

This now-closed Chevron station operated from the early 1940s in Templeton.

The River Lodge Motel at the south end of Paso Robles serves travelers at the junction of U.S. 101 and State Route 46.

The first of these is San Miguel, home of the 16th mission to be built along old El Camino Real (in 1797). If you get off the highway on Mission Street heading north, you'll be on the old highway, and you'll see a three-story stand-alone bell tower directly in front of you as you exit the off-ramp. Take your first right, and you'll be on the oldest section of highway in this area: concrete that now serves as a driveway to the Rios Caledonia Adobe. Built in 1835 by Native Americans, the adobe was once part of the mission property. The short drive, lined on both sides by shade trees, will give you an idea of what the old road was like in its earliest incarnation.

A building on the southwest corner of 12th Street, a business called the Coffee Station at this writing, is a pre-1940 Union Oil gas station; the building behind it was the garage.

the Avalon Motel from the same period, and the Town House Motel from 1959.

The 21st Street Drive-In and Foster's Freeze are surviving remnants of an era when "drive-in" referred to meals as much as to movies, and the 1941 Fox Theatre (which opened as the Hi-Ho) still stands—although it's closed as of this writing.

North of Paso Robles, the old road continues for a stretch as Monterey Road, and you can see some sections of the old concrete highway if you know where to look.

North of Paso, the highway heads through rural lands, and you'll have to get off the modern highway to see most of the towns along the way. Built along old alignments, these small communities seem to be almost withering away in the summer heat, dusty towns on what was once the beaten path but which now lie all but forgotten and, in a few cases, nearly abandoned away from the current flow of traffic.

Less than a block farther north on the same side of the street, you'll come to the Elkhorn Bar, the second-oldest

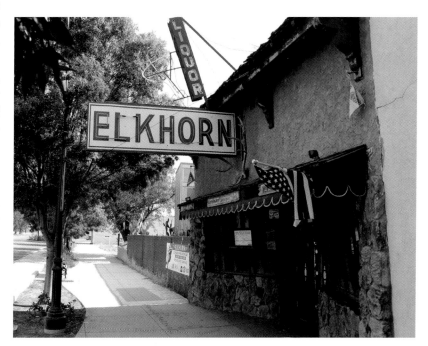

The Elkhorn has a long and colorful history in San Miguel.

watering hole in the state of California, dating back all the way to December 5, 1853. It was originally part of a tent city across from the mission, "at the site of an adobe frequented by Frank and Jesse James"—at least according to a plaque near the entrance. The original saloon burned down in 1925, after which it reopened at its current location.

Prohibition was in effect, but the bar remained open—customers just had to enter from the alley around back. The "front" to the place was a barbershop and candy store, and shipments of booze were lowered into the cellar through a trapdoor in the barbershop, then carried to the bar upstairs. The place got even more popular once Prohibition ended, especially during World War II, when the town became a gathering spot for troops stationed at nearby Camp Roberts. There were more than a dozen bars at that time in a once-sleepy town where the population had been just 300 a few years earlier.

Today, the establishment embraces its Old West heritage, with a woodstove and gun racks inside. Above the door is a more recent but still vintage neon sign featuring the standard, iconic tipped martini glass.

Next stop on the drive north is Bradley, which you can reach by exiting at Bradley Road and driving along the old alignment through town. It was bypassed by the current highway during the 1950s, and the town went rapidly downhill after that. There isn't much there now, and the population as of 2010 was shy of 100 people—less than what it was in the 1930s, before which an even older alignment took travelers down Meadow Street, south on Pleyto for a couple of blocks through the heart of town, and then west again on Dixie Street and across the Salinas River on a bridge that was torn down in 1933 and replaced with the current structure on Bradley Road. The concrete supports of the old bridge are still visible.

Many of the town's old commercial buildings are gone now, but a few remain. Notable among them is an old service station with a few pumps dating from the 1950s

The owner of the Sea Plane Inn, which dates back a century in Bradley, has amassed an odd and varied assortment of vintage collectibles large and small, including old gas pumps and (appropriately) a propeller.

still out front at Pleyto and Bradley. A block farther on, at Monterey, you can see the remnants of a pair of old motels: the Allen and the Sea Plane Inn.

The latter, on your right, is particularly interesting. Henry Veach bought out another business in town and moved it to its present location in 1916. He set up shop as a grocery store and gas station, but it was also known as "the Zoo" because Veach had, well, a zoo there that featured coyotes, foxes, deer, monkeys, alligators, and—the star attraction—a bear. You didn't want to get too close to the bear's cage, which is why Veach was rumored to have hidden his liquor stash there during Prohibition.

After you leave Bradley, keep going up the freeway until you hit Cattlemen Road, then turn east onto another section of the old alignment that will take you through San Ardo. This section of old road was 101 more recently than most: It was only bypassed in 1971. An older alignment ran parallel along Jolon Road to Main Street, which took you north to hook up with Cattlemen. An older trestle bridge carried Jolon across the Salinas River, but as with the old Bradley Bridge, all that remains are concrete supports, some still visible from the newer Cattlemen Bridge, which dates to 1930.

The fact that Cattlemen itself was originally a bypass is easy to tell from its long, gentle curve, which skirts the old downtown as its eastward heading changes to a north-south alignment along the railroad tracks.

One of the oddest sights in San Ardo is an old Shell gas station sign at the north end of this curve. It drew motorists to an old, single-bay station that was probably the "last chance" to get gas for a few miles. It stood next to the old Evergreen Camp restaurant, which was later replaced by the Evergreen Park (for mobile homes). There are still a lot of trees there, some of which partially obscure the Shell sign itself. The sign is interesting because it appears somewhat similar to the highway signs that tower beside modern freeways, but it's much lower to the ground, perhaps just 15 feet tall.

There's not much to see for the next several miles along Cattlemen, except the railroad tracks on the east and rows of crops on either side. You'll pass the abandoned buildings of an old labor camp on the west side of the road before you get to San Lucas, after which Cattlemen again joins the modern highway route. An old cattle ranching town, it was once known for raising fine thoroughbred horses, but today it's showing its age.

Before 1930, the highway went through town on Main Street, just east of the rail line; afterward, it ran on the other side of the tracks as Cattlemen. The most distinctive feature is three connected grain cylinders that rise above the highway at the south end of town, easily the loftiest structure on the landscape.

This Shell sign on Cattlemen Road at the north end of San Ardo is largely obscured by trees these days. The service station itself closed long ago.

**The King City Auto Camp offered Salinas Valley travelers
a place to spend the night, and fill up their tanks with Shell gasoline.**
Collection of Michael Semas.

over San Lorenzo Creek dates to 1924, when the section of road on either side was still unpaved.

The old highway next appears in Greenfield as El Camino Real, which was the main route until the bypass was finished in 1966. A short section of an even older alignment can be found at the north end of town, where a brief stretch of concrete is visible near Cypress Avenue just west of El Camino Real. As you enter the older section of town from the south, look on your right for a sign sticking up from the top of a blue gabled roof. From the north side, you can see the remnants of old Richfield lettering on the sign—at least you could as of this writing.

Once you leave Greenfield, it's on to Soledad, where you exit on Front Street, another old motel-and-gas-station row that's a dead giveaway you're entering another town along the highway.

Gonzales, the next town north, carries the old highway through town on Alta Street. At the north end of town, just before you rejoin the new highway, you'll pass the abandoned Rincon Café on the right. It's obviously been there (and closed) for a long time, but check out the distinctive step-pyramid design over the entrance. An

The heart of town was, for many years, the Bunte General Store on Main Street, a red, wooden structure built in 1886. The store's name dates back to Sam D. and H. D. Bunte, who operated the store until 1917. At one time, it sold "Big D" gasoline and housed an impressive collection of antiques. But the store burned down in July 2006 in a fire which investigators suspected was arson that spread from a dumpster next to the building. Nearby residences were spared, but the store was destroyed.

The Pit Stop is still there on Cattlemen Road: The building (which is a lot taller in front than it is in the back) was built in the 1930s and used to include a gas station, though the pumps are long since gone. Today it's a small diner.

From San Lucas, the modern highway—this section was built in 1962—heads north to King City, where the old alignment veers east from the current highway as First Street, then heads back toward it along Broadway. The First Street bridge

**It's hard to tell what they served at the Rincon Café near Gonzales, but it's safe
to say there's nothing but dust and weeds on the menu these days.**

Old concrete, foreground, leads motorists up the San Juan Grade, a winding old alignment of U.S. 101 east of Salinas that was bypassed in the early 1930s and survives as a scenic mountain road.

attached garage would seem to indicate it was once a service station, as well.

Chualar, site of an old Richfield Beacon station, is the last stop before you get to Salinas. Then, if you want an adventure—and a scenic one at that—take the old San Juan Grade up over the mountains northeast of Salinas.

The original alignment followed Old Stage Road, which skirts the city limits to the east before veering off into the foothills, away from the current road. If it seems out of the way, it is: If the road kept going in that direction, it would deposit you in Modesto (or thereabouts). But that was the path the state highway commission settled on back in 1913, when it chose to route travelers over the San Juan Grade rather than on a course beside the Pajaro River via Watsonville.

The debate over the route pitted Salinas against Watsonville, and in the end, Salinas won the day.

Why choose the tortuous, narrow path across the mountains instead of the less encumbered riverside route?

For one thing, the former was a little more direct, at least in terms of mileage. Besides, when the decision was made, cars couldn't have gone much faster on a straightaway than they could have over the mountains. They just didn't have the horsepower. But perhaps the most important factor was money: According to a report in the *Santa Cruz Evening News*, "the banks of Salinas and Hollister showed their faith in the highway by taking up road bonds in the sum of $75,000."

It was a decision they likely came to regret when cars started going faster but trucks continued to inch their way over the grade at a snail's pace. This was, after all, the main thoroughfare between L.A. and San Francisco, and no matter how scenic the drive might have been, travelers had little patience, then as now, for spending an afternoon stuck behind a sluggish convoy on a twisting mountain road.

A highway department report written in 1931—barely a decade and a half after the San Juan Alignment opened—cut to the chase: The grade had become "increasingly exasperating" for motorists traveling between Los Angeles and the Bay Area. Although it had been "entirely adequate for the prevailing traffic" in 1915, "due to the tremendous increase in motor vehicular travel, this grade has been obsolete for several years. Because of the long grades, narrow roadway and sharp curves, it is now a bottle neck on the Coast Highway and the scene of many unfortunate accidents."

So, the decision was made to forge a new alignment for U.S. 101 over flatter terrain, cutting more than a mile off the trip in the process. The million-dollar project, dubbed the Prunedale Cut-off, would cover just under 17 miles, and its highest point would be a mere 550 feet, barely half the altitude of the old grade. It's the route still followed by U.S. 101 today.

One by-product of the change was to bypass San Juan Bautista, an old mission town on the original El Camino Real that lay three miles east of the new alignment. Motorists hoping to reach the town now had to leave the federal highway in order to do so. To help them find it, the highway department placed a small, freestanding bell tower surmounted by a cross at the turnoff—and the 1930s-era campanile is still visible today at the junction of U.S. 101 and State Route 156.

It's still worthwhile to take the San Juan Grade north out of Salinas if you have some extra time for a scenic drive. Rolling foothills and shady stretches lined with trees will be your reward, along with some glimpses of old concrete from the original roadway. On the other side of the ridge, the road offers scenic views of the valley below before taking you down past rolling farmland and a couple of rectangular C-blocks. (These short concrete markers were placed along highway rights-of-way starting in 1914 and continuing, in some places, through the 1950s. If you look closely, you can find these two on the north side of the roadway as the land starts to level out.)

In short order, the old highway will deposit you in San Juan Bautista, traveling through town as 3rd Street just a block southwest of the old mission, where you'll find a distinctive El Camino Real bell on the grounds. Many of the buildings lining the two-lane street would seem right at home on an Old West Hollywood set. Don't blink, though. The business district is a mere ten blocks long.

Near the north end of town, the highway jogs right for two blocks, to First Street, then carries you out of this sleepy community (2016 population: 1,975) and off across rural flatland. You'll rejoin the modern 101 alignment about three miles up the road.

THE PACIFIC COAST HIGHWAY

Travelers can be forgiven for confusing State Route 1 with U.S. 101. For decades, lengthy segments of the road that's now called SR1 in the Los Angeles area were numbered as the 101 Alternate along the coast. This was before the San Diego Freeway (Interstate 405) was built and the state took over the route from the federal government.

Other sections, mostly where a single road is sandwiched between the Pacific and the coastal mountain ranges, remain signed as both State Route 1 and U.S. 101.

Much has been written about the Pacific Coast Highway—perhaps even more than about El Camino Real—probably because SR1 along the Central Coast is one of the most scenic drives you'll find anywhere. The Bixby Creek Bridge, with its majestic arch set against a backdrop of green hills on one flank and blue Pacific on the other, is one of the most photographed spans in California. The Piedras Blancas Light Station, Hearst Castle, Morro Rock, and the redwoods of Big Sur are among the sights you'll see along the stretch of winding road that's undoubtedly the "scenic route." In fact, it's officially designated as a state scenic highway.

This iconic, solitary cypress tree stands off the coast of central California, not far from State Route 1, on 17-Mile Drive in Pebble Beach.

By contrast, it parallels a segment of 101 about 30 miles inland that runs through the Salinas Valley, a straight shot at 65 mph across flatlands flanked by agricultural fields and often-brown hillsides.

U.S. 101 is the older of the two roads here, which makes sense when you consider how challenging it must have been to build a highway across the isolated, craggy cliffs that hug this section of coastline. Despite engineering that only gets better with new innovations, Mother Nature still plays havoc with the coast road, sending down mudslides and undercutting segments of the highway during heavy storms and El Niño-spawned rainy seasons. As I write this, a segment of State Route 1 to the north of me, between Ragged Point and Big Sur, remains washed out and impassible thanks to a recent mudslide.

It's no wonder that southbound traffic couldn't get any farther than Bixby Creek before the iconic bridge was built across it in 1932. And the town where I now live, Cambria, marked the end of the road for northbound travelers until as late as 1937 (there's even a book on the history of Cambria titled *Where the Highway Ends*).

You can still see the many sections of the first concrete road heading north from San Luis Obispo to Morro Bay. Much of it lies neglected on private property, with weeds sprouting up through cracks in the pavement. It runs north from the Cuesta College campus as Tomasini Road and crosses over the modern highway to its north side as Adobe Road, neither of which is accessible to the public. It crosses over again to the south side as Quintana Road just before you get to Morro Bay, and you can follow it here into that city for about two miles before continuing north on Main Street—another section of the old highway—to the point where it ends at the north side of town.

The stretch of highway from San Luis Obispo through Morro Bay, covering roughly 20 miles, was described as "newly paved" in a news article that appeared in the summer of 1925, and it wasn't long before the road would stretch farther than that.

A bond issue approved by the public in 1919 dedicated $1.5 million to completing the highway between Monterey and San Simeon, but it took nearly two decades for those plans to reach fruition. Inmates from San Quentin State Prison were enlisted to do much of the work—their reward being 35 cents a day and reduced prison sentences—and convict construction camps were set up along the course plotted for the road.

It wasn't until 1926 that workers began paving the section between Morro Bay and Cambria, and although that segment was completed by the summer of 1928, you had to settle for oiled gravel and dirt beyond that. Then, about eight miles north of San Simeon, you'd have to turn around and go back the way you came, because the road ended there, with one of those convict camps blocking the way.

But the biggest challenge was farther north, where steeper cliffs that plunged at impossible angles into the ocean below created daunting obstacles to highway builders. They had to bring supplies in by boat and lift them up via steam-powered engines to where the road was being built. The problem wasn't a new one. Charles Bixby, for whom the creek was named, owned the land around it and had asked Monterey County to build a road—only to be told that "no one would want to live there." He had to ferry goods in and have them hoisted up from ships anchored just offshore.

In the end, Bixby did manage to build a wagon trail from his ranch to Carmel that included 23 bridges but still had to be closed every winter. He built his road 11 miles inland to avoid the canyon Bixby Creek had carved between the mountains along the coast, but the builders of the new road decided to tackle the coastline head-on. They realized they'd need to carve an 890-foot tunnel to make the

Quintana Road near Morro Bay once served as a section of State Route 1.

The Bixby Bridge, which opened in 1932, is perhaps the most recognizable feature of Highway 1 between San Luis Obispo and Monterey.

work without realizing anything was amiss.

An account in the WPA to California, printed in 1939, recalled a particularly stormy winter night when slides had blocked the road: "The word spread that the wife of a man in the freeman's camp, about to give birth to a child, needed a doctor; of their own free will, men from both (work) camps poured out to work in the rain and pitch darkness, blasting open with dynamite a road to the community hospital."

As part of the project, more than 30 bridges needed to be built, the first of which was a timber span 19 miles north of San Simeon at Salmon Creek, which opened in 1928. The most impressive, of course, was the Bixby Creek Bridge, about 13 miles south of Carmel, which cost nearly $200,000 to build and was the longest concrete arch span in California's highway system at 716 feet. Concrete arch

inland route work for them, and ultimately decided that, despite its challenges, a route directly along the coast was safer.

Besides, the view was stunning.

As the project got under way, free men set up their own camps to build the road, along with those of the convicts. But despite the formidable manpower, progress on the road was anything but steady, with stormy weather producing the same sort of rockslides and mudslides that plague the road today. With the road still being built, one of these could damage or destroy equipment and put the workers all the way back to square one.

Once a boulder fell on a steam shovel, destroying the controls, just moments after the operator stepped away. In another case, earth gave way underneath a shovel, which somehow remained suspended 300 feet above the ocean, with just a few inches of soil holding it in place and the operator continuing to

This old bridge across Villa Creek lay on a section of old Highway 1 that was bypassed; the road used by the bridge now leads to a dead end a few hundred yards to the south.

This pink bead shop at the south end of Cambria was once a fuel stop for motorists, back when
Main Street through town was also Highway 1.

spans were also built across Garapata, Granite, Malpaso, Rocky, and Wildcat Creeks, with the Rocky Creek span carrying cars 150 feet above the waterway for a distance of nearly 500 feet.

Convicts from camps in the northern and southern construction zones met in the middle in 1934, but more work still needed to be done, and the road wasn't officially opened to the public until 1937.

Even though the section of the road between San Luis Obispo and Big Sur is largely rural, a few bypasses were built over the years. A new freeway replaced the Quintana Road-Main Street route in Morro Bay, and another section of freeway bypassed the old route through Cayucos, Ocean Avenue, in the 1960s. The older broad, two-lane thoroughfare passes a number of downtown buildings that look to predate the bypass, and the Borradori Garage at the north end of town dates to the earliest years of the highway. Built in 1932, it still stands at 455 Ocean Avenue.

To the north of Cayucos, just off Villa Creek Road, there's a bridge over the creek that's part of the old alignment, and farther north still lies Old Creamery Road in the village of Harmony. Once a dairy center and later a funky artists' colony, Harmony—perpetual population 18—now is home to a few businesses that include a glass-blowing shop and winery. The short strip of the old route that passes through it disappears onto private land behind a locked gate at the north end of the hamlet. If you look carefully, you can still see portions of that old road, although it's largely overgrown now. Another small bridge off to the right of the highway, just before you get to the junction of State Route 46, appears to have been part of that older road.

Cambria was bypassed, too, by the current highway in 1965, but vestiges of the old road remain. An old alignment there includes the south end of Green Street to the west of the current road, then dips eastward along Ardath and across the highway, where it becomes Main

Street. This will take you directly through town, past a number of historic buildings. Among them: the old independent Music Gas Station (Music was the family name; the historic family home is just down the street) that's been painted pink and was, as of 2017, home to a bead shop.

In the center of the old downtown—now known as the East Village—are Camozzi's Bar and Hotel, which dates to 1922 and these days is called Mozzi's Saloon; the old brick Bank of Cambria building (1931), later Bank of America and now an art gallery; and Soto's True Earth Market, built in 1939 as Cambria Meat Market & Grocery.

Following Main Street as it veers west on its northward journey, you'll reach the West Village, which has its own history. In 1995, it was submerged in a flood that turned the thoroughfare into something more closely resembling a river. More than eight inches of rain fell over the course of 24 hours, and the fact that the storm coincided with a high tide didn't help. The water measured 10 feet deep at the north end of Main Street, with the waters rising near the canopy of the gas station there.

The highway winds north through San Simeon, which is little more than a retail strip and a few scattered homes, and on past Hearst Castle, which is visible on a hilltop to the east. Newspaper mogul William Randolph Hearst hired architect Julia Morgan to create the 165-room mansion that included lavish indoor and outdoor pools, a grand dining hall, and a theater for movie screenings. It housed hundreds of antiques and works of art from across the ages, spanning the classical, medieval, and Renaissance periods, and Hearst used it as a showplace/playground for friends from Hollywood and Washington, D.C.

There was even an extensive zoo on the 127-acre site that, at one time, featured camels, llamas, emus, kangaroos, Barbary sheep, and even four giraffes. Although most of the animals were sold off in 1937 when the zoo was dismantled, zebras still roam the hillsides of the estate—now owned by the state of California—and can often be seen grazing beside Highway 1. Tours of the castle are available, and docents dress up as characters from the Hearst era for special occasions.

Main Street, formerly Highway 1, through Cambria's West Village.

Zebras descended from a herd brought to the San Simeon foothills by William Randolph Hearst can often be seen grazing alongside Highway 1.

About five miles farther north is an elephant seal rookery, where the marine mammals play and (mostly) sleep on the beach by the hundreds, and farther on is the Piedras Blancas Light Station, which dates to 1875.

One of the last pieces of civilization you'll hit before the road starts to ascend along the craggy coastline toward Big Sur is Ragged Point, site of the Ragged Point Inn. The current owners built a snack shack there back in 1961 after buying the land from a carnival owner who had left a bunch of rusting old rides and other attractions on the site. The simple roadside stop grew gradually, with the owners opening an upscale motor inn and developing a complex that came to include a restaurant, coffee bar, retail shops, and gas pumps. But the biggest attraction is the breathtaking panoramic view of the Pacific and the coastline you'll find there. If you look northward, you'll see the highway ascending up the hillsides, and there isn't much except wonderful scenery from there on till you hit the Big Sur redwoods.

8
THE BAYSHORE HIGHWAY

Before El Camino Real was a highway, before it was even paved, it was a narrow trail up the San Francisco Peninsula to Mission Dolores.

In the middle of the 19th century, all roads—or what few there were—led to the mission, which was then the epicenter of activity in the Bay Area. Foremost among those roads was El Camino Real, which carried travelers via stagecoach and on horseback in those days.

This was long before the era of gas stations (the motorcar had yet to be invented, after all), and modern rest stops were even further in the future. But travelers still needed to take a load off—even more so than today—on a rutted road that ranged from dusty during summer to mucky and muddy in the rainy season.

The Bayshore Highway in San Mateo offered liquor and lodging for weary travelers in 1963. © *California Department of Transportation, all rights reserved. Used with permission.*

The first stop on the County Road, as it was also called back then, was Abbey House in Daly City. Its distance from San Francisco accounted for its other name, 1 Mile House, and milestones farther down the road took on similar names based on how far they were from the mission. There was a 7 Mile House in Colma, a 14 Mile House in San Bruno, and a 16 Mile House on El Camino Real at Center Street. A mile farther south stood the 17 Mile House, at Millbrae Avenue.

The most significant of these was 14 Mile House, known as Thorpe's Place when it was built at the dawn of the Gold Rush in 1849. Like the other way stations along the trail, it wasn't much to look at: just a square cabin that measured a dozen feet in both directions, about the size of a modern bedroom. The proprietor (named Thorpe, naturally) also built stables where travelers could leave their horses as they stopped on their way to and from the city.

What was important about Thorpe's place was its location. It was there, in 1858, that a group of investors saw an opportunity to create a new road branching off from the main highway eastward toward the bay. The idea was to charge a toll for traveling along this shortcut, which would shave several miles off the journey to San Francisco.

There were reasons no one had created such a shortcut before: The chosen route traveled through marshlands and across the San Bruno Canal, which road crews conquered using a drawbridge. Workers were forced to cart in tons of dirt and gravel to fill in the marshes, and they also had to contend with thick stands of willow trees that lined the canal. Still, they persevered.

This ad invited travelers to patronize the Brisbane Auto Camp and Trailer Space, 15 miles from San Francisco on the Bayshore Highway.

The road they created, an arrow-straight cutoff that's known as San Mateo Avenue today, continued along the path of what would become Bayshore Boulevard and modern U.S. 101 on toward San Francisco. The toll section of the road came to an end in Visitacion Valley, east of San Bruno Mountain, at a tollhouse called 7 Mile House—not to be confused with the *other* 7 Mile House in Colma. Like Thorpe's at the other end of the toll road, it became a hub of activity, and it remains in business today, the only surviving mile house from the period.

The 7 Mile House, like other roadhouses, had a colorful history that included no small amount of wild doings and shady dealings. The so-called Hayes Valley Gang, which remained active into the late 1920s, paid the place a visit in August 1876 to harass passersby amid a rampage of theft, assault, and homicide centered on San Francisco's Mission District—an event that is believed to have helped inspire the terms "hood" and "hoodlum."

Then, during Prohibition, the area around the roadhouse became a hotbed of moonshining. The business has also housed a brothel, as well as a bookmaking operation described as the largest west of the Mississippi. (On two separate occasions, the FBI raided the 7 Mile House in response to illegal gambling and Mafia connections.)

Another roadhouse from the pre-highway era managed to hang on for nearly a century. The oldest building in Millbrae, the 16 Mile House at El Camino Real and Center Street, was demolished in 1970 after a group of preservationists failed to raise the $40,000 needed to move it from land targeted for a paint store. The city had declined to pay for the project, bowing to opponents who objected that it had once housed a brothel and a tavern and derided it as a "disreputable pile of junk."

The current 16 Mile House on Broadway reproduces the look and flavor of the original (minus the shady reputation), serving up a menu of steak and seafood.

It does, however, still offer a full bar.

The 14 Mile House, isn't around anymore either, but it had a long run of its own, well into the 20th century. Original owner Thorpe expanded it into a two-story hotel before selling it 1871, with the new owner—a man by the name of Gamble—adding a dining room and renaming it the Star and Garter. The new name, however, only lasted a few years. Gamble needed a cook for his new restaurant, and he found one in the person of Thomas Rolle, a former slave who was heading south to take a job in Searsville. He never made it that far, and it's probably just as well: You won't find Searsville on any modern map, because what remained of the town was inundated when

This pre-1914 photo shows a sign for Uncle Tom's Cabin along El Camino Real. *Public domain.*

APPROACHING THE GOLDEN GATE

Before the Golden Gate Bridge came along, San Francisco was all but a dead-end for motor vehicles. The city's geography, surrounded as it is on three sides by water, made it the equivalent of one giant cul-de-sac. Sure, you could take a ferry across the bay, but as more and more cars hit the road during the 1920s, the wait time increased.

At the dawn of the motor age, a single north-south thoroughfare funneled traffic into San Francisco: El Camino Real. But that artery, which generally followed the course set by today's Mission Street and State Route 82, soon became clogged as it strained to accommodate an ever-increasing number of motor vehicles. It was quickly clear that alternative routes would be needed, and thus began an era in which the label "Highway 101" bounced from one road to another so often it was hard to keep things straight—even with one of those handy road maps you picked up at your local Richfield or Shell station. At various points in time, there were even multiple alignments from which to choose. Do I take 101 East or 101 West? The 101 or the 101 Alternate? The 101 or the 101 Bypass?

the Searsville Dam was built in 1892. Instead, Rolle took a job from Gamble and, just four years later, parlayed it into ownership of the establishment—which he renamed Uncle Tom's Cabin.

The roadhouse retained its name after Rolle's tenure ended and became the site of some noteworthy historical events. In 1883, with the completion of a telephone line between San Jose and San Francisco, Uncle Tom's Cabin received the first telephone in northern San Mateo County. Later, in August 1912, workers right in front of the roadhouse dug the first shovel of dirt in the state's new highway system—which would help pave the way (literally and figuratively) for the network of federal highways that would put U.S. 101 on the map in 1926.

Uncle Tom's Cabin finally met its end in 1949, when it was torn down to make way for a Safeway supermarket.

The 7 Mile House, meanwhile, remains in business on Bayshore Boulevard just south of Geneva Avenue. It's mellowed significantly since its seedy heyday as a brothel, gambling haven, and biker bar. Today it's a sports bar and restaurant that serves up Filipino and Italian food along with performances by musical acts such as jazz trumpeter Al Molina. In late 2016, its website even touted a "Holi-Dog" photo contest, with a prize of a "Dog Birthday Party & Photo Session" to one lucky customer.

How times have changed.

It was easier to tell the players without a scorecard at a Seals game than it was to find the proper highway between San Jose and "the City." (Remember the Seals? They were San Francisco's baseball team before the Giants came along; they even had a player named DiMaggio on their roster.)

There'd been an early alternative to El Camino Real even before the age of the automobile. Because the state wasn't paying for roads in those days, a group of private investors set about clearing a path for a new thoroughfare, planning to recoup their money—and more—by charging a toll to the coachmen who used it. The San Bruno Toll Road was completed in 1860, veering north-by-northeastward from El Camino Real just south of San Bruno along what is now San Mateo Avenue. For a good

The Central Freeway in San Francisco, headed toward the Civic Center, in 1960.
© California Department of Transportation, all rights reserved. Used with permission.

portion of its length, it ran roughly parallel to the route that would be taken by the later Bayshore Boulevard—a future alignment of U.S. 101.

Roadhouses with practical names like 3 Mile House, 7 Mile House, and San Bruno House opened to cater to travelers along the length of the new road, which provided a more direct route into the big city.

But the explosion of roads in the area didn't occur until the advent of the automobile.

If you're not familiar with the Bay Area, imagine a three-pronged fork, and you'll have a very rough approximation of the road system that developed to take the burden off El Camino Real as the automotive age moved

into high gear. To the west was Skyline Boulevard, which became part of the state highway system in 1919 and morphed at its northern edge into the so-called Great Highway. Originally numbered as State Route 5, it became SR35 in 1964 to avoid confusion with the new Interstate 5, but it was never part of U.S. 101.

The central prong in the fork was El Camino Real, while the eastward prong was Bayshore Boulevard (later Highway and still later Freeway), which ran along the western edge of the San Francisco Bay.

U.S. 101 originally split into two branches at San Jose, with 101W heading northward into San Francisco on the western peninsula. Meanwhile, 101E took a parallel

The double-decker freeway with parking at Fell Street in San Francisco in 1961.
© California Department of Transportation, all rights reserved. Used with permission.

course on the east side of the bay, moving up through Oakland and across the Carquinez Bridge before veering westward along modern State Route 37 to rejoin the western branch near Novato. The federal highway system dropped the 101E designation in the 1940s, with that route subsequently becoming State Route 17 and, later, Interstate 880.

But that's not the end of the confusion.

El Camino Real was signed as U.S. 101 until 1937, when signs were removed from that route and transferred to the newly completed Bayshore Highway. El Camino Real was relegated to the status of U.S. 101 Alternate (101A)—a development that didn't please merchants along that route who feared the second-class

status would mean a loss of business. To their way of thinking, the federal highway planners were sacrificing the merchants' financial fortunes on the altar of the need for speed.

"It is the purpose of the highway maintenance division to speed the motorist to San Francisco by the shortest route," Judge Charles Carlstroem of Sunnyvale said, showing off pictures of directional signs diverting motorists to the new Bayshore Alignment—and away from the established route. "They are preventing the tourist from reaching El Camino Real."

The political pressure apparently worked: Two years later, the 101 designation had been restored to the old alignment, with Bayshore getting a new designation: the

U.S. 101 Bypass. But even that didn't turn out to be permanent, because in 1964, the Bayshore Alignment went back to being just plain U.S. 101 again, with El Camino Real moving over to the California highway system as State Route 82.

But back to the Golden Gate.

As traffic grew by leaps and bounds in the roaring twenties—and even, despite the Great Depression, into the 1930s—the ferries that took drivers across the water to the north side of the bay struggled to keep up. In 1936, the year before the Golden Gate Bridge opened, as many as 60 million people crossed the bay on nearly 50 ferries, and 250,000 passengers each day made their way through San Francisco's Ferry Building.

Traveling on a ferry was, in a way, like being caught in rush-hour traffic. The massive vessels, powered by steam engines until the advent of diesel in the 1920s, moved at a leisurely pace—barely 17 miles per hour.

The concept of relieving that congestion by building a bridge to span the bay wasn't a new one. In fact, the bridge idea even predated the automobile. As far back as 1872, a railroad executive had suggested building a span for trains across the water, but the cost even then was prohibitive. Estimate: $100 million.

Fast forward to 1919, when San Francisco officials asked city engineer Michael O'Shaughnessy to revisit the idea—this time, with the automobile in mind. But it would have to cost far less than the $100 million price tag that had been bandied about for more than four decades. O'Shaughnessy consulted with other engineers on various approaches and attracted the attention of Joseph Strauss, who insisted that such a bridge could, in fact, be built for somewhere between $25 million and $30 million.

In 1921, he did even better: He submitted a design for a cantilever-suspension bridge hybrid that he said

The Golden Gate Bridge under construction. *Public domain.*

could be built for $17 million. "In the simplest language," according to one newspaper report, "the proposed structure will consist of two cantilever bridges sustaining between them a suspension bridge."

The idea was to have the best of both worlds. By reducing the length of the suspension section, engineers could overcome what they believed at the time to be an insurmountable problem: No suspension bridge had yet been built that was more than 1,600 feet long, and the distance that had to be covered across the bay was nearly four times that length. The hybrid design would reduce the length of the suspension portion to a more manageable (if still unprecedented) 2,640 feet, with the cantilever design bearing more of the load on either end. Two towers were envisioned even then, as they were in the final plan, and the newspaper report boasted that the design had "the endorsement of the leading bridge engineers in the country."

There was just one problem: It was ugly as hell. One local writer said it "seemed to strain its way across the Golden Gate," describing it as "a ponderous, blunt bridge that combined a heavy tinker toy frame at each end with a short suspension span."

Fortunately for the San Francisco skyline—and those of us destined to admire it—the hybrid design was scrapped in the late 1920s when engineers demonstrated that a suspension bridge spanning the entire length of the crossing was, in fact, feasible after all.

But engineering wasn't the only hurdle that had to be overcome. By 1930, the proposal had attracted 2,300 lawsuits seeking to stop it. Famed Yosemite photographer Ansel Adams and the Sierra Club thought the bridge would be a blot on the area's natural scenery. And the Southern Pacific Railroad had a very big stake in the game: It owned majority stock in the ferry company that transported cars from one side of the bay to the other.

But the ferry itself was part of the problem. The public was getting fed up with enduring the long waits and jam-packed boats that were the by-product of ever-increasing vehicle traffic across the bay. A 1930 campaign pamphlet for the bond measure that would fund the Golden Gate Bridge lamented that the ferry system had "reached its saturation point" even with ferries "closely packed" to an average capacity of 73 vehicles.

"The congestion at the Marin shore due to inadequate transportation across the bay has caused thousands of motorists great delay and inconvenience on Sundays and holidays," the brochure declared. "The ferry schedules cannot be increased without immense cost and even then the inadequacy of ferries as compared with a Golden Gate bridge is apparent to all."

So, after a decade of planning, they built that bridge—and it wasn't just any bridge, either. The orange suspension bridge with its instantly recognizable twin towers became the symbol of San Francisco, photographed more than any other bridge in the country, its silhouette emblazoned on everything from souvenir T-shirts to the uniforms of the NBA's Golden State Warriors. It didn't come cheap, though: It cost a whopping $74 million (including $39 million in interest), and it also cost 11 construction workers their lives.

It could have been worse: Safety netting broke the fall of 19 other workers who lost their footing and plummeted toward the bay—creating what was known as the "Halfway to Hell Club." Of the 11 who did perish, 10 of them died when a scaffold fell and ripped through the netting, leaving nothing between them and the water below.

When it was built, the Golden Gate was taller than any building in San Francisco, the roadway itself suspended by a pair of cables more than 7,600 feet long. More lives were lost, tragically, but not because of any safety problems with the bridge. Instead, the fatalities—an estimated 1,600 of them as of 2012—were due to suicide leaps from the bridge's lofty

Workers toil on the partially completed Golden Gate Bridge in 1935. *Public domain.*

span. When it comes to safety, though, the engineers got it right: The bridge not only survived the 1989 Loma Prieta earthquake unscathed, it withstood an unprecedented number of vehicles that crossed in the wake of the disaster. On October 27, 1989, a record 162,414 cars traversed the bridge heading both directions.

In all, more than 2 billion (yes, *billion*) vehicles have crossed the bridge during its history. And not only that, the bridge isn't the eyesore it might have been had the original design been implemented, but a soaring monument to grace and style.

One interesting note: Even though traffic on both sides of the bridge enters it from U.S. 101, the bridge itself isn't technically part of the highway, which ends at the north abutment of the bridge and 1,000 feet south of the bridge toll plaza. Still, it's a key part of the highway's history, providing a vital link from north to south and from past to present.

9

THE REDWOOD HIGHWAY

Just a little north of San Francisco, U.S. 101 reaches the northernmost of California's 21 missions—San Francisco de Solano in Sonoma County—and stops being El Camino Real. Northward, it's the Redwood Highway.

It's not hard to see why.

The heart of that drive takes you through one of the most breathtaking stretches of countryside you're likely to see, featuring views of old-growth redwoods whose history far predates that of the road itself or the motorcars that traverse it.

In 1922, P. A. McFarland of Concord told the *Oakland Tribune* of the beauty he found on the northern section of this road, between Eureka and the Oregon state line: "From Eureka to Crescent City, the route winds through virgin redwood forests much of the way. In many places the road is cut out of the side of the cliffs which drop off, almost sheer into the ocean. On the one side is a great forest of redwood and on the other the sea pounding against the cliffs."

That estimation hasn't changed today, with travelers and road enthusiasts remarking at the highway's beauty throughout the Redwood Empire, as it is known.

The Redwood Tree Service Station is still an eye-catching sight in Ukiah.

The road itself, however, wasn't always easy to drive.

Harvey M. Harper was reportedly the first man to see the redwoods from the front seat of his car when he drove his Model T from Phoenix to Eureka in 1912. It took him 40 days to get there, but he must have liked what he saw, because he founded one of the country's oldest Ford dealerships in Eureka that same year. His son, Harvey G. Harper, who inherited the business, recalled what his

A car traverses the old road in Del Norte County in 1925.
© California Department of Transportation, all rights reserved. Used with permission.

father had told him about the trip, made six years before the younger Harper was born.

His father, he said, used a shovel to clear a path around the giant trees so his car wouldn't get stuck on the muddy trail.

Later, his father took the family on picnic trips some 70 miles south to Twin Trees, near Benbow on the Eel River. Even then, in the 1920s, the road was little more than a dirt-and-gravel path that spewed forth clouds of dirt and dust as the car traversed it.

"My mother said she could never live in southern Humboldt [County because] it was too dusty," the younger Harper said. "Further south, Mendocino County even had a law against automobiles for a while, when noisy engines spooked horses."

Harper added that his father "sold tractors and road equipment to the Highway 101 crews that improved the road over the years: It was tough country, and they went through a lot of equipment to build the road back then."

Another section of the old highway between Ukiah and Willits was so narrow and winding that "you could get stuck behind a truck for what seemed like forever," Harvey G. Harper recalled.

Farther south, dirt wasn't the problem; marshland was. According to *A History of Corte Madera*, roadbuilders laid in a section of U.S. 101 directly across the North Bay marshes of Marin County. When waters sometimes rose with the tide on both sides of the thoroughfare, worried drivers were eager to get to the other side. A quarter-mile bridge across Richardson Bay was built in 1931 using, appropriately enough, redwood.

"It was built out of redwood timbers, supposedly to last hundreds of years," Caltrans historian Alicia Whitten said of the Redwood Bridge, "but just 25 years later, in 1956, it was replaced with a much wider steel and concrete structure."

A trip up the coast from the North Bay to Eureka would take you a couple of days in the early 1920s—compared to maybe six hours today—but with so much scenery to take in, it wasn't a trip most travelers were inclined to rush. A. J. Beckett, one of the proprietors of an Oakland distributing company, sang the praises of the roadway in 1922:

"From Willits north the scenic country begins. The road climbs up and down among the mountains there with easy grades and fine traveled roads all the way to Eureka. … From Cummings, about 40 miles above Willits, the road follows the Eel River most of the way to Eureka, and the scenery is well worthwhile.

If you take along a camping outfit you should be sure and have enough blankets, because the nights are chilly there, even if the elevation is not so great.

There are many places to stop along the road. Most of the resorts run the year round. They are really hunting lodges, because there always is some sort of game in season in Mendocino and Humboldt counties."

The old highway through the heart of Petaluma.

PETALUMA TO WILLITS

Of course, the road wasn't the same as it is today. As with other highways, alignments were upgraded and bypassed with straighter, wider roads.

Traveling north, the old highway went straight through Petaluma on Petaluma Boulevard until it was bypassed in 1956. Among the sights of note there are the old Mystic Theatre, a vaudeville house that opened in January 1912 and played host to a scene from *American Graffiti*, and the Hotel Petaluma, which welcomed its first guests 12 years later.

The hotel was Petaluma's love letter to the world. More than 1 in 10 of the town's residents—850 in all—pooled their resources and came up with $250,000 of the $350,000 needed to build the establishment, which served not only as a hotel but a hub of social activity in the community. A bronze placard at the hotel declared, "It stands as evidence and proof of the faith which the people of Petaluma have in each other and in their city."

Petaluma was known as "the World's Egg Basket" for good reason. The 1939 WPA Guide noted that the roads leading into town were "often clogged by trucks heavily loaded with crates of eggs and white leghorns," adding that "the slopes around town echo with the cackle of hundreds of thousands of chickens." So devoted was the town to its fowl pursuit that it even had a chicken pharmacy.

The highway was a perfect location for shipping the town's most renowned product to the world at large. So, in 1927, Bill McCarter chose a spot just north of town in

The historic Mystic Theatre and Music Hall in downtown Petaluma was built in 1911 and is still open.

Penngrove as the site for his new "electric hatchery." By the time he sold the brick building in 1944, McCarter's Penngrove Hatchery had a laying capacity of about 360,000 eggs in a day. Mechanical incubators turned the eggs, a trayful at a time, and the chicks hatched there were nurtured in heated brooders. The building ceased being used as a hatchery sometime in the late 20th century and later became a saddle shop.

In the same area was the Green Mill Inn, which started out as a roadside stand selling (surprise) chicken, along with fruit pies. It soon expanded to include a dining room that hosted various social functions. A 1932 ad in the *Petaluma Argus-Courier* said you could get either chicken and dumplings or a roast goose dinner for 75 cents.

"By the 1940s, it was a popular spot for upscale dining and dancing," said U.S. 101 historian Dan Young. "In the '60s, I loved going there with my family, because every meal included unlimited trips to the generous smorgasbord. Couples looking for a romantic evening could take advantage of two private dining rooms."

Young said the restaurant closed in the 1980s and has stood idle ever since, but "if you stop and peek through the curtains, you'll see the tables in the dining room still laid for dinner."

The Old Redwood Highway heads north into Cotati, another old poultry town, after which the it makes its way through Santa Rosa as Santa Rosa and Mendocino Avenues. As you entered town from the south, you'd come upon the inevitable row of motels, auto courts, and service stations eager for your business. Most are gone, but at least one, the 1950s-era Monte Vista Motel, was still open for business as of this writing.

On the right, just before you hit downtown, is the Santa Rosa Marketplace, a modern outdoor shopping center anchored by various big-box stores. In earlier times, though, it was the site of the El Rancho Tropicana (did every town along the highway have an inn called the El Rancho?). With 180 "deluxe hotel units," 14 banquet and meeting rooms,

and the requisite 24-hour coffee shop, it billed itself in a 1966 newspaper ad as "the finest deluxe hotel, restaurant and cocktail lounge in the Redwood Empire."

Whether that claim was true or hyperbolic, the Oakland Raiders weren't about to argue. In fact, they had a hand in making the El Rancho what it was.

From 1963 to 1984, the motel served as the pro football team's summer headquarters. The team was still a member of the upstart American Football League, and Al Davis—who was just 33 at the time—had just taken over as the team's head coach and general manager when he drove up Highway 101 and came upon the El Rancho Tropicana. Other teams held their summer training camps on college campuses, but Davis wanted his players to get out of Oakland as they prepped for the coming season, and the El Rancho seemed to him like the perfect place.

The Raiders set up a locker room and had practice fields behind the hotel (where an Office Depot now stands), and they studied films of the practices in the motel's conference rooms. They had their own section of the motel: An annex out back with a central courtyard, it was dubbed "the Zoo." The players were encouraged to stay away from the guests in the main area of the motel, but they'd ignore that advice to hang out beside one of the three pools—where swimsuit-clad female guests were, not coincidentally, also known to congregate.

Look closely: This home a couple of blocks off U.S. 101 in Santa Rosa is actually a converted Richfield Beacon station.

"I worked at a gas station across the street, which has since been demolished," Dan Young recalled. "Some of the team used to come in to the store—not the first-string guys, though. But anyone could go behind the motel and watch them practice, there was no security or anything."

The motel grew during the Raiders' tenure there from a 25-room horseshoe-shaped motor inn to a 275-room complex. The Raiders kept training there for three years after Davis moved the team south to L.A. in 1982, then looked to the El Rancho again when he moved the team back to Oakland in '95. But the old motel had been torn down just months earlier.

The old highway's name changes from Santa Rosa Avenue to Mendocino Avenue near the center of town. For a quick detour, head east for a block on Chanate Road and turn right on Lomitas Avenue. One house down from the corner on the west side of the street is a house whose architecture might look familiar. That's because the house is actually a converted Richfield Beacon station (in the southern Spanish mission style). No gas pumps. No tower. Just your standard landscaping out front and an SUV in the driveway.

The Old Redwood Highway continues north of Santa Rosa and morphs into Healdsburg Avenue through the community of the same name. Before you get to town, you'll pass what's left of a 1920s-era roadhouse called Windsor Castle. It just looks like a two-story residence these days, but the old-style wooden overhang in the front betrays what used to be the gas pump island. It also gives the place its "castle" feel.

"Like most nightclubs at that time it was a speakeasy, with liquor available if you knew the password," Dan

This 1920s-era roadhouse in Healdsburg, north of Santa Rosa, was known as Windsor Castle.

Young said. "It continued to operate into the '50s, with a coffee shop and some cabins in the back. Today all that's left is the building which once housed the gas station."

A mile and a half farther north, the road passes under a 1915 railroad crossing, one of the few landmarks in the area that predate the 101 designation. Another bridge—one that carries the cars on the old highway across the Russian River—marks the entrance to Healdsburg. The 1921 Pennsylvania truss bridge was renovated at a cost of $12 million in 2015, with the upgrade including bridge lamps made in the style used during the Roaring Twenties.

Pick's Drive In in Cloverdale has been operating since 1923.

The bridge nearly didn't make it to the 21st century: Caltrans gave it a poor safety rating in 1979, and there was talk of tearing it down. But the agency eventually withdrew that rating, saying it had been faulty and the bridge was safe to carry legal loads.

From Healdsburg north, the highway grows more rural, with fewer subdivisions and more farms and vineyards lining the road, called Geyserville Avenue through that small community and Cloverdale Boulevard farther on. When you hit Cloverdale, you'll get a look at a couple of old eateries on the old alignment through the downtown area. The Owl Café is closed now, but when I drove by, it still sported a vintage neon sign in the shape of its avian namesake, and the tables inside were set as if the next lunch crowd was about to arrive.

Pick's Drive In at First Street in the center of town has been around even longer, dating back to 1923, and is still in business.

If you go another mile north, you'll hit the junction with State Route 128, where you'll want to turn left, away from the current highway. This road will take you northwest up into the hills to Mountain House Estate, at which point you'll veer north again on the winding Mountain

House Road. While it may seem unlikely, this was the U.S. 101 Alignment until roughly 1934. Dan Young describes the drive:

> For the next nine miles, you will experience motoring as it was almost one hundred years ago. This is a lightly traveled route. In fact, you may not meet another vehicle until you reach Hopland where the old route converges again with the modern highway. You'll enjoy some pretty scenery, including cow pastures, vineyards and acres of moss-laden trees.

You'll cross a couple of old bridges, too, although they don't stand out and it would be easy to drive on through without even noticing them. One dates to 1913 and another, near the entrance to the Red Barn Ranch, was built a year earlier and upgraded in '32. Both dates are stamped into the bridge's concrete, and Young says it's the only bridge he's ever seen with two dates stamped in the same place.

North of Cloverdale, the two main stops before the redwoods are Ukiah and Willits.

In Ukiah, the old alignment follows State Street, where you'll find such landmarks as the Ukiah Theater and the Redwood Tree Service Station.

The Willits sign welcomes U.S. 101 travelers to the northern California city, which has since been bypassed by a new freeway alignment that opened in late 2016.

Willits, a few miles north of Ukiah, offers proof that highway bypasses are still being constructed, even into the 21st century. The Willits Bypass finally opened to traffic in November 2016, six decades after it was originally proposed. Construction began in 2012, and the project cost $300 million to complete. You can still take the old alignment through town, of course, passing beneath the distinctive neon-lit Willits arch just south of the junction with State Route 20.

INTO THE TREES

Heading north into the hills, it was more of a challenge to build the highway. If you want evidence, all you have to do is look at a couple of viaducts that hug the hillsides—sections of highway no longer in use. One's still mostly intact, and the other is now mostly not.

The first one—the "mostly intact" one—is the Sidehill Viaduct, which Young also referred to as "The Tilt-A-Whirl," "the Roller Coaster," "the Slab" and "the Rock Star of Old 101." It's about 90 years old, and it's been out of service for the last 30 years of that. You might have to walk over or past some rocks that have slid down from the hillside, but you can still walk the length of it

at this writing. Much of the old concrete railing is still intact, and you can peer out beyond it to the Eel River below and the modern highway. You can also tell how difficult it would have been for two-way traffic, especially trucks, to pass this way.

"Imagine driving out onto this narrow viaduct on a pitch black rainy night, coming around the bend and finding a lumber truck bearing down on you," Young said. "I experienced this myself in the 1970s multiple times."

The second old viaduct is just a mile farther north. Turn off the highway at the longtime tourist stop called Confusion Hill and keep going to the end of the parking lot. You're actually driving on the old highway here, but there's a gate at the far end that keeps you from going any farther. If you want, though, you can get out and walk past the gate. You can go a short distance on foot along the old highway pavement before it starts to disappear beneath sticker-filled grass (if you do this, be sure to bring extra shoes and socks), along with newly planted trees in the middle of the old route that are being used to reclaim the land—and help hold it in place.

There's a reason this mountainside is called the "Confusion Hill Slide": In the days when the highway used this route, the rainy season caused frequent mudslides and road damage—and closures. Between 1997 and 2006, Caltrans spent an estimated $33 million clearing away debris that had fallen down onto the road. Today, much of the old viaduct is gone, having slid down the hill into the canyon below, but you can look across from this vantage point and see the bridge that carries the modern highway, towering over the south fork of the Eel River below.

The majestic south bridge towers 255 feet above the river. Two bridges were actually built to span the river over a quarter-mile distance, with the pair being completed in 2009 at a cost of $67 million.

Despite its impressive height, the south span isn't the highest bridge on Old 101. An open-spandrel concrete arch called the Cedar Creek Bridge actually rises 291 feet, farther above the creek for which it's named than the Golden Gate is above San Francisco Bay. It's part of a section of highway—now State Route 271—through Leggett that dates back to 1917, when prison laborers from San Quentin were conscripted to do the work.

To get a better look at the abandoned Confusion Hill viaduct, your best bet is to drive to the north end of the bridge, take an immediate right onto the other end of the old highway, and follow it back south as far as you can. It eventually stops, and from there, you can hike out onto a section of the abandoned viaduct that's still intact. You'll see where some of the aforementioned trees have been planted, and runoff has cut into the flat area in at least one place. Farther on, some of the old railing is still in place. But a word of warning: This is nothing like the Sidehill Viaduct, and I wouldn't recommend going too far. You'll see plenty of rockslides on the hill, and you don't want to end up at the bottom of a new one. At a certain point, you won't be able to make it any farther without losing the road entirely, and it may not be many years before the entire area is impassible on foot.

FLOOD OF THE MILLENNIUM

The Confusion Hill Viaduct hasn't been the only victim of geology and the elements along the Redwood Highway.

Entire portions of the highway built during the first half of the 20th century are gone for good—not only because of bypasses and new alignments but, in some cases, because they were literally washed away.

In the winter of 1964, Mother Nature came calling before Santa could get his sleigh packed up and delivered

This photo taken from the Confusion Hill Viaduct shows the stone guardrail from the old, overgrown alignment in the foreground and the new, state-of-the-art span in the distance.

the kind of "gift" North Coast residents would never dream of putting on their Christmas lists. This wasn't any ordinary lump of coal. It was a full-on tirade, the likes of which no one in the area had ever seen.

Nine years earlier, almost to the day, the area had endured "the storm of the century."

If that was the case, this was the storm of the millennium.

The 1955 storms were still fresh in the memories of local residents. They remembered the flood warnings issued on December 18 of that year, followed in short order by the floods themselves. It was worst along U.S. 101, which ran parallel to the Eel River, and the Redwood Empire stood defenseless against the river's onslaught as it escaped its banks and inundated the highway.

A federal report on the flood of '55 tallied the damage:

Splintered wood and debris lie strewn alongside the highway in Klamath after the catastrophic flood of 1955. © *California Department of Transportation, all rights reserved. Used with permission.*

"The high-velocity flow carrying heavy debris either flattened buildings or swept them from their foundations," the report read. The lumber industry took the heaviest damage, "as facilities were destroyed and large stocks of logs and finished lumber were swept away." A photo taken near Fernbridge showed the Eel River having taken a Godzilla-sized bite out of old Highway 101, at one point consuming the entire southbound lane of asphalt.

The communities of Stafford, Elinor Pepperwood, Shively, South Fork, Myers Flat, Phillipsville, and Bull Creek were "devastated," the report read.

Word arrived of people clinging to the rooftops of houses and even barns that were being swept away by the river's fury. The torrent did even more damage by sweeping up cut logs and slamming them into the sides of buildings that still clung to their foundations. Roads were so severely damaged that communities found themselves isolated for weeks after the storm, and residents couldn't even get word out to family members because the phone lines were down, too. Even the

massive redwoods were no match for the floodwaters. Trees as thick as 15 feet in diameter collapsed, unable to stay upright in the saturated earth, with as many as 500 fallen trees clogging Bull Creek.

Livestock was swept away and perished by the hundreds. A skating rink in Scotia was destroyed, never to be rebuilt, and a similar fate was feared for the historic Stafford Inn, which had been built as a bunk house in the late 19th century by lumber mill owner (and town founder) Percy Brown. Before the flood, the inn had advertised "the finest cuisine in a traditionally hospitable setting," with a complete dinner of pork chops in charcuterie sauce with water chestnuts for a mere $3. But afterward, a New Year's Eve headline in the *Humboldt Times* had to reassure its readers: "Stafford Inn Still There."

"All during the big flood, and even afterwards, stories continued to filter out that the Stafford Inn had disappeared," the *Times* reported. "Topping off its experience of having the river all around it, the Stafford Inn is holding its final night of the current season this evening."

The inn did, indeed survive the flood of '55—only to be destroyed nine years later in a deluge that made its predecessor seem gentle by comparison.

There were warning signs before the big storm hit. Earlier storms had moved through the area in November, softening up hillsides and feeding rivers and streams around the area. A high-pressure system had choked off the flow of storms in early December, but then it began to weaken, and as it did, it gave way to a new storm track nearly 500 miles wide, extending from Hawaii to Northern California.

The band of clouds heading in from the tropics was flush with precipitation just waiting to be delivered to the north end of the state.

The first rains fell from December 15 to 20 and on December 18, the National Weather Service sounded the alarm, issued flood warnings for the days ahead, and urged area ranchers to evacuate their livestock.

Then the second storm hit December 21 to 24.

The results were devastating.

In 1955, the highest single-day rainfall total in Garberville had been 3.23 inches in 1955; the top figure in '64 was more than 2½ times that amount: 8.29 inches. More than 4 inches fell in '64 near the mouth of the Smith River, just off the highway a few miles south of the Oregon border. That was significantly more than the 2.74 inches recorded there nine years earlier, but also much less than fell in the mountains, where swollen headwaters fueled the frantic floodwaters' rush downhill to meet the ocean.

By midday on December 21, water from the Eel River was 8 inches over Fish Creek Bridge near Benbow, site of the historic Benbow Inn. The Tudor-style lodge just off the highway that opened in 1926—the same year the highway was designated U.S. 101—and attracted the likes of Basil Rathbone, Joan Fontaine, Clark Gable, Herbert Hoover, Alan Ladd, Charles Laughton, Eleanor Roosevelt and Spencer Tracy in its heyday.

The inn itself survived the flood, even as mud and debris choked off the highway.

An Arcata High School teacher named Erling Daastol watched events unfold from a trailer at the H and H trailer park in Stafford, just below U.S. 101, on September 22, 1964. He and a friend had spent the previous night in the

trailer, taking a "wait and see" approach, but when they awoke the next morning, the water was rising steadily—about a foot and a half each hour.

"At about noon, the river water seemed to be breaking through the woods over by Stafford Inn, heading for the trailer court and the area around Kemp's grocery store," Daastol wrote. "My friend and I hooked up the trailer and headed up the hill toward the P. L. logging road. It was high time. The water was right below the pan of our pickup."

Their wheels were stuck in the mud, but a red-haired gentleman, known to Daastol only as "Red," managed to pull them out using a four-wheel-drive Jeep and parked it up the hill. He repeated the procedure with two other trailers and a Lincoln. But by the time he got to the third and final trailer at the park, he didn't have enough time to secure it using the trailer hitch. So, he "threw a heavy chain around the tongue of the trailer and floated the trailer out of the water," Daastol recalled. "The water was so high that the top of the wheels of the Jeep was under water. The top of the river was approaching the highway now. Kemp's grocery and the homes immediately below the road were filling with water."

Daastol joined others in rushing to remove the owners' belongings.

"Want us to get anything?" he asked Kemp, the owner of the grocery store.

"There are some clothes on top of the TV. Get them."

"How about the TV?"

"Let the river have it."

A short time later, the red-haired man returned, this time in a motorboat, carrying a family to safety. By late afternoon, Daaston said, the water was well above the highway in front of Kemp's and was continuing to rise.

"Into the evening and night we could hear the eerie boom-boom—sounds as logs and houses hit the two bridges crossing 101 below Stafford," he recalled. "At about 10 p.m., we heard a tremendous crash, and we assumed that one or both of the bridges had collapsed."

The river crested during the night, and the next day, Daaston and his friend were airlifted from Scotia to Eureka in time to spend Christmas Eve with their families.

The Douglas Memorial Bridge, with its iconic bear guardians, was closed after a massive flood destroyed the 1926 span. A new bridge was later rebuilt, with new bears. *Library of Congress, public domain.*

By then, five people had been killed and 5,000 others evacuated in the flooding, as Gov. Pat Brown declared disaster areas in Mendocino, Shasta, Del Norte, and Humboldt Counties. The highway was so badly damaged that the president of the Redwood Highway Association predicted it would take a month to reopen it to traffic and twice that long to make it suitable for trucks. A Christmas morning photo on the front page of the *Humboldt Standard* displayed evidence of the floods' brutality. The caption declared that "the new highway from Fernbridge to Ferndale is demolished, completely ruined by the Eel and Van Duzen Rivers, which flooded this week."

Ginger Nunes of Fortuna later recalled the experience of sitting in her Fortuna home along the Eel River as a log smashed through a window and debris threatened to cave in the kitchen wall. Two men in boats managed to rescue her family, but not before one of the boats nearly capsized in the effort.

When the rains finally stopped during the first week in January, residents and highway workers alike surveyed the damage. In Pepperwood, a town of about 400 people along the highway, just two or three ruined buildings were still standing by the time the waters receded. Several thousand logs had been swept away from the Pacific Lumber Company in Scotia, and railroad boxcars were "tossed around like dice thrown from a cup," according to a California Highways report.

The final toll: 29 people killed and nearly 1,700 injured, along with 5,000 head of livestock. More than 4,700 homes destroyed, in addition to 374 businesses and 800 farm buildings. Some 4,000 lumber mill employees were out of a job.

Seven bridges along the Redwood Highway were among the eighteen destroyed. One casualty was a concrete arch bridge over the Klamath River famous for its statues of California bears on either end. The town

The Fortuna Theatre, built in 1938, is still open, housing six theaters in downtown Fortuna.

This undated historical photo shows a car pulled over at the side of the Redwood Highway. © *California Department of Transportation, all rights reserved. Used with permission.*

of Klamath itself lost its entire business section to the floodwaters. Mudslides—some containing half a million yards of earth—buried the highway at numerous points. Still, thanks to a herculean effort from state highway workers, it took a little less than a month to reopen the road: On January 16, a highway patrol truck convoy dubbed Operation Lifeline cleared U.S. 101 to one-way traffic between San Francisco and the Oregon state line.

"Highway construction crews cut out a road in raw mud along the hillside to bypass the slides and hauled in rock to give the vehicles some degree of traction," California Highways engineer Sam Helwer said. "We have equipment there, four-wheel-drive motor graders, to pull out vehicles if they get stuck, and our people will continue to improve the one-way road so we can lift restrictions."

AVENUE OF THE GIANTS AND BEYOND

Most of the communities nestled among the redwoods aren't full-blown cities; some are towns, some are villages, and others still are little more than road stops. Along the Avenue of the Giants, a 30-mile stretch of road that used to be 101, you'll pass through places like Phillipsville with its 140 residents and Miranda (formerly known as Jacobsen's), a community of 520 people. Later, you'll hit Myers Flat, population 146, and Redcrest, population 89. But the most notable residents along this area of two-lane highway are the redwoods themselves, bathing the road in dappled sunlight in some places and shading it entirely in others.

Back on the new highway, you'll hit Fortuna, where the old alignment veers due north from the Kenmar Road turnoff as Fortuna Boulevard, east of the freeway, then curls back east as Main Street through the old downtown. Tomkins Hill Road, which provides access to the College of the Redwoods just south of Eureka, was also once a section of the main highway. Now, it parallels the modern 101 to the east.

An old alignment of U.S. 101, Endert's Beach Road, enters Crescent City from the south. *Library of Congress.*

From Eureka, the road heads north through Arcata, a city of some 17,000 people with a name that sounds suspiciously like Arcadia—which is also in California, but way down in Los Angeles County, close to the other end of the state. It's easy to be tricked into thinking Eureka's right on the Oregon border, but it's not. There're nearly 90 miles more to travel before you get there, and Arcata's your first stop. Originally known as Union Town, it's home to Humboldt State University. G Street, which swings west as you're traveling northward, is just a two-lane road but is probably the original routing of U.S. 101.

North of Arcata is McKinleyville, an unincorporated town of about 15,000 that includes an old alignment of 101 called Central Avenue. It crosses under the modern freeway north of town and continues on the ocean side as Clam Beach Drive.

Scenic Drive, a two-lane, heavily wooded, and winding road that morphs into Patrick's Point Drive, may be another remnant of Old 101.

Crescent City, the only incorporated city in Del Norte County, is the last major stop before the border. Its population, which is shy of 8,000, includes the inmate population of Pelican State Prison. A segment of Old 101 enters town from the south as Endert's Beach Road, while the modern 101 splits in two through the center of town, with northbound traffic heading one way on three-lane M Street and southbound traffic a block west on L Street. The town itself is so small that this bifurcation lasts just about a mile before the two sides reconverge and head on to Smith River, a community of fewer than 1,000 people just this side of the state line.

There, U.S. 101 crosses into Oregon as the Oregon Coast Highway, and there we end our tour. There's plenty more to discover northward, but that's another story, another journey, another road.

REFERENCES

"About the BCWRR," Bitter Creek Western Railroad, www.bcwrr .org.

ACR 97, Amended in the California Assembly, Jan. 4, 2006, relative to Alex Madonna Memorial Highway, www.leginfo.ca.gov /pub/05-06/bill/asm/ab_0051-0100/acr_97_bill_20060228 _amended_asm.html.

Allan, Lon. "Century Plaza was built on holey ground," *San Luis Obispo Tribune*, p. B1, Oct. 3, 2006.

"All-Year Highway on Oregon Coast Urged," *Oakland Tribune*, p. 45, Mar. 23, 1919.

"Andersen's pea soup puts small city on map," *Tuscaloosa News*, p. 41, Mar. 2, 1982.

Anderson, Frank. "Stars of Jungleland Just Animals Again," *Long Beach Independent*, p. 13, Oct. 10, 1969.

Anderson, Glenda. "Willits Highway 101 bypass finally opens to traffic," *Santa Rosa Press Democrat*, Nov. 3, 2016. www .pressdemocrat.com.

Arellano, Gustavo. "How Doritos Were Born at Disneyland," *OC Weekly*, Apr. 5, 2012, ocweekly.com.

"Atlantic Richfield Company History," www.fundinguniverse.com.

"Auto Falls Off the Conejo Grade," *Bakersfield Californian*, p. 1, Nov. 3, 1910.

"Backgammon title to Stephens," *Long Beach Independent Press-Telegram*, p. S-4, July 11, 1976.

Baney, Lisa. "The great flood of 1955," *Scotia Independent*, p. 1, Oct. 28, 2014.

Barber, Phil. "When Raiders Ruled," *Santa Rosa Press-Democrat*, Aug. 19, 2007. www.pressdemocrat.com.

"Barnsdall-Rio Grande Oil Company," Primarily Petroliana, Apr. 7, 2006, www.oldgas.com.

"Barricade Is Erected at Ice Company," *San Bernardino County Sun*, p. 2, Sept. 12, 1936.

Bartlett, James. "Hollywood Bowl's Secret Backstage History," *LA Weekly*, June 3, 2011, www.laweekly.com.

"Benbow Inn—About Us," www.benbowinn.com.

Benson, Lee. "About Utah: Old barn still stands, ad and all," *Deseret News*, Nov. 3, 2011, www.deseretnews.com.

Billiter, Bill. "City Looking Up Ways to Seize 'Encyclopedia Lots,'" *Los Angeles Times*, Oct. 28, 1990, articles.latimes.com.

"'Black Rain' from Fire in Oil Field," *Frederick* (Md.) *News*, p. 2, Apr. 9, 1926.

Blitz, Matt. "The Bum Brigade," Today I Found Out, Aug. 15, 2014, www.todayifoundout.com

Blocker, John. "Luther Gage: Father of Carlsbad's Flower Fields," Growing Grounds, July-Aug. 2010, www.sdfloral.org.

"Boutique Paso Robles Area Hotel History," www.the-carlton.com.

Bowers, H. Dana. "Stately Campanile Erected on Highway in Honor of Old Mission," *California Highways and Public Works*, p. 6, January 1938.

Brakken, Suzi. "Can't see the trees for the forest," *Ukiah Daily Journal*, p. 3, Oct. 19, 1986.

Brenoff, Ann. "Dig into history, you'll strike snake oil," *Los Angeles Times*, Feb. 10, 2008.

Bridgehunter.com.

"Bridge Plan Colossal," *Los Angeles Times*, p. 1, Dec. 28, 1922.

Brigandi, Paul. "Breaking New Ground: The Early Years of Knott's Berry Farm," *The Branding Iron*, Summer 2008, www .orangecountyhistory.org.

Broggie, Michael. *Walt Disney's Railroad Story*, p. 195, Pentrix/ Donning, 1997, 2005, 2006.

"Build Aerial Road: Toboggan Railway for Ocean Park," *Los Angeles Herald*, part 3, p. 8, July 17, 1904.

"Building of Highway One, The," Cambria Historical Society, cambriahistoricalsociety.com.

"Bum Blockade, The—Stopping the Invasion of Depression Refugees," California Legends, www.legendsofamerica.com.

"Calabasas Garage is Looted by Bandit Gang," *Oxnard Press-Courier*, p. 1, May 13, 1921.

"California, Oregon Roads Still Blocked," *Humboldt Standard*, p. 1, Dec. 25, 1964.

"Camino Robbed of Auto Traffic by Plot, Claim," *San Mateo Times*, p. 1, Dec. 23, 1937.

"Campbell Bros. World Famous Confusion Hill," www.confusionhill .com.

Capon, Sally. "Ellwood shelling caused wartime panic," Roadside Attractions, *Santa Ynez Valley News*, Mar. 22, 2012, syvnews .com.

Capra, Paglo. "Topanga Ranch Motel Residents Get 30-Day Notice," *Topanga Messenger*, July 29, 2004, topangamessenger.com.

Carneytrain.com.

"Carrousel Chronology, A" *Los Angeles Times*, Mar. 24, 1985.

Caskey, Melissa. "La Salsa Mexican Restaurant Closing Next Week," Feb. 5, 2015, www.malibutimes.com.

Chandelier Drive-Thru Tree, www.drivethrutree.com.

Cheney, Jim. "Dr. Pierce's Golden Medical Discovery," activerain, May 13, 2010, www.activerain.com.

Christine, Bill. "Jockeying for Position," *Los Angeles Times*, Aug. 12, 1988. articles.latimes.com.

Cinematreasures.org.

Clovis, Margaret E. *Salinas Valley*, Arcadia Publishing, 2005.

Cole, D. L. *The Beacon Story*, Olive Press Publications, 2000.

Connell, Sally Ann. "Plan to Remake Roadside Strip Means Santa Better Watch Out," *Los Angeles Times*, p. 38, May 30, 1999.

Coombs, Gary B. and Olsen, Phyllis J. "Sentinel at Ellwood: The Barnsdall-Rio Grande Gasoline Station," Institute for American Research, 1985.

Cornejo, AnnMarie. "Plans for Tank Farm property near SLO include open space, business park," *San Luis Obispo Tribune*, Sept. 3, 2014.

———. "Public market envisioned at historic Long-Bonetti Ranch in San Luis Obispo," *San Luis Obispo Tribune*, Sept. 6, 2014. sanluisobispo.com.

"Cowboy Vigilantes Patrol Strike Area," *Santa Ana Register*, p. 1, Sept. 12, 1936.

Cuda, Heidi Siegmund. "New Ups and Downs for Santa Monica," *Los Angeles Times*, p. F1, May 23, 1996.

De Turenne, Veronique. "Santa Monica's pier and carousel: a long and circular tale," *Los Angeles Times*, July 26, 2009. articles .latimes.com.

"Den vs. Hollister Case,, The" Price, Postel and Parma LLP, www .ppplaw.com.

"Diamond Tires Are Sold in Tustin, Too," *Santa Ana Register*, p. 13, Jan. 16, 1929.

Diehl, Phil. "Oceanside natives sell historic 101 Café," *San Diego Union-Tribune*, Mar. 11, 2016, sandiegouniontribune.com.

"Donated Backbone Fossil Being Studied at SAC," *Los Angeles Times*, part IX, p. 10, Jan. 2, 1955.

Dorothea Lange, International Photography Hall of Fame, www .iphf.org.

Dotson, Bob. "American Story: 'Moa Lisa' of Dust Bowl 'never lost hope,'" www.today.com.

"Double-Barreled Probe Into Bus-Train Tragedy," *Santa Cruz Sentinel*, p. 18, Sept. 19, 1963.

"Dr. and Mrs. Pillsbury killed on Casitas Pass," *Oxnard Courier*, p. 3, Sept. 8, 1911.

"Dr. Pierce's Alternative Extract or Golden Medical Discovery," The National Museum of American History, americanhistory.si.edu.

Drake, Jerry. "Lion Training: All in Day's Work for Lass," *Naples Daily News*, p. D1, Mar. 7, 1976.

Drive-ins.com.

"Early Views of the Hollywood Bowl," Water and Power Associates, waterandpower.org.

"Eight Killed, 40 Injured In Bus, Auto Collision," *Santa Cruz Sentinel*, p. 11, Aug. 18, 1964.

"1880—San Diego's County Fair is born," delmarfairgrounds.com.

"El Camino Real a Fake," *Oakland Tribune*, p. 6, Aug. 21, 1906.

"Evolution of the Conejo Grade in Ventura County Over the Last 100 Years," Conejo Valley Guide, conejovalleyguide.com.

"Eye-witness Story From Stafford," *Humboldt Standard*, p. 6, Dec. 28, 1964.

"Face that symbolized Depression now dying," *Paris News*, p. 7, Aug. 24, 1983.

Facebook.com/pg/Fjords-Smorg-ette.

Feldman, Ellen. "Lights Out on an Era," *Los Angeles Times*, Nov. 19, 1991, articles.latimes.com.

Ferrell, David. "St. Nick May Be Evicted From Santa Claus Lane," *Los Angeles Times*, p. B2, Sept. 20, 2001.

"Fire and Surf Victim Had Dread of Ocean," *Los Angeles Times*, p. 27, Sept. 5, 1912.

"5 Killed, 4 Hurt in San Diego Head-on Crash," *Los Angeles Times*, p. 2, Aug. 3, 1964.

"5,000 flee northern floods," *Pasadena Independent*, p. 1, Dec. 23, 1964.

"Fossil Of Large Prehistoric Animal Unearthed at Tustin Garage," *Tustin News*, p. 1, Nov. 5, 1954.

Fredricks, Darold. "Bayshore Freeway on the peninsula," *Daily Journal*, Jan. 2, 2012, archives.smdailyjournal.com.

———. "'Mile Houses' of the Peninsula," *Daily Journal*, Feb. 16, 2009, archives.smdailyjournal.com.

Fredricksen, Justine. "Escrow closes on former Fjord's building in Ukiah," *Ukiah Daily Journal*, June 25, 2016. www.ukiahjournal .com.

"Frostie Freeze Meets La Salsa," Jan. 22, 2011, www.experiencingla .com.

Fullwood, Janet. "Nature serves up a tall order along Redwood Highway," *San Bernardino County Sun*, p. E11, Mar. 4, 1990.

Garberville Theatre History, www.garbervilletheatre.com.

"Gas Barrage Routs 2,500 in Salinas; Children Overcome," *Fresno Bee*, p. 1, Sept. 15, 1936.

Gast, Ross. "Efficient Methods Bring Success on Big Berry Farm," *Los Angeles Times*, Farm and Tractor Section, July 27, 1924.

Gaviota Pass, www.geocities.ws.

Geggel, Laura. Livescience, Oct. 17, 2014, www.livescience.com.

Genzoli, Andrew. "Redwood Country," *Eureka Times-Standard*, p. 21, Dec. 4, 1969.

Geoghegan, John J. *Operation Storm*, Crown Publishers, N.Y., 2013.

Giant Orange Stands of California, www.weirdca.com.

Gibson, Lester H. "La Cuesta Realignment Opened, 59 Steep Curves Eliminated," *California Highways and Public Works*, p. 6, December 1938.

———. "New Cut-off Highway Route to End Dangers of San Juan Bottle Neck," *California Highways and Public Works*, p. 14, October 1931.

Gold, Scott. "In quaint Avila Beach, oil firm plans resort where crude once spilled," *Los Angeles Times*, Nov. 29, 2013, articles.latimes.com.

Golden Gate Bridge bond pamphlet, 1930, www.sfmueum.net.

Golden Gate Bridge, history.com.

Golden Gate Bridge, sftravel.com.

"Golden Lotus Temple, Coast Landmark, Sliding Into Ocean," *Los Angeles Times*, p. 16, July 22, 1942.

Goodrich, Chauncey Shafter. "Billboard Regulation and the Aesthetic Viewpoint with Reference to California Highways," *California Law Review*, vol. 17, no. 3, Mar. 1929, scholarship.law.berkeley.edu.

Graffy, Neal. *Historic Santa Barbara: An Illustrated History*, HPNbooks, 2012.

Graffy, Neal. "Summerland's Oil Wells in the Sea," May 21, 2011, www.edhat.com.

Greenson, Thaddeus. "Confusion Hill bypass set to open next weekend," *Times-Standard*, June 27, 2009. www.times-standard.com.

Gruen, John. "Son of Cheetah Goes West," *Los Angeles Times*, p. 92, Mar. 12, 1967.

Gudis, Catherine. *Buyways: Billboards, Automobiles, and the American Landscape*, 2004, Routledge, New York.

"Guests Welcomed at Milestone Inn," *San Luis Obispo Daily Telegram*, p. 1, Dec. 12, 1925.

Gunn, Douglas. *Picturesque San Diego*, Knight & Leonard Company, 1887.

Gutman, Richard. *American Diner Then and Now*, p. 142, HarperCollins, 1993.

Gyllstrom, Paul. "Rincon Sea-Level Road Soon Completed," *Motor Age*, p. 24, Oct. 17, 1912.

Harrison, Ken. "You can't run, but you can hide Papa Burger in Oceanside," *San Diego Reader*, Apr. 19, 2016, www.sandiegoreader.com.

Haverlin, Carl. "State Highway to the South is Scenic and Historical," *Oakland Tribune*, p. 43, June 7, 1925.

Haymes, Lefty. "Outdoor Writer, Wife Visit Famed Jungleland," *Winona Daily News*, p. 22, Jan. 26, 1969.

Hicks, Peggy. *The Ghost of The Cuban Queen Bordello*, Peggy Hicks, 2011.

"Highway Associations, Again," *Reno Evening Gazette*, p. 4, Mar. 15, 1924.

"Highway Details Sent to Salinas," *Oakland Tribune*, p. 3, Sept. 11, 1936.

Hinman, Ralph. "Collisions in Fog Snarl 5,000 Cars," *Long Beach Independent*, p. 1, Feb. 22, 1966.

Hissong, J. E. "Whirlwinds at Oil-Tank Fire, San Luis Obispo, Calif.," *Monthly Weather Review*, p. 161–162, Apr. 1926.

History, www.peasoupandersens.net.

History of Highway 101 through the redwoods, Feb. 24, 2005, discovertheredwoods.com.

History of Lincoln Park, www.lincolnheightsla.com.

History of Traffic Signing in California, The, www.caltrafficsigns.com.

"Hollywood to Rescue its Sign," *San Bernardino Sun-Telegram*, p. 2, July 1, 1978.

Hollywood Sign, The, www.daviesignarama.com.

Horn, Donna. Lots & Encyclopedias, SeaGate Landing, www.donnahorn.com.

Hotel Petaluma History, hotelpetaluma.com.

Hough, Robert. "Cat Woman," *Guardian*, Apr. 4, 2003, www.theguardian.com.

How Bob's Big Boy got his name, Original Retro Brand Blog, Aug. 9, 2013, originalretrobrand.com.

Jacobson, Will. "No desire? Streetcars move to Morro Bay," *Santa Ynez Valley Journal*, June 21, 2012, syvjournal.com.

James, Goldie. Benbow Inn—Hollywood's Golden Age Elite Hotspot, Aug. 9, 2015, goldiejames.com.

"Japanese Sub attacks Oilfield," American Oil & Gas Historical Society, aoghs.org.

"Japanese to Buy California Oil," *San Francisco Call*, p. 7, Dec. 14, 1906.

Japenga, Ann. "Santa Claus Lane Persists," *Los Angeles Times*, p. V1, Dec. 23, 1980.

"Jayne Mansfield remains at bedside of young son," *Redlands Daily Facts*, p. 9, Nov. 28, 1966.

"Jayne's son, Zoltan, home from hospital," *Redlands Daily Facts*, p. 7, Dec. 26, 1966.

"Jayne Sues Jungleland for Lion's Attack on Her Son," *Valley News*, p. 3A, Jan. 17, 1967.

Jepsen, Chris. "In Walter Knott's Footsteps: Shandon," Nov. 27, 2009, ochistorical.blogspot.com.

"Jobless Worker Forced to Sell His Pet Hippo," *Bridgeport Post*, p. B-20, Nov. 9, 1969.

Johnson, Bruce. "The days when Thousand Oaks was a jungle," *Ventura County Star*, July 2, 2011, www.vcstar.com.

Johnson, John. "Newly Rebuilt Avila Beach Faces an Identity Crisis," *Los Angeles Times*, p. 1, July 5, 2000.

Jungleland of Thousand Oaks, Stagecoach Inn Museum, www.stagecoachinnmuseum.org.

Jungleland Skates, www.junglelandskates.com.

Jungleland, Thousand Oaks California, Gorillas Don't Blog, Sept. 24, 2007, gorillasdontblog.blogspot.com.

Kay, George W. Final Years of Frustration, doctorjazz.co.uk.

"Knott Berry Farm Radio Rumor Blasted by F.B.I." *Los Angeles Times*, page 2A, Feb. 7, 1945.

Koelzer, Bill. "Meet Me at Tommy's: New Owners Reclaim the '50s Diner," San Clemente Journal, May 19, 2014, www .sanclementejournal.com.

Kopp, Phoebe S. *California Vieja: Culture and Memory in Modern American Place*, pp. 52–70, 2006, University of California.

Koppel, Lily. "Alex Madonna, 85, Creator of a Colorful Inn, Dies," *New York Times*, Apr. 26, 2004, www.nytimes.com.

"L.A. Anti-Aircraft Guns Roar, But Knox Says Mystery Plane Scare 'False Alarm,'" *Oakland Tribune*, p. 1, Feb. 25, 1942.

Lady Bird Johnson: The Beautification Campaign, www.pbs.org.

Las Cruces Adobe, Weird California, www.weirdca.com.

"Last stoplight blinks off," *Santa Cruz Sentinel*, p. A-6, Nov. 21, 1991.

Ledonne, Rob. "Remembering the glamorous history of party town Encinitas," *Del Mar Times*, July 29, 2014, www.delmartimes.net.

"Leggett Valley Facts," *Ukiah Daily Journal*, p. 30, Aug. 27, 1971.

Lelyveld, Nita. "A Hollywood tragedy, a neighborhood remembrance," *Los Angeles Times*, Sept. 17, 2014, www.latimes.com.

"Lettuce Growers Refuse to Give Union Preference," *Santa Cruz Sentinel*, p. 1, Sept. 1, 1936.

Leovy, Jill. "Bowling Alley May Fade Into Memory," *Los Angeles Times*, Mar. 16, 1994.

Levin, Floyd. *Classic Jazz: A Personal View of the Music and Musicians*, University of California Press, 2000.

Levy, Joan. "Millbrae's 16 Mile House lives on," *Daily Journal*, Aug. 2, 2004, archives.smdailyjournal.com.

"Lightning Hits Oil Tank Farm; Starts Big Fire," *Oxnard Press-Courier*, p. 1, Apr. 7, 1926.

Linn, Sarah. "The Dunites: Building a Utopia in the Oceano Dunes," KCET, July 8, 2013, www.kcct.org.

Linn, Sarah. "Excavating the 'Ten Commandments' in the Guadalupe-Nipomo Dunes," KCET, June 10, 2013, www.kcet.org.

"Lion Farming is Latest," *Eugene Morning Register*, p. 3, Aug. 19, 1928.

Lomax, Alan. "Jelly Roll Morton," transcript of the 1938 Library of Congress Recordings of Jelly Roll Morton, 1938. server2.docfoc .com.

Looff Hippodrome, www.smconservancy.org.

"Louis Goebel, 84, Animal Trainer; Ran Jungleland Compound," *New York Times*, Apr. 25, 1981.

Lovret, Juanita. "Tanks for the Memories," Tustin News/Tustin Area Historical Society, tustinhistory.com.

Lynem, Julie. "Motel Inn in SLO could be brought back to life," *San Luis Obispo Tribune*, Aug. 20, 2015.

"Mabel Stark: The Lady with the Tigers," Mental Floss, July 2, 2013, mentalfloss.com.

"Mabel Stark, tiger trainer, dies at 79," *Redlands Daily Facts*, p. 2, Apr. 22, 1968.

Mai-Duc, Christine. "The 1969 Santa Barbara oil spill that changed oil and gas exploration forever," **Los Angeles Times**, May 20, 2015.

Manual and Specifications for the Manufacture, Display and Erection of U.S. Standard Road Markers and Signs, first edition, Jan. 1927.

Marceline: Where Walt Found the Magic, Walt Disney Hometown Museum, www.waltdisneymuseum.org.

Mason, Clark. "After big retrofit, Healdsburg's Memorial Bridge to open next week," *Santa Rosa Press-Democrat*, Oct. 15, 2015, www.pressdemocrat.com.

Masters, Nathan. "From Daisy Dell to the Hollywood Bowl, a Little Musical History for the Summer," June 23, 2011. www.kcet.org.

———. "When Orange County Was Rural (and Oranges Actually Grew There)" Lost L.A., KCET, Feb. 7, 2014, www.kcet .org.

"Materials rushed for great amusement pier." *Los Angeles Times*, part 2, p. 11, Mar 1.2, 1916.

Maulhardt, Jeffrey Wayne, *Jungleland*, Arcadia Publishing, 2011.

McCarty, Ellen. "Waves of Time," *Huntington Beach Independent*, Nov. 11, 1999. articles.hbindependent.com.

McCormack, David. "I never lost hope," *Daily Mail*, Mar. 9, 2013, www.dailymail.co.uk.

Meares, Hadley. "The Origin Story of Tarzana, a Neighborhood Named After an Ape Man," *LA Weekly*, July 2, 2016. laweekly .com.

Merritt, Christopher and Priore, Domenic. *Pacific Ocean Park*, Process Media, Port Townsend, Wash., 2015.

Meyer, Ferdinand V., "Looking at Dr. Pierce's Barn Advertising," Peachridge Glass, Dec. 20, 2012, www.peachridgeglass.com.

Meyers, Carole Terwilliger. "10 wild and crazy North Coast Redwoods," *Press-Democrat*, Nov. 20, 2015, www.pressdemocrat .com.

Middlecamp, David. "Cuesta Grade a Formidable Foe—Photos from the Vault," http://sloblogs.thetribunenews.com.

———. "Madonna Inn Fire of 1966—Photos from the Vault," *San Luis Obispo Tribune*, Feb. 17, 2012.

———. "Motel Inn in San Luis Obispo, the world's first 'mo-tel,'" *San Luis Obispo Tribune*, Dec. 4, 2014.

Middlecamp, David. "Oilport, before it was Shell Beach," *San Luis Obispo Tribune*, Aug. 6, 2010, https://photosfromthevault .wordpress.com.

———. "Remembering SLO County's floods of 1995," *San Luis Obispo Tribune*, Nov. 14, 2014, sanluisobispo.com.

———. "The San Luis Obispo Tank Farm Fire," *San Luis Obispo Tribune*, https://photosfromthevault.wordpress.com.

Migrant Mother, 1936, eyewitnesstohistory.com.

Miles, Kathleen. "Pacific Electric Red Car in LA Covered 25 Percent More Mileage than NYC's Subway Today," Huffpost Los Angeles, Jan. 31, 2013.

Miller, Martin. "The Oil Spill That Sparked the Green Revolution," *Los Angeles Times*, Nov. 30, 1999.

Modugno, Tom. "Architectural Influence," Goleta History, Apr. 25, 2015, goletahistory.com.

——— "Attack on Ellwood," Goleta History, Oct. 19, 2014, goletahistory.com.

———. "Bishop Ranch," Goleta History, Oct. 19, 2014, goletahistory.com.

———. "Gaviota Pass, The," Goleta History, Sept. 15, 2015, goleta-history.com.

———. "Gaviota Village," Goleta History, Apr. 7, 2016, goletahistory.com.

———. "Kate Bell's Cactus," Goleta History, Oct. 19, 2015, goletahistory.com.

———. "Tecolote Cut, The," Goleta History, July 27, 2015, goletahistory.com.

Morrow, Tom. "Ed Frazee was a big part of local history," *San Diego Union-Tribune*, July 30, 2004, www.sandiegouniontribune.com.

"My Picture And I Get Nothing For It," *Santa Cruz Sentinel*, p. 8, Nov. 17, 1978.

"New Field of Oil Found in S. Barbara," *Oakland Tribune*, p. 38, July 31, 1928.

Newman, Bruce and Melendez Salinas, Claudia. "Bracero Memorial Highway dedicated to celebrate contributions of Mexican field workers and railroad builders," *San Jose Mercury News*, Sept. 16, 2013, www.mercurynews.com/immigration.

Nickell, Joe. "Dr. Pierce: Medicine for 'Weak Women,'" *Skeptical Inquirer*, www.csicop.org.

"1962 Trees of Mystery Paul Bunyan & Blue Entrance Photograph Slide," www.timepassagesnostalgia.com.

"North Coast Loss Is Worst In History," *San Rafael Daily Independent Journal*, p. 4, Dec. 24, 1964.

"Not-So-Famous Products Were Radio Sponsors, Part I," www.old-time.com/commercials.

"Oakland Goes Down Side of Hill; Four-Wheel Brakes Halt Disaster," *San Bernardino Daily Sun*, p. 17, Dec. 30, 1923.

Oaks Drive-In, cinematreasures.org.

"Ocean Park Fire Loss is $1,200,000," *San Francisco Chronicle*, p. 3, Sept. 5, 1912.

"Ocean Park: The Home of Fraser's Million Dollar Pier," *Arizona Daily Star*, p. 18, June 11, 1911.

Oceanside-Carlsbad Freeway: Carlsbad Portion, www.gbcnet.com/ushighways/US101/carlsbad_fwy.html

"Oil and Gas Production History in California," ftp://ftp.consrv.ca.gov/pub/oil/history/History_of_Calif.pdf.

"Old Spanish Highway, The," *Santa Cruz Evening Sentinel*, p. 5, Sept. 30, 1901.

One Log House Espresso & Gifts, www.oneloghouse.com

101cafe.net.

"101 Café Oceanside, a 50s Diner with a Past," west-coast-beach-vacations.com.

"'Operation Lifeline' Goes Through to S.F. Over 101," *Humboldt Standard*, p. 1, Jan. 16, 1965.

Ordway, Cary. "A Look Back At This Years California Adventures," *Crescenta Valley Sun*, p. A17, Dec. 30, 2005.

"Oregon Line Trip One of Rare Beauty," *Oakland Tribune*, p. 0-5, Aug. 20, 1922.

"Otono Fans Signing Up," *Los Angeles Times*, p. 1, July 19, 1936.

Overaker, Ken. "Slaughter Alley Death Rate Cut by Improvement," *Los Angeles Times*, p. C1, Mar. 16, 1969.

Pacific Electric Subway, www.westworld.com/~elson/larail/PE/tunnel.html.

Paddock, Richard C. "A Long-Buried Oil Spill Casts Beach Town Adrift," *Los Angeles Times*, Sept. 28, 1994, articles.latimes.com.

Pastras, Phil. *Dead Man Blues: Jelly Roll Morton Way Out West*, University of California Press, 2003.

"Patricia, Fritz United After Santa Ana Show," *Oxnard Press-Courier*, p. 1, Sept. 5, 1929.

Pavlik, Robert C. "Historical Overview of the Carmel to San Simeon Highway," dot.ca.gov/dist5.

Pereira Octagon Barn, National Register of Historic Places Registration Form, Nov. 29, 2013, https://www.nps.gov/nr/feature/places/pdfs/13001068.pdf.

Pfingsten, Tom. "101 Café proprietor, Oceanside go way back," *San Diego Union-Tribune*, Aug. 17, 2014, sandiegouniontribune.com.

Phelan, Ben. "The Story of the 'Migrant Mother,' Antiques Roadshow, Apr. 14, 2014, www.pbs.org.

"Picketing Peaceful in Lettuce Industry," *Daily Capital Journal*, Salem, Oregon, p. 8, Sept. 9, 1936.

Pool, Bob. "Tarzana Film Fest to Honor Swinging Namesake," *Los Angeles Times*, part II, p. 8, Oct. 29, 1987.

"Port Hartford Hard Hit," *San Bernardino County Sun*, p. 5, Mar. 6, 1907.

Powell, J.F. "Service Town, U.S.A.," *California Highways and Public Works*, p. 1-7, Sept.-Oct. 1949.

"Pretty Old Barn, A," The Bookshelf of Emily J., Mar. 25, 2014, thebookshelfofemilyj.com.

Primarily Petroliana: Gas Station Shop Talk, Mar. 11, 2006, www.oldgas.com.

Provost, Steve. "Knott's Berry Farm preserves now made by Linn's in Cambria," *Cambrian*, Jan. 8, 2015, www.sanluisobispo.com.

"Prunedale Cut-off, By-passing San Juan Grade, Opens in July," *California Highways and Public Works*, p. 17, Apr. 1932.

Pulley, Tom. "The Huntington Beach Encyclopedia Lots," *County Courier*, Oct. 2009, www.orangecountyhistory.org.

"Raiders of the Lost Set: Excavating DeMille's City of the Pharaohs, 1923–2014," Barrelhouse, May 27, 2014. fromthebarrelhouse.com.

Rasmussen, Cecilia. "Curse of the Cahuenga Pass Treasure," *Los Angeles Times*, Jan. 23, 2000.

Ray, Nancy. "Yogi's Followers Keep the Faith at Scenic Retreat on Encinitas Bluff," *Los Angeles Times*, San Diego County section, Mar. 9, 1986.

Redmon, Michael. "Las Cruces Adobe: History of the Once Thriving Ranch," *Santa Barbara Independent*, June 18, 2013, www.independent.com.

———l. "Rincon Point Road," *Santa Barbara Independent*, Nov. 21, 2011, www.independent.com.

"Redwood Forests Saved for State," *San Bernardino County Sun*, p. 22, June 28, 1928.

"Refuse $15,000,000 For Gaviota Oil Lease," *Oxnard Press-Courier*, p. 1, Aug. 10, 1928.

Reich, Howard, and Gaines, William. "The Great Jazz Swindle," "Down And Out In New York," "A Jazz Man's Revival," *Chicago Tribune*, Dec. 12–14, 1999, articles.chicagotribune.com.

Reinhardt, Emil. "Winter Travel to L.A. Heavy," *Oakland Tribune*, p. 37, Nov. 19, 1922.

"Rejected Film Career Leads Young Actress to Spectacular Death Leap," *San Bernardino Daily Sun*, p. 3, Sept. 20, 1932.

"Remember Santa's Village and Santa Claus Lane?" Dec. 16, 2013, http://thesoutherncalifornian.blogspot.com.

Reynolds, Julia. "Historic Store Burns Down: Investigators, Firefighters Suspect Arson," *Monterey County Herald*, July 12, 2006, www.highbeam.com.

Richman, Jan. "Outlaws And Burgers And Clowns, Oh My!" SFGate, www.sfgate.com.

Richmond, Peter. "The 1970s Oakland Raiders: Boozin' and Coozin' Through El Rancho," Deadspin, http://deadspin.com.

"Ride's About Over at Old-Time Carnivals, The," *Los Angeles Times*, p. 36, June 30, 1968.

Rinehart, Katherine J. "Old Redwood Highway: Penngrove poultry boomtown," http://town.blogs.petaluma360.com.

"Road From San Luis In Shape To Arroyo," *San Mateo Times*, p. 3, June 2, 1928.

Roadside Architecture, www.roadarch.com.

Roe, Cherie. *Santa Margarita*, Arcadia Publishing, 2016.

"Route Bypassing Slaughter Alley to Open Tuesday," *Los Angeles Times*, p. 3, June 20, 1966.

"Sam Bunte, Native of Santa Cruz, Dies In King City," *Santa Cruz Sentinel*, p. 2, May 18, 1943.

"Sam, the hippo, costs and eats a big bundle," *Montana Standard*, p. 8, Nov. 5, 1969.

"San Bruno's toll road was the main thoroughfare," *Daily Journal*, May 19, 2008, archives.smdailyjournal.com.

"San Diego Fair," *Los Angeles Herald*, p. 4, Oct. 2, 1881.

"San Diego Fair, The," *San Francisco Chronicle*, p. 8, Oct. 8, 1886.

"San Juan Grade Chosen Definitely For the State Highway; Decision Public," *Santa Cruz Evening* News, p. 1, Apr. 29, 1913.

Santa Maria Inn, Weird California, www.weirdca.com.

Santa Monica Pier History: The tale of two piers, www.westlandtraveler.com.

Saperstein, Susan. "San Francisco's Old Clam House on the Lost Waterfront," *Guidelines*, www.sfcityguides.org.

"Scenery of North Trip is Praised," *Oakland Tribune*, p. 11, Oct. 22, 1922.

Scott, Quinta. *Route 66: The Highway and its People*, University of Oklahoma Press, 1988.

Seireeni, Rick. "20th Century Canyon History," laurelcanyonassoc.com.

"Sennett Breaks Ground, First In Valley Studio Center," *Van Nuys News*, p. 1, 4, June 21, 1927.

"7 Mile House," 7milehouse.com/history.

Shallert, Edwin. "Hertz Opens Bowl Season," *Los Angeles Times*, part 2, p. 9, July 7, 1927.

Sheeran, Owen. "Parade on over to Santa Claus Lane," *San Bernardino County Sun*, p. D1, Dec. 21, 1991.

Sherman, Pat. "Road stop is on memory lane," *San Diego Union-Tribune*, May 23, 2010, www.sandiegouniontribune.com.

Signor, Bob and Ann. "Lost Treasure of Cahuenga Pass," *Long Beach Independent Press-Telegram*, p. 7, Sept. 14, 1958.

"Sign is Born, A: 1923," The Hollywood Sign, hollywoodsign.org.

"Signs May Disfigure Lovely Rincon Road," *Oxnard Courier*, p. 5, Mar. 7, 1913.

Sim, Nick. "Mickey Mouse Park: The Story of Walt Disney's Lost Theme Park," Theme Park Tourist, May 3, 2015. themeparktourist.com.

Simon, Richard. "It's a Billboard Jungle Along L.A. Freeways," *Los Angeles Times*, Oct. 22, 1995, articles.latimes.com.

"Slaughter Alley Deaths Hit Record," *Long Beach Independent Press-Telegram*, p. 31, Jan. 10, 1965.

"Slaughter Alley To Become 8 Lanes," *San Mateo Times*, p. 4, Feb. 28, 1966.

Sleeper, Jim. "How Orange County Got Its Name," ocarchives.com.

"Small Boy Has Fun By Blowing Up An Oil Tank," *San Francisco Chronicle*, p. 5, Jan. 22, 1903.

Songfacts.com

Songmeanings.com

St. John, Allison. "New Carlsbad Sign Goes Up Over Highway 101," KPBS, www.kpbs.org.

Stanton, Jeffrey. "Amusement Pier Fires," Apr. 6, 1998, www.westland.net.

Stanton, Jeffrey. "Fraser's Million Dollar Pier," Apr. 6, 1998, www.westland.net.

Stanton, Jeffrey. "Ocean Park Pier," Apr. 6, 1998, www.westland.net.

———. "Pacific Ocean Park," Apr. 6, 1998, www.westland.net.

Stanton, Jeffrey. "Prior and Church—Roller Coaster Designers," Apr. 6, 1998. www.westland.net.

———. "Roller Coasters & Carousels," Apr. 6, 1998. www.westland.net.

———. "Santa Monica Pier," www.westland.net.

Stewart, Robert W. "Doom of Development Hanging Over Topanga Canyons," *Los Angeles Times*, part VII, p. 1, Dec. 23, 1982.

Stratford Square, Del Mar Village, visitdelmarvillage.com.

Strawther, Larry. *Seal Beach: A Brief History*, History Press, Charleston, SC, 2014.

"Strike Battle Rages in Downown Salinas," *Oakland Tribune*, p. 1, Sept. 16, 1936.

"Strike Threatens Lettuce Harvest," *Roseburg News-Review* (Oregon), p. 1, Sept. 4, 1936.

"Summerland Steal," *Los Angeles Herald*, p. 9, Aug. 13, 1898.

"Taco Shop founder Robledo dies at 70," *Las Vegas Sun*, June 18, 1999. lasvegassun.com.

"Tarzanans Considering Name Change," *Van Nuys News*, p. 1, May 30, 1949.

Tejeda, Valerie. "Is the Hollywood Sign Haunted?" VFHollywood, Oct. 31, 2014, www.vanityfair.com.

"Temple and Hermitage Completed Near Encinitas," *Los Angeles Times*, p. 9, Nov. 2, 1937.

"10 Millions Lost in Oil Fire," *Santa Ana Register*, p. 1, Apr. 7, 1926.

Thomas, Bob. "$10 Million Park Readied To Honor King of the Seas," *Circleville Herald*, p. 4, May 31, 1958.

Thomas, Haley. "Elkhorn bar, est. 1853, plans to ink history," *Paso Robles Press*, July 16, 2010.

Tom, Donna. "A 'grand gentleman': Eureka business icon Harvey G. Harper dies," *Times-Standard*, Nov. 4, 2010, www.times-standard.com.

"Treadwell's Wharf," *Los Angeles Herald*, p. 9, Aug. 12, 1898.

Trees of Mystery, www.treesofmystery.net.

"Trees of Mystery" (advertisement), *Eureka Times-Standard*, p. 9-B, May 25, 1954.

Treffers, Steven. "How a Visionary Scoundrel Created Woodland Hills in the 1920s," Apr. 16, 2014, lacurbed.com.

"Tustin Garage Used As Pre-Race Base For Balloon," *Tustin News*, p. 1, May 31, 1979.

"12 Movie Animals Die in Fire; Many Shot by Trainers," *Oakland Tribune*, p. 5, July 10, 1940.

"20 Awesome Facts About the Golden Gate Bridge," mentalfloss.com.

"28 Are Killed In Bus-Train Accident," *Pampa Daily News*, p. 1, Sept. 18, 1963.

"28 Braceros Killed," *Salinas Californian*, p. 1, Sept. 18, 1963.

"28 Killed In Worst Vehicle Accident In State History," *San Rafael Daily Independent Journal*, p. 1, Sept. 18, 1963.

"#29—The Eternal Tree House," 101things.com. "Two Dead and One Dying From Oil Fire in San Luis Obispo," *Oxnard Press-Courier*, p. 1, Apr. 8, 1926.

"Uncle Tom's Cabin in San Bruno," *Daily Journal*, Nov. 16, 2009, archives.smdailyjournal.com.

Urseny, Laura. "Iconic Dust Bowl woman Florence Owens Thompson lived in Oroville," *Chico Enterprise-Record*, Nov. 16, 2012, www.chicoer.com.

Vaught, Steve. "Lighting Up the Coast," Mar. 16, 2011, paradiseleased.wordpress.com.

Wagner, Stephen. "The Ghost of the Hollywood Sign," About entertainment, paranormal.about.com.

Wallace, E. E. "San Diego Celebrates Completion of Million Dollar Highway into City," *California Highways and Public Works*, p. 6, Jan. 1933.

"Walt Disney's Proposed Theme Park in Burbank," D23, Official Disney Fan Club, d23.com.

"Water Over Road At Benbow; Many Slides in Area," *Humboldt Standard*, p. 1, Dec. 21, 1964.

"We did not think we would survive: Ginger Nunes," www.times-standard.com.

Weingroff, Richard F. "From Names to Numbers: The Origins of the U.S. Numbered Highway System," www.fhwa.dot.gov.

"Wershaw Industrial Auction Calendar," *Los Angeles Times*, p. C6, June 23, 1968.

Wetzel, Tom. "What explains the demise of the Pacific Electric Railway?" 2009, www.uncanny.net.

"Wharves Damaged by Storms," *Santa Cruz Evening News*, p. 6, Dec. 12, 1907.

What's My Line (video), Aug. 27, 1961, youtube.com

"Wild Lion Kills Woman Trainer In Cage; Children Try Rescue," *Cape Girardeau Southeast Missourian*, p. 16, Dec. 21, 1949.

"William Reed, Discoverer of Bowl Site, Dies," *Los Angeles Times*, p. 13, Aug. 28, 1946.

Williams, Amy. "The Del Mar Race Track: 75 Years of Turf and Surf," sandiegohistory.org.

Williams, Lauren. "Finding owners of Huntington Beach's 'encyclopedia land' property is tough," *Orange County Register*, Apr. 1, 2015.

Wilson, Don. "Highway 101 Project," www.historic101.com.

Wise, Barry. "The History of Studio City," www.studiocitychamber.com.

"Women Pickets Jeer Workers, Salt Lake Tribune, p. 7, Sept. 13, 1936.

Wood, Jim. "History of a Highway: Marin's 101 was first established in 1909," *Marin Magazine*, May 2009, www.marinemagazine.com.

Wright, Lawrence. "Lady Bird's Lost Legacy," *New York Times*, July 20, 2007, www.nytimes.com.

"Yellow Cars—L.A. Railway," www.oerm.org.

"Young Actress Ends Life at Hollywood," *Lewiston Daily Sun*, pp. 1, 11, Sept. 20, 1932.

Young, Heather. "Nonprofit forms to save Atascadero Printery," *A-Town Daily News*, Jan. 11, 2016. atowndailynews.com.

Zarakov, Barry N. "A History of the Las Cruces Adobe," www.corderofamilyhistory.com.

"Zoo oughta be in pictures," astimesgobye.com.

INDEX

About the Author

STEPHEN H. PROVOST is an author and journalist who has worked as an editor, columnist, and reporter at newspapers throughout California. His previous books include *Highway 99: The History of California's Main Street*, the first book in his *California's Historic Highways* series; *Fresno Growing Up: A City Comes of Age 1945–1985*; and the fantasy novels *Memortality* and *Paralucidity*.

The Pat Hunter and Janice Stevens Collection
Breathtaking artwork of California's most beautiful places

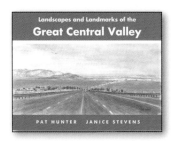

Landscapes and Landmarks of the Great Central Valley
$29.95 • ISBN 978-1-61035-362-5

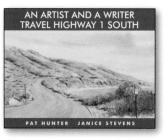

An Artist and a Writer Travel Highway 1 South
$26.95 • ISBN 978-1-61035-297-0

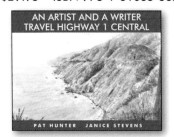

An Artist and a Writer Travel Highway 1 Central
$26.95 • ISBN 978-1-61035-219-2

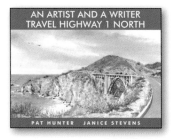

An Artist and a Writer Travel Highway 1 North
$21.95 • ISBN 978-1-61035-053-2

Remembering the California Missions
$26.95 • ISBN 978-1-884995-64-4

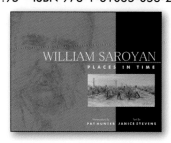

William Saroyan: Places in Time
$26.95 • ISBN 978-1-933502-24-3

Fresno's Architectural Past Volume I
$26.95 • ISBN 978-0-941936-97-2

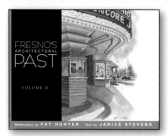

Fresno's Architectural Past Volume II
$26.95 • ISBN 978-1-933502-13-7

Available from bookstores, online booksellers, and CravenStreetBooks.com, or by calling toll-free 1-800-345-4447